10.17.18

Withdrawn

CUSTOMERS THE DAY AFTER TOMORROW

STEVEN VAN BELLEGHEM

CUSTOMERS THE DAY AFTER TOMORROW

How to attract customers in a world of AI, bots and automation

LANNOO
CAMPUS

Second edition: Januari 2018

D/2017/45/352 – ISBN 978 94 014 4521 4 – NUR 802

Design: Karl Demoen
Translation: Ian Connerty

© Steven Van Belleghem & Lannoo Publishers nv, Tielt, 2017.

LannooCampus Publishers is a subsidiary of Lannoo Publishers,
the book and multimedia division of Lannoo Publishers nv.

LannooCampus Publishers
Erasme Ruelensvest 179 box 101
3001 Leuven
Belgium
www.lannoocampus.com

TABLE OF CONTENTS

THE DAY AFTER TOMORROW MINDSET

THE DAY AFTER TOMORROW INVESTMENT AXES

CHAPTER 7.
FIGHTING THE COMMODITY MAGNET

CHAPTER 8.
INTELLIGENCE AUGMENTED

THE DAY AFTER TOMORROW CONSEQUENCES

INTRODUCTION

An eight-year-old boy is sitting eating a cheeseburger with his sister in a McDonald's in Ohio. Just as he pops the last bite into his mouth, the police arrive to question the two children. "Have I done something wrong?" the boy asks the policemen politely. He certainly doesn't think so. As far as he can remember, he followed all the rules of the road perfectly when he drove here in his dad's car. "So where did you learn to drive, kid?" asks one of the cops. "Me? On YouTube, of course!"[1]

A murder trial is going nowhere. The defendant protests his innocence, but there are no witnesses to support his story. His only chance for acquittal is his Amazon Echo – the virtual assistant that more and more consumers are using to make their lives easier. The device is effectively the world's first computer with no keyboard, and people have quickly started to use it for everyday tasks like checking the news, buying products or listening to music. The interface is operated by the user's voice, but it is not just the owners' words that are registered by Echo; the device also picks up every other spoken word within its range. In this ground-breaking case, the police asked Amazon to release the data from the defendant's Echo, in the hope that this might move the murder trial forward. Initially, Amazon refused, but later changed their mind, at the explicit request of the defendant. So, the key witness in the trial became a machine. Not a person.[2]

Google Translate is getting better every day. Artificial intelligence is helping the translation tool to work faster and more efficiently. Google Translate can now translate from Japanese to English and vice versa; and also from Korean to English and vice versa. So the next logical question is this: can the computer teach itself to translate from Japanese to Korean and back again? The obvious way to do this is to translate first from Japanese to English and then from English to Korean. However, artificial intelligence software discovered that it was more effective to develop its own intermediary language for this intermediary step, a language that gave much better results than English. But the developer of this intermediary language was not a human engineer. The computer, Google DeepMind, decided for itself that this was the best route to follow.[3]

Children learning to drive with YouTube. A machine testifying in court. Computers that can think and learn for themselves. Ten years ago, it would have sounded like science fiction. Today, it is reality. In just ten years, YouTube has grown to become the second largest search engine in the world. Amazon Echo is the most popular gadget of the moment: more than 10 million American families currently have this virtual assistant in their living room.[4] Google DeepMind is widely regarded as the smartest computer in the world. And this is just the tip of the iceberg.

The third phase in digital evolution

All signs are pointing in the same direction. We are at the start of a new phase in digital evolution. The first stage was about making information available via the internet. The second phase was about mobile technology and new forms of communication. The third phase will be about automation and artificial intelligence.

In this book you will be offered far-reaching insights about the influence of this third phase of digitalization on customer relations. What impact will artificial intelligence (AI) and rapidly-advancing levels of automation have on the relationships between businesses and customers? That is the core of this book. For customers, we are entering a period where we can expect an unrivalled quality of service. Smart technology now allows companies to identify and solve their customers' problems before they even know that it is a problem. Faster than real-time customer service is quickly becoming the new norm. The level of personalization of products and services is also increasing rapidly, based on a dramatic improvement in the quality of data management. Last but not least, user interfaces are becoming more intuitive than ever before, with the way we operate devices and software changing beyond recognition in recent years.

To make all these benefits available to their customers, companies are now making the strategic shift from 'mobile first' to 'AI first'. Initially, it will be unclear to some why certain brands are successfully improving their customer service, while others are not. The reason being that, in most cases, artificial intelligence is invisible technology. A website (phase 1 of digitalization) and an app (phase 2 of digitalization) were investments that were highly visible to everyone – customers and competitors. The unseen nature of AI means that businesses that are quick to embrace it

Digital   **Mobile**   **AI**

can quickly gain a significant competitive advantage. Customers won't understand it. It will simply seem as though company A has better staff than company B, but in reality, the staff in company A are being assisted by smarter software. In the first part of this book I will describe in detail this transition from 'mobile first' to 'AI first'.

Customers The Day After Tomorrow

My first two books, *The Conversation Manager* (2010) and *The Conversation Company* (2012), were both guides for marketing in the second phase of digitalization. The books described how companies could adjust their culture and communication in a new world of social media and smartphones.

Today, the second phase of digitalization has reached maturity. That is not to say that it isn't still vital to continue investing in mobile and social media communication. The third phase of digitalization has already started, but this does not mean that consumers no longer have a need for good communication and service provision based on technology from phase 2. In fact, it is more ingrained into consumer behaviour than ever before.

When Digital Becomes Human (2014), my third management book, focused on the initial shift from phase 2 to phase 3. It is the period in which digital transformation became *the* buzzwords, as companies asked themselves how the relationship between people and machines could be enhanced. Three years later (2017), the basic conclusion of *When Digital Becomes Human* is still relevant: computers should add value primarily through the automation of operational processes while people should focus on the more emotional tasks. People and machines are highly complementary when it comes to offering added value to customers. This will not change in the years ahead. All that will happen is that the role of the machines will become more prominent and the role of the people will be given an even sharper focus.

Customers The Day After Tomorrow, as the title implies, is all about customer relationships in the medium-term future. In this book, I will make clear where companies need to invest if they want to be successful in phase 3. The challenge is to combine this investment for The Day After Tomorrow with the further development of evolutions from phase 2. In other words, working to improve customer relations The Day After Tomorrow runs parallel with continued efforts to improve customer relations today and tomorrow.

This book is not an appeal to end investment in your current day-to-day relations. On the contrary, it is an appeal to continue investing in today, but also to set aside resources for what your customers will expect in the future. A future that will arrive much faster than you think.

Today, there is so much hype around so many emerging technologies that it can be difficult for companies to know where their focus should be. The answer is that the most important focus should always be the customer, and as this book will explain, if you take the customer as your starting point, the specific technology becomes less crucial.

To make this as concrete as possible, the second part of the book describes four axes of investment for the customer relationship of the future. Firstly, there is a need to *increasingly see customer relations as a science*. Data must be used as a lever for developing new customer benefits, and consequently, the need for data in the third phase of digital development is greater than ever. Artificial intelligence can only work effectively if it has enough data.

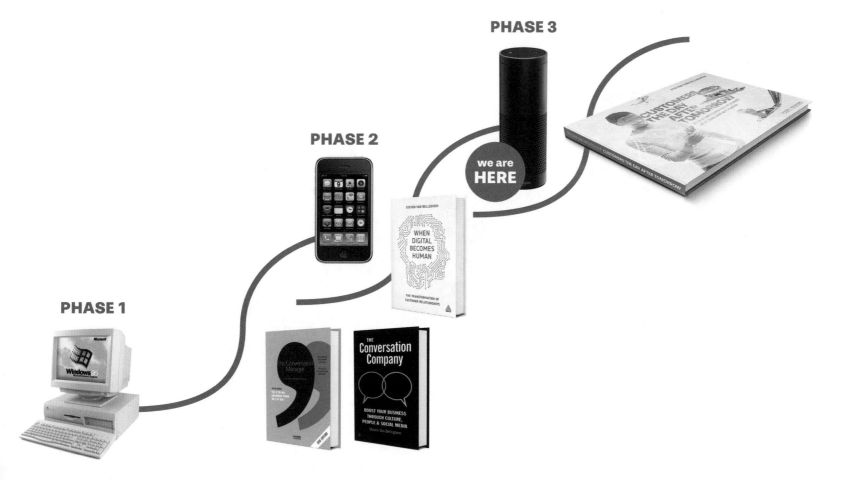

PHASE 3

we are
HERE

PHASE 2

PHASE 1

Secondly, there is a need for *new interfaces* to automate communication and interaction with customers more efficiently. Customers are no longer willing to wait an hour for an answer. Real time is the new expected minimum for communication, and it must be via user-friendly interfaces. Reducing the amount of effort the customer must make is the priority. In The Day After Tomorrow people will not be looking for a flawless customer experience; they will be more interested in an automated or very simple customer relationship.

Thirdly, there is the *battle against the commodity magnet*. Because customers will be taking more and more decisions based on algorithms and the power of the major digital platforms continues to grow, there is a risk that every product will become a commodity where price is the most important factor. As a business leader and a marketeer, it is vital to find ways to add value and differentiate to counter this risk.

The data lever

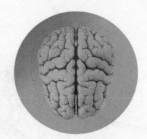

New user interfaces

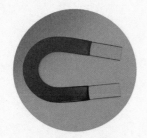

Fighting the commodity magnet

Intelligence Augmented

Fourthly, The Day After Tomorrow requires investment to *improve the performance of people via technology*. How can speed be increased and the number of errors reduced in the most personal manner possible? How can we help our team to meet the wishes and expectations of the customers of the future? This fourth axis is focused on 'augmented intelligence': enhanced human performance with the assistance of technology.

In short, customer relations The Day After Tomorrow will use data as a lever for additional customer benefits (1), employ the most user-friendly interfaces (2), succeed in escaping from the commodity magnet (3) and bring in new technology to optimize human skills (4).

The structure of *Customers The Day After Tomorrow*

Over the past five years, I have had the pleasure of following the evolution of the most innovative companies in the world from the front row. These companies include the biggest names in the field of technology (Google, Facebook, Amazon, Tesla, Tencent, Alibaba, Microsoft, etc.), established market leaders (Cisco, Oracle, Autodesk, etc.) and disruptive rising stars (Planet Labs, Fyusion, etc.).

The story of this book is based on more than 300 company visits spread across New York, Los Angeles, San Francisco, Silicon Valley, Seattle, Barcelona, London, Berlin, Dublin, Belgium, the Netherlands, Singapore, Shanghai, Shenzhen and Hangzhou.

I have also carefully selected and interviewed nine experts, whose thoughts add further insights to the most important aspects of my story. All the interviews were filmed and can be viewed on *www.youtube.com/stevenvanbelleghem*. You will, of course, also read their comments and opinions throughout the book.

Feedback

I would be delighted to receive your questions and comments. My email address is *Steven@VanBelleghem.biz*. It is always a pleasure to read your feedback.

I hope you enjoy my book *Customers The Day After Tomorrow*. Steven Van Belleghem

www.stevenvanbelleghem.com
www.youtube.com/stevenvanbelleghem

Bringing the book to life via Augmented Reality

This book is about the future. One of the technologies that looks set to boom in the years ahead is Augmented Reality (AR). I will be talking about it a lot in the next few pages. But I want to do more than just talk about it; I want to use it as well. So, this is one of the first books in which AR applications have been integrated.

This is what you need to do to bring this book to life:

Download the 'Aurasma' app on your smartphone

Create an Aurasma-acount

Find me, 'stevenvanbelleghem' via 'Discover Auras' and follow me on Aurasma

Look for pages with the 'Aurasma' logo (take a look at the cover if you are not sure)

Scan the page or the image with your smartphone

Watch how the book comes to life

CHAPTER 1

CUSTOMER EXPERIENCE IN THE THIRD PHASE OF DIGITALIZATION

Success today? Process — Measuring — Culture

Before we look forward into the future, I would first like to look back at the recent history of customer experience management, using three seminal books as examples. Each of the three books added fundamental insights to the customer experience debate.

The first is *The Disney Way*[5] (Bill Capodagli, 2001). Since its earliest days, Disney has been a reference for customer experience. This book describes the entertainment company's service philosophy. In short, it is a story of perfectly designed processes to make the life of the customer as enjoyable as possible. The first step towards satisfied customers is to make sure that all your transactions run smoothly. And if you visit one of the Disney parks, you will immediately notice that each and every one of their processes is still thought out to the very last detail. They have even set up a separate division, the Disney Academy, to share this philosophy with other companies.

The second book is *The Ultimate Question*[6] (Fred Reichheld, 2006). It was this book that introduced the Net Promoter Score (NPS). To calculate your Net Promoter Score, you ask your cus-tomers to give you a score between 1 and 10 to reflect how willing they would be to recommend your company to others. Whoever gives a score of 9 or 10 is a promoter. If you give a score of 0 to 6, you are a detractor. By subtracting the number of detractors from the number of promoters, you end up with your Net Promoter Score. The central proposition of this book is simple: if you measure your NPS, this single score will tell you whether your company is performing well or not. If the score is higher than zero, your company will grow faster than the market. If the score is lower than zero, you have a problem. The most important impact of NPS was felt in the boardroom. Many top executives now suddenly had a way to measure and interpret how custom-ers saw them. The concept has always had its supporters and opponents, but it is impossible to deny that it had a huge effect on the business world. Customer experience evolved from some-thing you had to 'believe' into something you could 'measure'. As a result, it brought customer experience management higher up the agenda.

The third influential book was written by Tony Hsieh, the CEO of Zappos. *Delivering Happiness*[7] (2010) tells the story of one of the world's largest online shoe stores, which is now generally regard-ed as a leading pioneer in the development of enhanced custom-er experience. They first became famous as a result of a number of seemingly extreme decisions, which all worked to the benefit of the customers, but at times appeared detrimental to the com-pany. However, Tony is convinced that if you choose what's best for the customer, you will also be choosing what's best for the company. So just how extreme were these decisions? Here's an example. Imagine that you are looking for a specific pair of shoes but can't find them on Zappos.com. What do you do? You call the Zappos contact centre and they will search with you to find the shoes you want. First on Zappos.com, but if that doesn't work they will trawl the websites of at least five of their competitors to help you track down the shoes of your dreams. What's more, you have up to 365 days to return any shoes you buy from Zappos if you don't like them, and if the day you make a purchase happens to fall on 29 February, you have a full four years before you need to return them! Once Zappos had a customer on the phone for more than 5 hours. In most contact centres, this would be seen as a sign of failure. But not at Zappos. They proudly announced to the world in a press release: "We have just broken the world record for the longest telephone call with a client!" *Delivering Happiness* is an outstanding book. At first glance, it seems to be about customer experience, but it's actually about company culture, which is the third pillar you need to make customers happy. The Zappos story is a very popular story, and one that sent the debate about a customer-oriented company culture into hundreds of boardrooms all around the world.

A good process, measuring the right feedback and a culture that puts the customer first are still keys to success in customer experience today.

Process

Measurement

Culture

Are these the only three books to have contributed something significant to the customer experience debate? Of course not. This is just my personal choice based on the important nature of their contributions. Each of them added a core element for the creation of a truly fantastic customer experience. A good process (1), measuring the right feedback (2) and a culture that puts the customer first (3). These are three vital building blocks for anyone searching for customer satisfaction. Do the test for yourself. Think of a company you regularly do business with. You will soon see that they score well on each of these three aspects. A good process, listening carefully to feedback and a customer-oriented culture are *today's* keys to success in customer experience.

Social media pushes customer experience into the boardroom

Over the last decade, customer experience management has increased significantly in importance. The growth of social media has played a big part in this. Many companies found that the customer now had a voice, often for the very first time. Thanks to social media, customer feedback became visible – and not only for the company. Social media made great, less good and even downright bad customer experiences visible for other customers and for the traditional press. As a result of this external pressure, customer policy has evolved in a positive direction over the last ten years.

In the future, consumer pressure will continue to increase. The number of social media platforms, the level of their use and the impact they make are all still on the rise. At the time of writing (mid-2017), it is clear that Facebook is the most important player in this virtual world, with more than 2 billion active users. People with an iPhone spend 48% of their screen time on Facebook. They spend just 4% of their screen time on all their other apps put together. Android users spend a third of their screen time on Facebook.[8] In addition, Facebook also controls Instagram (600 million users), Messenger (1 billion users) and Whatsapp (1.2

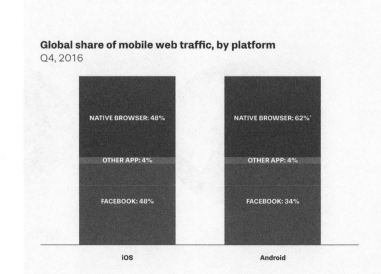

Global share of mobile web traffic, by platform
Q4, 2016

NATIVE BROWSER: 48%

OTHER APP: 4%

FACEBOOK: 48%

NATIVE BROWSER: 62%

OTHER APP: 4%

FACEBOOK: 34%

iOS

Android

billion).[9] The power of Facebook was confirmed with the launch of Instagram Stories at the end of 2016. At the start of that year, Mark Zuckerberg wanted to buy Snapchat, but his offer was rejected. Since then Facebook has copied just about every functionality of Snapchat and has rolled them out to its billions of users. When Instagram Stories was launched in October 2016, Snapchat had about 150 million active users. Nine months later (June 2017), this figure had risen to 170 million, but Instagram Stories already has 250 million. From 0 to 250 million active users in just nine months – that's the power of Facebook.

Little wonder that everybody is keeping a close eye on the approach and plans of Mark Zuckerberg at the moment. Not least because of the role Facebook played in the election of Donald Trump, which has finally woken up many senior policy makers and managers. The impact of social media on the perceptions of the average consumer or citizen is massive. Positive or negative customer stories on Facebook have a major impact on the public's perception of a company.

Alongside the dominance of Facebook, there are a number of other impactful online platforms. YouTube has a strong community of influencers. Snapchat remains popular with young people. Twitter is going through difficult times, but is still an important communication channel for public figures. LinkedIn continues to attract its own group of professional followers. Quite simply, social media channels have become a part of our everyday life, and we all know and feel their impact.

The customer relationship is the TOP priority for companies

The conclusions of the previous paragraph are not new. Early adopters already understood the impact of social media back in 2009. My book *The Conversation Manager* described that philosophy in detail. We are now almost ten years further on and the biggest resulting change is in the priority list of senior managers.

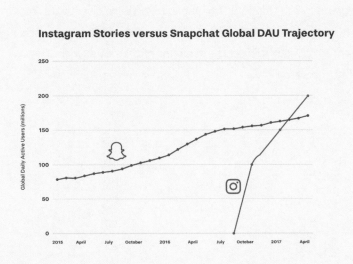

Instagram Stories versus Snapchat Global DAU Trajectory

89% of company leaders now see customer experience as their biggest differentiator.

In the past, company leaders were focused first and foremost on the development of innovative products and operational excellence. Today, customer satisfaction is the absolute number one priority – a point confirmed by almost every recent survey of top managers. 89% of company leaders now see customer experience as their biggest differentiator.[10] Product, price and communication are no longer the big winners. It is the way companies treat their customers that makes all the difference. More and more CEOs see customer strategy as an important part of their own direct responsibility.[11] Moreover, it is becoming ever more difficult to differentiate your company on the basis of product and price. The differentiator with the biggest potential in today's marketplace is customer experience. To me, this is a great evolution.

In short, we now live in a world where companies see customers as their highest priority. That's great, but let's be honest: despite this higher priority and the availability of better tools, it is still only a minority of companies that wholeheartedly embrace this new philosophy. 80% of companies think that they score well on customer satisfaction; yet unfortunately, only 8% of customers agree with them.[12] For example, United Airlines sees itself as being so customer-oriented that they made their motto: 'Fly the friendly skies'. Even so, the company has been known to drag passengers (sometimes violently) off their planes when they are overbooked, and it is this kind of horror story that makes headline news and shows to everyone that there is still plenty of room for improvement.

The star performers in customer satisfaction lead the way with an outstanding process, a good feedback dashboard and a fantastic culture in which the customer is central.

However, the question is whether or not these three building blocks will still be enough for brands to successfully navigate the turbulent years ahead. What new elements will be necessary in the following decade(s) to win the hearts, minds and business of consumers? In this book, I will search for the answer to this most crucial of conundrums: *where do companies need to invest if they want to be ready to meet the demands of their Customers The Day After Tomorrow?*

The third digital wave: Connectivity, Artificial Intelligence and Automation

We are currently at the start of the third digital wave. In the next few years we will all experience a new tidal wave of innovation, which means that in your business, you already need to be looking for your own particular answer to the above question.

The first digital wave was about making information more freely available via the internet. From the moment when Marc Andreessen introduced Netscape to the world in 1994, everyone suddenly had the ability to consult a massive range of information online via a user-friendly web browser. This was the beginning of the internet hype. Andreessen is still regarded as an icon in Silicon Valley. He founded a company that changed the world, but that company no longer exists after losing the

Phase 1
information

Phase 2
mobile and
communication

Phase 3
artificial
intelligence

1995   2007   2017

browser war with Microsoft. The day Microsoft Explorer was made freely available within Windows, the fate of Netscape was sealed. But it was thanks to the battle between Netscape and Microsoft that the internet became accessible and popular. Just a decade later, you could find almost anything online. There was even talk of an information overload! But nobody continued to question (as they once had) whether or not the internet was really necessary. Everyone realized that any company that wanted to survive would be forced to follow this new information highway.

The second digital wave began in 2007 with the launch of the iPhone. This was a device that changed the world. From that moment on, digital information started to become available anywhere and everywhere. Today, we all have the same single priority whenever we enter a new building: what's the Wi-Fi code?! Deprived of our external source of knowledge, we feel uncomfortable. For the current generation of teenagers, the internet is what electricity was for us: something indispensable that is always just there. My grandfather remembers watching how electricity was first installed in his village. He can recall what it was like to live in a world without electricity. Even when he was 80 years old, he was still amazed that electricity was available everywhere. Of course, my parents, myself and my children regard this as the most normal thing in the world. In fact, we rely on it. If the electricity is cut off for whatever reason, no matter how briefly, we cease to function. This is the way that anyone born after 1995 now regards the instant and universal availability of the communication and information network.

The biggest winner of the first digital wave is clear. It was Google. Google made online information accessible to everyone. The winners of the second digital wave were even clearer: Apple and Facebook. Apple 'only' has a 20% share in the smartphone market, but they net 80% of the profit from that market. I have already described the power of Facebook, but to put it into context, in 2016, Facebook and Google combined received some 20% of the global advertising budget.[13]

We are now at the start of the third digital wave. The key words for this phase are connectivity, automation and artificial intelligence. Ten years ago we could not have imagined how completely mobile technology would change our lives. But the impact of this third wave will be greater than the first two waves put together. The first two waves were about the optimization of communication. The third wave is about the automation of the world.

Artificial intelligence will have a double impact on relations with customers. On the one hand, numerous processes that take place behind the scenes will improve the output to customers. This will include better search results, better recommendations from e-commerce sites and a faster and more personal customer service. The customer will no doubt notice that performance output has improved, but he will not really understand what is going on. In this sense, artificial intelligence is an invisible technology that makes magical experiences for the customer possible.

On the other hand, the customer will also come into direct contact with new and tangible user interfaces. In 2017, we have already made acquaintance with the first 'bots'. Bots are programmes that to a large extent automate the company's conversation with the customer. Bots can answer customer questions in real time. They can also be used to help solve simple problems. (If you'd like to try out a bot, just find my Facebook page and press the Facebook Messenger button. You'll get to meet my bot, and discover the strengths and weaknesses for the technology.) But that's just the start. Within a few years, conversations with bots will be part of all our daily lives. In a business context, artificial intelligence facilitates the development of man-machine interfaces that will guide and assist customers through each phase of the customer journey.

The main driver of this third digital wave is data. Artificial intelligence feeds itself with data. Without data, automation is not possible. The rapid growth in the use of data-collecting devices in both our personal and professional lives has made an important contribution in this respect. In 2017, each consumer has on average four connected devices (smartphone, smartwatch, tablet, Nest thermostat, etc.).[14] By 2020, it is estimated that this number will have risen to seven or eight. This will mean a total of some 31 billion connected devices around the planet.[15] This evolution

The main driver of this third digital wave is data.

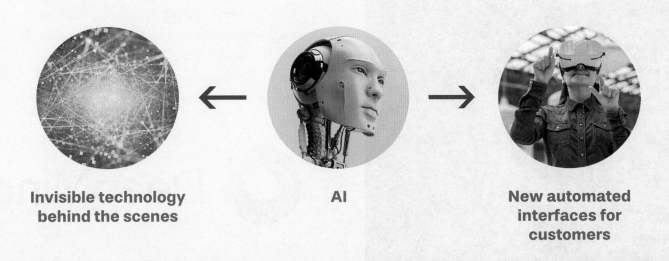

Invisible technology behind the scenes   **AI**   **New automated interfaces for customers**

will unquestionably change the position of us humans in the digital world. During the first two digital waves, people looked at information. We consumed data. During the third digital wave we will live amongst data. We will be surrounded by it, and we will become the largest source of further data creation.

The opening shot? DeepMind beats the Go world champion

The third digital wave started in March 2016, when Google Deep-Mind beat the world's best Go player. DeepMind is a specialized AI and machine learning department within Alphabet (Google). DeepMind was set up in 2010 by Demis Hassabis, Shane Legg and Mustafa Suleyman. The founders succeeded in teaching the DeepMind computer to play games via a neural network. This form of machine learning is comparable with the human

Demis Hassabis
Founder and CEO of DeepMind

learning process. The computer tests out various strategies and investigates which of them will result in the highest score. Once the computer knows which strategy will give the best outcome, it can implement it to perfection time after time, eventually crushing the best human high score. In January 2014, Google bought DeepMind for 500 million dollars[16], and since then the machine has gone through 'life' as Google DeepMind.

In 2016, this impressive subsidiary of the Google empire challenged the world champion of Go to a duel. Man played machine five times over the course of a weekend. The machine won 4-1. In the following months, DeepMind played another 50 duels with Go players. The score was easy to remember: 50-0.[17] Game over for the humans! Many AI scientists have agreed for a long time that once a computer is capable of playing Go, this represents a tipping point in the evolution of artificial intelligence. However, most of the experts predicted that this would only happen between 2025 and 2030, so we are ten years ahead of schedule! Back in 1997, an earlier generation of scientists was predicting that this couldn't possibly happen until the year 2100[18], so perhaps we are actually more than 80 years ahead of schedule...

Many people ask about the difference between a computer that can play chess well and a computer that can play Go well. Deep Blue, the supercomputer of IBM, beat the chess grandmaster Gary Kasparov already in 1995. But the key difference is in the number of possible combinations in the game. Go is the most complex board game in the world. There are 10 to the 170th power (10^{170}) possible combinations of moves in Go, whereas in chess, the number of combinations is much more limited. This means that all the possible combinations in a game of chess can be pre-programmed, so all you need is a fast computer to make the right choice from all these combinations. IBM's Deep Blue was just the fastest computer of its kind in 1995. But the number of combinations in Go is so immensely large that it is impossible for humans to pre-programme them. The day that a computer can play Go to a high standard, you know that it has taught itself how to do it.

Game over for humans!

During an interview after the tournament, the losing finalist explained that the computer made moves he had never seen any human player make. As a result, the human champion was repeatedly surprised by the computer's inventiveness in playing the game. DeepMind does not imitate; DeepMind creates.

From Go to poker to dogfights to business impact

Since that spectacular day back in March 2016, we have seen reports about the rapid evolution of artificial intelligence on an almost daily basis. It was the beginning of a renaissance for AI. The start of a new spring. Scientists have known since the 1940s how artificial intelligence works. The theory is not new, but it is only now that we have computers powerful enough to put the theory into practice. But don't get carried away: this is just the first day of a very early spring.

Even so, in recent months we have seen the power and reputation of AI increase still further. Smart computers do more than just play Go. They play poker as well – and they can beat the best players in the world. Why? Because a computer never gets tired and doesn't have any inconvenient emotions – both of which are big plus points when you are locked in a gruelling poker session. The poor humans never stood a chance.[19] Game over! For its next challenge, artificial intelligence took on the best pilots in the American army in a simulated dogfight. The result? What do you expect? Game over![20] And I could go on for a while. There is even a golf robot that can hit a hole-in-one every time – something that Tiger Woods has never achieved.[21] Game over! Game over! Game over!

AI is evolving at lightning speed. The power of DeepMind now goes far beyond the playing of games. For example, Google have used the computer to cut the cost of their own data centre. If DeepMind is operating, these costs fall by 42%.[22] The computer traces and removes all the imperfections from the system and optimizes performance. DeepMind's next objective is to cut the total energy bill in the UK by 10%.[23] How? Because it is widely expected that DeepMind can manage the supply and demand of energy more efficiently than the existing systems. This would be a truly spectacular achievement: reducing a nation's energy bill by a tenth without any investment in new infrastructure. It's all done by smart software.

In this way, we can see the impact of artificial intelligence on our daily lives steadily increasing. It began with a chess computer and has now reached the level of optimizing a nation's basic economic infrastructure. And I repeat: we are still only in the embryonic phase of AI.

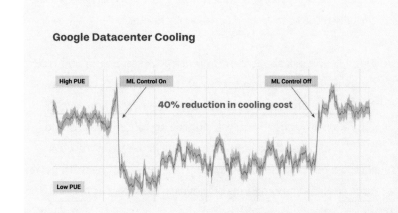

From stupid to smart in five years time

The evolution in drones is equally spectacular. A few years ago drones were very expensive, difficult to operate and stupid. In our home, several of them were flown into our neighbour's trees! This type of 'old' drone was heavily dependent on the skill of the pilot. In my case, that skill was fairly limited. However, the drone industry has made huge strides forward during the past five years.

In May 2015, a video was posted on the Kickstarter crowdfunding platform that immediately attracted thousands of views. The video announced the launch of a new drone: Lilly. Drone Lilly amazed the world. All you need to do is throw it (her?) into the air. After that, Lilly just follows you around during your sporting adventures. And when you have finished for the day, Lilly simply lands on your hand. It doesn't matter whether you are skiing downhill in the Alps or surfing the breakers off Hawaii: Lilly will film it all. It's a great way to impress your friends – or give them a good laugh. Thousands of the new drones were ordered on the basis of the video alone, before the device was even in production. Sadly, none of these enthusiastic customers ever got to see their Lilly. In October 2016, I visited the company that planned to make them. It was cool to see their R&D unit, but you could feel the uncertainty. The designers felt that they weren't making enough progress with the necessary improvements, and at the start of 2017, the company went bust. Drone Lilly was smart, but not smart enough. Lilly followed the owner, but if the owner ran under a tree, Lilly smashed into it. In today's market, consumers

want self-steering drones.

Skydio is a start-up trying to develop this kind of fully autonomous drone. In 2016, the CTO of Skydio was Frank Deallaert, a Belgian professor. Frank has wide experience in the world of self-driving cars and artificial intelligence. "But self-driving cars are so very 2015," he says. Allowing drones to fly autonomously is much more complex than letting cars drive on their own. Even so, the Skydio drones don't crash into anything: it's almost as if they have eyes. The self-steering drone is a fact. In 2012, I crashed my dumb drone into a tree. Five years later, the drones can 'see' the tree and avoid it. From stupid to smart in five years time. Not bad.

Drones are just one example. When Google launched their PR video for the first self-driving car back in 2011, many people thought that it was some kind of stunt. The majority of the population had no idea that technology had already advanced so far and so fast. Six years later, in 2017, several countries

are already preparing for the new era of the driverless car. At the start of the year, Latvia approved a law that would allow self-driving cars on its roads.[24] In May 2017, South Korea did the same.[25] At the end of 2016, Uber began operating with driverless cars on the streets of San Francisco and other American cities. From fiction to reality in just six years. Again, not bad. And who knows where we will be in another six years...

This evolution from stupid to smart will continue in the years ahead. In fact, almost every aspect of our daily lives will become smart. Clothing will be fitted with RFID chips, which will not only help stores to better monitor and protect their stock, but also help recognize their customers more easily. Household devices will have chips installed to optimize performance and consumption. Ordering coffee or picking it up from the local supermarket will be a thing of the past. Your coffee machine will order it for you and it will be delivered to your front door, probably by drone. Rubbish bins in city centres will also have a chip, so that they can be emptied before they get full.

But first prize in the digitalization stakes goes to Palo Alto, the most digital city in America, located in the heart of Silicon Valley. There, each individual tree has its own chip and its own data profile. If something happens to the tree, the city authorities know it immediately. What's more, all this data is made available online. If we want, we can all check up on the status of the trees in Palo Alto. So, if even the trees in a small American town can get smart, just think what this kind of technology could do for your company or industry... If you want to know more about the Palo Alto vision, take a look at my interview with Jonathan Reichental, CIO in Palo Alto, on *www.youtube.com/stevenvanbelleghem*.

We are reaching the point of convergence

All the stars are aligned for the third digital wave to unleash its full force upon us. Many technologies that were no more than a

from dumb to smart

hype just a few years ago are now approaching a more mature phase. Scientists have been talking for years about promising technologies like the Internet of Things, virtual reality and augmented reality, but ordinary consumers are increasingly discovering that these technologies can have a positive daily impact on their lives.

When the hype of Pokémon Go exploded in the summer of 2016, this was the first real mass adoption of an augmented reality application. Some people thought it was the most ridiculous game ever, but the huge majority were hooked from day one. In just four weeks, more than half a billion people were hunting Pokémons all over the world. If the interface is easy enough, consumers are usually ready to give most things a try. And Pokémon Go is augmented reality in its simplest form. Future applications will be much more impressive. In mid-2017, Mark Zuckerberg launched his virtual reality platform. The aim was to acquaint more people with this interface which allows you to enter a new world where you are not physically present via a computer.

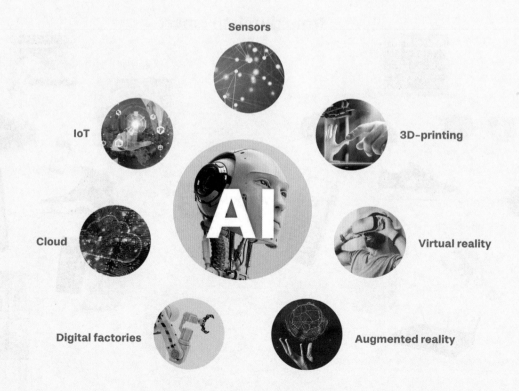

The Internet of Things is also making rapid progress. More and more cities are installing sensors in their streets to optimize their service provision. A growing number of manufacturers are putting chips into their domestic appliances to ensure that they can be repaired before they ever break down or wear out. The Internet of Things, VR and AR are just a few of the examples of technologies that have made the transition from hype to everyday reality. And to these you can add 3D printing, digital factories, the cloud and many others.

We are approaching a point of convergence. Different technologies are becoming mature at the same moment and are strengthening each other. This convergence will increase the speed at which new technologies and applications are made available to

AI is at the centre of this (r)evolution, with the new applications revolving around it. It's like a solar system in which AI is the sun and the other technologies are the planets that are only able to exist because of the sun.

the public. Just imagine: a shop has sensors, the clothes of the customer also have sensors, the customer has a smartphone and the shop has smart mirrors that allow customers to try on new virtual outfits. This combination of technologies can provide a highly personalized shopping experience. The shop will immediately be able to recognize the individual customer and pass information about him/her to its sales staff. On the basis of this information, the staff can then offer the customer tailor-made advice. If the customer wants to try on a new pair of trousers but the shop doesn't have the colour he/she wants in stock, the virtual mirror can help. If the mirror confirms that this is the right colour, it will order the trousers from another store and arrange for their delivery to the customer's home the very next day. It is important to remember that it is not just one specific technology that makes this experience possible. It is the combination of different technologies that is so powerful, and it is reaching the point of convergence that is necessary to take service to the next level.

In the third digital wave, we will experience the combination of artificial intelligence and the convergence of many new technologies. AI is at the centre of this (r)evolution, with the new applications revolving around it. It's like a solar system in which AI is the sun and the other technologies are the planets that are only able to exist because of the sun. But the sun's light is of little value without the planets orbiting around it. The power is in the convergence.

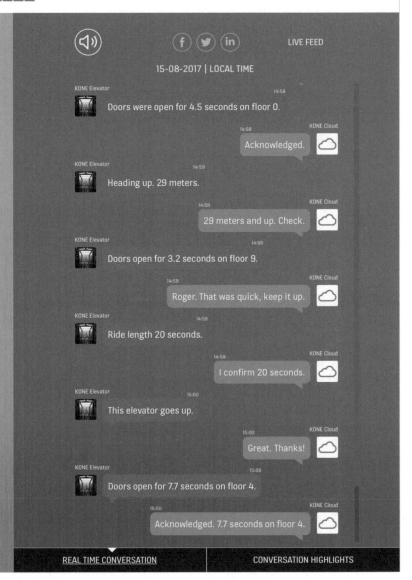

The talking Kone lifts

Kone is a Finnish company that is active in the elevator market. For some people, the idea of getting trapped in a lift is one of their greatest fears. I even get a little nervous myself. When my children jump up and down in a lift, my immediate reaction is "DON'T: the thing might jam!" Kone wants to develop a perfect passenger experience by making sure that its lifts never get stuck. The idea is that potential problems can be solved before they become real ones, and to make this possible they have made clever use of digital convergence.

The lifts are fitted with sensors that register all movement and measure all relevant environmental factors. There is also an artificial intelligence interface that analyzes all of the resulting data. Effectively, it is almost as though the lifts are able to talk with each other and with the central operating computer. This has been visualized in a brilliant manner on the Kone website. Via the online interface, you can quite literally follow the conversations between the lifts and the AI interface. Lift A suddenly says: "The temperature in my lift is much higher than average. Is this a normal situation?" The AI interface checks its data briefly and answers: "This is not a problem. It is currently 28°C outside. This explains the high temperature in your lift." A short time later, lift B questions the accuracy of its finishing position when it reaches the ground floor. This time the AI interface concludes that the lift

does indeed stop a few millimetres lower than it should and so decides to call in some human assistance. It sends a message to a Kone technician that lift B requires urgent maintenance – and, in this way, the problem is repaired before it becomes really serious.

This is yet another instance where the effectiveness of the experience or system is based on the power created through the convergence of different technologies: the sensors, the automatic data analysis, the AI interface and the communication interface between man and machine.

ISS uses algorithms for better and more efficient service

The Danish company ISS is one of the largest facility management companies in the world. They have more than 500,000 people on their payroll. The majority of them are employed on the premises of ISS customers, where their tasks include cleaning office buildings and maintaining food-and-drink machines.

In Denmark, ISS has started an experiment. They have placed sensors in various office premises, aiming to bring the buildings to life. Amongst other things, they measure which meeting rooms, toilets, etc. are underused or overused, and they know how early and how late activity in parts of the building starts and finishes. All this information is then provided to the customers, so that they can know exactly what is happening in their buildings and perhaps make better use of them.

Of course, ISS also make use of the data themselves to work in a more targeted manner. Via the sensors, they know when the toilets need to be cleaned. In the past, that might have happened at regular intervals every few hours, but now it happens on the basis of the information from the sensors. It is almost as if the toilet 'asks' its human partner to be cleaned. In the past, the ISS technicians came either too early or too late to refill the coffee machines. Now they come at exactly the right time. Thanks to the data analysis and the algorithms, ISS has improved its customer service and works more efficiently. Win-win.

The manner in which customers take decisions in the future will also be increasingly influenced by algorithms.

Algorithms direct decisions

The third phase of digitalization is about artificial intelligence, automation and connectivity. Data is the raw material of this phase. The second phase of digitalization already created large amounts of data, but the third phase will absorb and expand this data to automate the world. The more data that becomes available, the greater the number of elements in the customer journey that will be influenced by AI.

In the examples of Kone and ISS, algorithms direct the decisions that need to be made during the process. The Kone lifts decide amongst themselves when they need human assistance. The toilets and coffee machines do much the same for ISS. In other words, the algorithm takes an active part in the process. According to Wikipedia, an algorithm is a finite series of instructions that precisely define a sequence of operations to lead from a given starting point to a given objective. Algorithms make use of a series of steps that are either repeated (iteration) or require decisions to be taken (logic or comparison) in order to complete the task. For example, simple algorithms can solve simple mathematical problems. To calculate the average of two numbers, the algorithm is: ((number 1 + number 2) divided by 2). If you then input two numbers, the algorithm will automatically work out their average. An Excel spreadsheet is an example of a table where many algorithms are used to automate calculations.

As more and more data becomes available and more and more processes become capable of rationalization, the impact of algorithms will increase.

The manner in which customers take decisions in the future will also be increasingly influenced by algorithms. The necessary data is already available for many aspects of daily life. Our digital footprint (agenda, communication, mobility, etc.) makes it possible for algorithms to simplify and facilitate many of our day-to-day tasks. Over the course of the last 20 years, consumers have been gradually 'trained' to allow algorithms to participate in their decision-making. Think back to the first time you bought something from Amazon. I remember how amazed I was when I bought a book that I immediately received recommendations for other books I might like to buy. This was something that had never happened to me in a bookstore. Since then, I have bought dozens of books based on Amazon recommendation. This means that on each occasion my purchasing decision was based on input from an algorithm. The same is true of Netflix. Whenever you watch a series or film suggested to you by Netflix, you are responding to an algorithmic calculation. In the near future, there will be smart packaging in the shops to tell you whether or not the fruit you want to buy is the right level of ripeness you like. You no longer need to act on your gut feeling; the algorithm will make the decision for you.

These are just a few practical examples of how algorithms can help us in our daily lives, but their real impact will be much greater and more widespread. 5% of married people in the US say their relationships began online, but as many as one in three of the most recent marriages started on the internet.[26] Finding the love of your life is no longer something you do at a party or in a pub. You do it at home in front of your computer. Algorithms will search for your perfect match, so that you increase your chance of a successful relationship.

Algorithms are also taking more and more decisions in the field of health. There are already vending machines where you can only buy a bar of chocolate if you have already walked your recommended 10,000 steps that day. The machine is linked to the data in your smartphone and makes a decision based on this input. This may be one of the moments when many of us will curse algorithms, but at a more serious level they can have a crucial impact in the healthcare sector. The supercomputer Watson has already proved its added value in making diagnoses. When assessing patients with potential lung cancer, the number of correct diagnoses increases from 50% to 90% when Watson is involved in the process.[27]

But perhaps one of the most powerful examples is the case of Angelina Jolie. Back in 2013, she wrote a breathtaking article for *The New York Times*: 'My medical choice'.[28] Data analysis had shown that she had an 87% chance of developing an aggressive form of breast cancer. To deprive the disease of its opportunity to develop, Angelina decided to undergo preventative surgery. Naturally, this was a brave and deeply emotional decision, almost certainly the most difficult in her life – but it was one that she took on the basis of input from an algorithm.

If people are capable of taking such traumatic personal decisions on the basis of data analyses and algorithms, it is easy to imagine how inclined we might be to make our daily purchasing decisions based on the recommendations of smart computers. We are moving towards a world where algorithms will become the decision-maker for (part of) our purchases and life choices. Some people might find this analysis unsettling. The idea that a machine might know better than we do is something not many of us want to hear, but it is the reality. Researchers at Cambridge University have discovered that Facebook scores better in analyzing your personality than your family and friends.[29] Even more remarkable, the Facebook algorithm knows the user better than the user knows him- or herself. After 70 interactions on Facebook, Facebook already knows you better than your friends. After 150 interactions, Facebook knows you better than your family. After 300 interactions, Facebook knows you better than your partner... In many cases, we are not aware of certain aspects of our personality, and as a result we may sometimes make the wrong choices in our lives. So, for many things, the added value of advice from an impartial machine can be a big help.

A new customer journey

The customer journey has been evolving for years. During the past two decades, the way in which consumers reach their decisions has been changing. In pre-sales, sales and after sales, things are no longer what they were.

During the first digital wave, the customer journey was a kind of tunnel. Consumers found information about their planned purchase on maybe four or five websites online. After that, the purchasing process moved into the offline world, where they perhaps visited two or three suppliers to make comparisons. These offline investigations were the key determining factor in the final purchasing decision.

The second wave saw the advent of digital word-of-mouth. Sites like TripAdvisor made a breakthrough, while the positive or negative comments on Facebook and Twitter became an influential factor in customer choice.

During the third phase, word-of-mouth will remain important, but there will also be a huge increase in the importance of personalized recommendations made by algorithms. Their input in decision-making will increase dramatically, so that our purchases become more rational. Decisions based on feedback from other customers or on your own intuition are essentially emotional decisions, which can sometimes lead to the wrong choice. Accepting the purchasing suggestions of a machine based on facts is a much more reasoned – and reasonable – approach.

In the third digital wave, the role of e-commerce will increase significantly. Today, half of consumers still have their doubts about online purchases.[30] They are worried about their data, about the quality of the delivery and about the safety of the transaction. Even so, in the next few years more and more people will switch to e-commerce. In the United States in 2017, the growing power of this sales channel was already evident in the streetscape of many American cities: by the middle of the year, no fewer than 3,500 major retail outlets had closed their doors.[31] The classic American shopping malls are getting emptier and emptier.

The impact of e-commerce is already huge. Companies like Alibaba and Amazon continue to develop their dynamic business models that bind customers like never before. Amazon invests astronomical sums in virtual assistants. Their Echo product range is the clear leader in this new market. Alexa is Echo's virtual assistant. Alexa helps people with many different practical matters in their lives. By mid-2017, more than 10 million American families have an Amazon Echo in their homes.[32] One in three of them purchases goods and services by giving their orders verbally to Alexa.[33] What's more, the major online players are also looking for ways to leave a strong footprint in the physical world. Online remains their main platform, but they can supplement their online presence with premises at strategic locations. This idea became clear to all when Amazon purchased the retailer Whole Foods in June 2017. Amazon didn't just buy their stores – they were more interested in their strategic localities.[34]

It is not only pre-sales and sales that will evolve during the third digital wave. After sales will also discover new interfaces. In the first and second digital waves, the telephone continued

	First digital wave: information	Second digital wave: communication and mobility	Third digital wave: automation, connectivity and AI
Most important customer information source in purchasing process	Website company + offline sales conversation	Word-of-mouth of other customer + website information	Word-of-mouth + algorithms
What determines the final choice	Emotion	Emotion	Reason – algorithm
Purchase channel	Offline still the main channel, e-commerce very limited	E-commerce gets a huge boost, offline falls dramatically	E-commerce large, sales via virtual assistants
Most important customer service channel	Telephone, email	Telephone, email and increasingly social media	Bots in combination with human interface
Best price-quality advertising model	Google Adwords	Facebook promo-messages	Partnerships with personal virtual assistants

to be the most important service channel for customers. At one point during the second wave, it seemed that social media was likely to take off in after sales, but the volume of tweets and Facebook messages eventually stagnated at a level that was still much lower than the number of telephone requests for help. The reason for this is the relative slowness of social media. People sometimes moan about waiting times on the phone. But even if you have to wait 15 minutes, this is still quicker than a Facebook message, which often only arrives after an hour. In The Day After Tomorrow, people will expect real time feedback. They are tired of waiting: they want their answer, and they want it now! This will only be possible with the help of computers, and bots are destined to play an important role in solving this issue. Bots are artificial intelligence interfaces that can communicate automatically with customers via Facebook Messenger and other chat platforms. Bots are available 24/7 and can assist customers in real time. Today, bots are still too limited to answer all questions. But the combination of bot + human interface is a powerful team. In a later phase, bots will undoubtedly be able to answer more complex questions, so that the role of the human interface will steadily decrease. Gartner predicts that by 2020 more than 80% of customer service interactions will take place via AI tools.[35]

Finally, the communication mix will also change. The evolution from offline advertising to online advertising has been ongoing for some time. Gary Vaynerchuck, the American social media guru, has a brilliant philosophy for using online publicity. He says that you should always start advertising early on a new platform. In that way, you get maximum attention for the lowest cost. Once everyone starts using the platform, prices rocket and your advert gets lost amongst all the rest. People who were smart enough to advertise with Google Adwords in the 1990s got real value for their money. At that time, the price for Adwords was still relatively low and, because the number of companies using the platform was also low, the advertising impact was correspondingly high. Adwords still works today, but the prices are now much higher than 20 years ago. During the second digital wave, advertising on Facebook was the new big thing. In the United States, almost everyone did it (and most still do). Companies large and small recognized the importance of a strong presence on the most dominant social network. This has inevitably led to a steep increase in prices, the effects of which remain to be seen. In Europe, we are still a few years behind on the US, so that advertising on Facebook is still highly relevant. During the third digital wave, Facebook posts and Google Adwords will continue to be important, but potential users are going to need a serious advertising budget to compete.

An example of a channel that is yet to be fully exploited is communication via the virtual personal assistant. The trick to this is to make sure that the Amazon, Google and Apple bots find and connect with your own company bot. If someone is looking for new insurance and asks for help from a virtual assistant, it is crucial that the assistant's bot proposes your insurance products to the potential customer. For example, Uber works closely with Echo. Every time a consumer asks for a taxi, Uber is automatically chosen. Just Eat, a food delivery company in the UK, also has a partnership with Amazon, so that every meal ordered via Echo is delivered by Just Eat. Domino's Pizza has the same deal in the United States. This type of early partnership currently offers outstanding advertising value for money.

Process — Measuring — Culture is no longer enough

AI

Process

Culture

Measurement

Companies that score strongly with customers in today's marketplace stand out because of their efficient processes, good feedback instruments and excellent customer-based culture. These three elements are currently enough to make your company a customer-oriented company. But will they be enough to keep you customer-oriented in The Day After Tomorrow?

No, they will not. The third digital wave makes it imperative for companies to add a fourth element: artificial intelligence and automation. Without strong investment in these new technologies it will be very difficult to meet the future expectations of your customers.

In the rest of my book, I will examine what steps you need to take to prepare yourself for customer relations in The Day After

Tomorrow. In the first part, I will discuss the strategic impact of The Day After Tomorrow. What mindset will you need to succeed? That is the most important question. In the second part, I will look at the key axes of investment, so that you can start preparing for the future today. In part three, I will outline the consequences for the customer relationship in the years and decades ahead. This includes a guest chapter by Peter Hinssen about the new organizational model that will be necessary to make a successful transition. Finally, I round off the book with some thoughts about the ethical consequences of the evolution of AI. Ending on a philosophical note, you might say.

I hope you enjoy the rest of my book. *Customers The Day After Tomorrow* is a motivating story for every manager and entrepreneur who wishes to embrace the changes that are inevitably coming and wants to start taking concrete steps in response. It would be foolish to delay. The Day After Tomorrow starts NOW.

THE
DAY
AFTER
TOMORROW
MINDSET

CHAPTER 2

FROM MOBILE FIRST TO AI FIRST

Faster adoption and higher impact

When the internet first came into our lives, most people had to think twice about whether or not they wanted to incur the extra monthly expense of a subscription to an internet service provider. In the beginning, it was only the technology freaks who were prepared to pay for internet access. The masses followed later.

When the iPhone was introduced (and the wave of other smartphones that followed), once again there was a classic adoption curve. First the dedicated fans, then the rest of the world. After all, buying a smartphone was quite a big investment, so most people first wanted to see how things would pan out. In fact, the reaction to the launch of the smartphone from the majority of consumers was that they would never buy such a device, but of course, things turned out differently. The reality is that if the relevance is great enough, the masses will always follow the technology lovers in a later phase.

The use of artificial intelligence will become part of our daily lives more quickly than any previous technology. Why? Artificial intelligence has a sublime distribution channel: our smartphone. During the first two digital waves, the consumer had to make a purchase decision before the technology became part of everyone's everyday life. But artificial intelligence is already in our smartphone. The Facebook app uses artificial intelligence every second to decide which updates we see. If you use a smart navigation tool in the car, you are using AI. It is already here. In the near future, almost every product we buy will contain smart applications that are driven by AI. As a consumer, you no longer need to buy 'something special' to make use of AI. Of course, you can always buy extra add-ons like Google Home, but you don't need to: without it, you can still use Google's AI services.

Because of this fast adoption curve, it is impossible for companies to say: 'We're not playing'. When the internet exploded onto the scene, many business leaders thought the hype would soon pass. They didn't see the use of investing in a website. When the iPhone arrived, many in the business world quickly concluded that the use of apps was again being over-hyped. Investing in mobile technology was therefore not a priority. Sadly, even today you can still find commercial websites that haven't been adjusted to mobile browsing. It is a pity, but not a disaster. Even in today's market, if your company has no website and no mobile app it is certainly a missed opportunity, but you are unlikely to go bust as

Artificial intelligence has a sublime distribution channel: our smartphone.

a result. In most cases, it simply means missing out on new ways to communicate to and engage with your customers.

But it is different with artificial intelligence. Not only will artificial intelligence be adopted faster, it will also have a bigger impact on customer relations than both the previous waves of digital. Artificial intelligence will speed up and improve user experience. In short, AI is going to be at the heart of all customer experience in the future. This time it's not just about optimizing communication; it's about revolutionizing the core operations of your business. Both behind the scenes and in front of the customer, automation will raise service levels to previously unseen heights. Quite simply, if you don't play, you can't win.

Invisible technology leads to magical experiences

When we think about artificial intelligence, many people will think of the science fiction movies in which robots and humans are scarcely distinguishable. In our mind's eye, we see all different kinds of walking-talking machines and gadgets. And believe me, these things are on the way.

In business, however, companies adopting the AI-first mindset will be less visible than the ones who moved to a mobile-first mindset. Mobile-first resulted in apps and responsive websites appearing, meaning that not only every customer but also every competitor could immediately see what kind of mobile strategy a company was adopting. It is going to be a very different story in the AI-first world. Artificial intelligence is an invisible technology. This time, customers and competitors will not see what is going on. The visible robots and gadgets are just the tip of the iceberg – the real power is hidden beneath the surface.

Invisible technology provides magical experiences for consumers. Uber is perhaps the best example. The most impressive thing about an Uber ride comes right at the end. You thank the driver, you step out of the car, and before you know it you've already paid! You don't know how. And you don't know how much. Everything has been settled automatically. It is invisible technology creating a magical experience.

One of my favourite apps is Magisto. When we go on holiday, I always make Magisto movies so that the rest of the family can also share our adventures. Magisto is a brilliant interface to edit and compile your photos and videos in a really simple and fun way. When I installed Magisto for the first time, I received an email from them the very same evening. The subject line read: 'Enjoy this video about the best day of your year'. Of course, I was curious and so I clicked on the video. The result was incredibly impressive. It was a video of our family during our holiday in Disneyworld. I saw my children with Disney characters. I saw myself

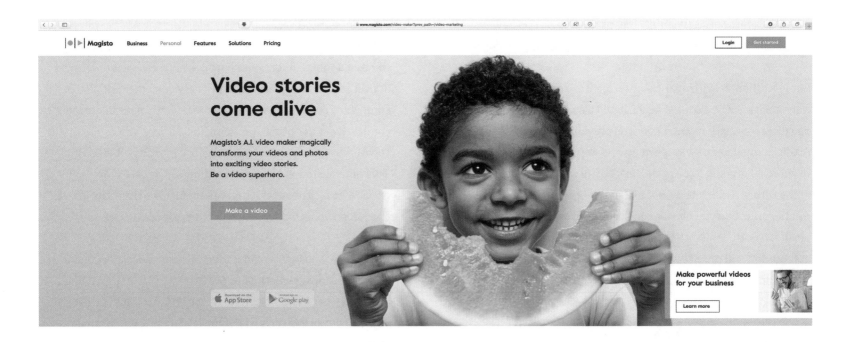

Video stories come alive

Magisto's A.I. video maker magically transforms your videos and photos into exciting video stories.
Be a video superhero.

Make a video

App Store   Google play

Make powerful videos for your business

Learn more

Magically transform your videos and photos

Magisto is the fastest way to turn your everyday videos and photos into inspired video stories and the easiest way to share them everywhere. It's not *actually* magic, its Magisto.

and my wife Evi enjoying the atmosphere in the different parks. The accompanying music was perfect. I was sold immediately and since then I have used the app regularly.

But I still couldn't understand how they did it. How can an almost free app assess what my 'best day of the year' might be? How could the app know who the Disney figures are? Who my children are? The video was perfect. There wasn't a single

photo I didn't love. I was blown away. It was only later that I discovered how the system works. It's all done using a simple algorithm. For this first film, Magisto identifies and uses the point when you took the most photos in the shortest time. They probably know from their research that this is a good predictor of enthusiasm – and they are usually right. With a simple algorithm, they create a magical moment thanks to invisible technology.

Artificial intelligence is not the only technology that is invisible. Various other technologies in which digital meets the outside world are also hidden from view. Think of sensors. Think of Wi-Fi. Think of robots that work behind the scenes. Think of data analyses. All these elements can contribute to a magical customer experience, without anyone knowing how they really work.

When I recently took a group on an innovation visit to Singapore, we were all impressed by the efficiency of their airport. We were off the plane quite quickly. Passing through customs control also went smoothly. Ten minutes later, we arrived at the luggage carousel, and to our amazement our luggage was already waiting for us. This was a wow-experience! At the time, we didn't stop to think about the operational processes that made this possible. We just said: "What a pity it isn't like this everywhere."

Invisible technology provides magical experiences for consumers.

A few days later we visited Singtel, the largest telecoms company in the region. Singtel is *the* telecoms operator in Singapore. Although Singapore only has a population of 5.5 million, Singtel has more than 500 million customers. They are market leader in large parts of Asia and Oceania. During our tour of their offices, they explained how the airport is able to work so efficiently. Using data analysis based on input from smartphone sensors and

Invisible technologies

 Data analytics

 Sensors collecting data

 Behind-the-scenes robots

 Machine learning

 WiFi everywhere

security cameras, they monitor which passengers are moving most quickly toward the carousel. This analysis is then relayed to the baggage section, who make sure that the luggage of the quickest passengers is put on the carousel first. They even have self-propelled robots to speed up the process. And it's all done with invisible technology that results in an outstanding customer experience.

Wi-Fi is a fine instance of invisible technology. Tech company Radiomaze discovered that Wi-Fi signals reflect off water. People are made up of 90% water. Combining these two facts allowed the company to develop a new product. From now on, every home with Wi-Fi can add a new alarm function without the need for extra hardware. If the home owners are away and someone reflects the Wi-fF signal, it means there is a burglar in their house! The system also has additional built-in safety functions. For example, Wi-Fi can 'see' if someone has fallen. If this person stays still for too long, it is possible to call the emergency services automatically. Radiomaze is also working on a digital lock that they can open at a distance when the emergency services arrive.

Automation of everyday life

Faster than real time service

Hyper-personalization

IMPACT ON USERS

INVISIBLE FOR USERS

Data analytics

Sensors collecting data

Behind-the-scenes robots

Machine learning

WiFi everywhere

The CEO of Radiomaze told me that their most frequently asked question is: "I have a dog. Will your system work in my house?" Their answer is brilliant. "If your dog is less than 50 centimetres tall, yes, our system will work. If your dog is more than 50 centimetres tall, you don't need the system!" Radiomaze integrates Wi-Fi signals and data analysis to create invisible technology.

In each of these examples, AI analysis is the invisible driver behind the customer outcome. And this AI is driven by the hidden technology that surrounds it. Magical customer experience is the perfect output of the AI-first mindset. It leads to greater efficiency, speed, personalization and ease of use, both for the customer and for companies. For companies, AI first offers a huge boost in efficiency. For the customer, it offers a much better user experience, without understanding or even being aware of the technology that makes it possible.

The AI-first mindset

Until just a few years ago, most companies were still working with a digital-first mindset. Facebook's recent history has shown the world that this is no longer enough. When Facebook was launched on the stock market in 2012, its shares were hammered because the company had no mobile strategy. At the moment of the launch, Facebook had no form of income from mobile adver-

tising. The stock market gurus even predicted that this might mean the end for Facebook. Mark Zuckerberg was forced to make a drastic choice – and he decided that the company had to switch to a mobile-first mindset. All improvements and innovations had to be developed from that perspective. New tools that only worked in a desktop environment were immediately vetoed by the CEO.

Within three years, more than half of Facebook's turnover came from mobile advertisements. In 2017, no less than 84% of their revenue now comes from this source.[36] During the same period, the share price has risen from 18 dollars to 150 dollars.[37]

This remarkable comeback inspired many other companies to also adopt a mobile-first mindset. Other technology companies followed the Facebook example, and many financial organizations followed suit. Most banks quickly realized that the number of mobile customer transactions was far higher than the number on their online banking modules. And, as far as the customers were concerned, the perception of banks was largely based on the quality of their mobile banking solutions.

In the meantime, Facebook has switched its mobile-first mindset to an AI-first approach. Other major technology companies like Microsoft, Google, Amazon, Tencent and Baidu are doing the same. The top management at Google can only see a future for their company if they can lead the way in AI.

Aside from the tech-giants, today there are thousands of small start-ups trying to grab their share of the AI market. This means that all the world's top AI talent is currently either working for one of the giants, or have their own company, or are carrying out fundamental AI research in the world of academia. This is perhaps the greatest challenge facing all other companies. The scarcest resource in the AI world is AI talent. As a result, the companies without the expertise will often collaborate with the various

From digital first to mobile first.
From Mobile first to **AI first**

Digital → **Mobile** → **AI**

players in the AI world, rather than trying to do everything themselves in-house – especially since most things connected with AI are still fairly expensive. In the future, however, there will be a lot more 'off the shelf' technology available, so that even smaller companies can quickly jump on board the AI train. The technology will become cheaper and more accessible for everyone.

This combination of fast adoption, high impact on customer experience and the focus of technology companies on AI means that other companies have no choice but to adopt the same focus.

The shift from mobile-first to AI-first is the next big step in the never-ending challenge of meeting customer expectations. The majority of top managers already understand this. According to

a recent survey by the consulting company PWC[38], 72% of CEOs regard AI competencies as the most important asset of a company. But a worldwide study by McKinsey revealed that just 20% of large companies are currently investing in AI. What's more, these investments are not equally distributed in geographical terms. The United States lead the way with 66% of all AI investment, followed by China. At this stage, Europe is still some way behind.[39]

AI is necessary for governments to meet their financial targets

Artificial intelligence provides new possibilities to make machines work more efficiently. Nowadays, most governments are frantically searching for new ways to eliminate their budget deficits. Linear savings have reached their limit. For example, Germany has a huge GNP, but Europe's largest economy is also facing serious challenges, not least of which is a rapidly ageing population.

This means that even a rich and powerful country like Germany will need AI if it wants to balance its books in the long-term future. A recent McKinsey report[40] examining the German situation revealed that around one-third of the required growth

Facebook, Inc. Common Stock
NASDAQ: FB - 31 Oct, 06:24 GMT-4

179,87 USD ↑ 1,99 (1,12%)
After-hours: 180,57 ↑0,39%

| 1 day | 5 day | 1 month | 3 months | 1 year | 5 years | max |

Open	179,26
High	180,69
Low	177,61

Mkt cap	522,38B
P/E ratio	39,07
Div yield	-

in Germany's GNP is dependent on efficiency improvements. Automation driven by AI has the greatest potential to realize these efficiency benefits. In fact, if Germany was one of the first countries to invest heavily in AI, it could even exceed its GNP targets by 4%. The AI investment would also increase annual productivity from 0.8% to 1.4%. But if the country fails to invest sufficiently in AI-driven automation and so becomes a laggard, it risks missing its GNP target by a staggering 30%, according to McKinsey. The more a country is dependent on repetitive processes in its service provision, the greater the need for an AI-first mindset in government circles.

How a single self-driving car can reduce traffic jams

Artificial intelligence optimizes certain elements of business processes. It is not necessary to immediately automate everything in your company – an AI strategy starts with the selection of clearly defined processes that have potential to be successfully automated. AI first does not mean automating everything that can be automated. It's about setting smart priorities. Just optimizing part of your operations can make a huge difference.

This 'all or nothing' discussion regularly crops up in relation to the use of self-driving cars. Between 2020 and 2030 more and more vehicles will be driving more and more autonomously. Mercedes wants to have self-driving trucks by 2025. Volvo has a driverless car in its planning for 2030. Tesla wants to be first and envisages a fully autonomous commercial model by 2020. In May 2017, Ford selected a new CEO with the specific intention of underlining its commitment to autonomous vehicles. The man who heads their driverless car programme was appointed as the new leader of the entire company. It shows Ford's determination to reach its objective: mass production of self-driving cars by 2021.[41]

In other words, the next decade will see a transition period in which some cars are still driven but an increasing number are driverless. Whether we like it or not, it is going to happen. It seems like it is only a matter of time before governments start to ban people from getting behind the wheel of their own car – my guess is that it will happen in about 2035. Until then, man and machine will still be seen in collaborative harmony on our roads.

But what happens after that? Some people have a problem with this whole idea. They believe that a semi-automated world will be more complex than a world with only human drivers, but the reality is actually very different. A study by the University of Illinois has proven the benefit of even a very limited introduction of self-driving cars for reducing traffic congestion.[42]

For the research, the team at the University of Illinois created a 'phantom traffic jam'. They made 30 cars drive on a circular track and then asked one of them to brake fairly hard. This one movement brought all the other 29 cars to a standstill. The idea of this phantom jam is to simulate situations that occur on our roads. And it is certainly true that if drivers hit their brakes too hard during the morning rush hour, the result is a huge stop-go snarl-up. But when the researchers added a single self-driving car to the experiment, everything changed. Self-driving cars apply their brakes more intelligently and keep their distance better than human drivers. As a result, the other cars in the row also break less, so that the traffic flow continues and a jam is avoided.

The figures produced by the research are impressive. The addition of just this one self-driving car reduced the standard speed deviation of all the cars in the jam by about 50%. The number of abrupt braking manoeuvres per vehicle fell from nine per kilometre to between 2.5 and zero. And because vehicle speed remained more constant, petrol consumption was also down – by as much as 40%!

Artificial intelligence is too often depicted as science fiction. Everyone imagines a world in which it is no longer possible to tell the difference between men and machines. In 2014, Stanford University launched a 100-year study into AI.[43] It is the world's largest study of its kind so far. The researchers have covered every possible element of AI in their study design. To date, there has not been a single result to indicate the existence of a computer with its own will and its own objectives. AI is not about a world full of terminators. Nor is it about a world taken over by megalomaniac computers. AI is about the automation and duplication of human processes. People combine intelligence with consciousness. AI is intelligence without consciousness.

As mentioned previously, a good AI strategy is based on the identification of the processes that can be automated most meaningfully. The next step is to collect as much data as you can about these processes. This data is the raw material for your algorithm. It is this combination of data and algorithm that makes the automation possible. And automation leads to greater efficiency for both the company and the customer. AI-first does not mean that you will immediately automate everything in your business, but just automating a single aspect of your operations can have a massive impact on the rest of the organization. Just like the introduction of a single self-driving car had a massive impact on 29 others. AI-first is not an 'all or nothing' option.

Trust in machines > trust in people

Will customers trust AI? Will they take the predictions and recommendations of their virtual assistant seriously? Will they – will you – be prepared to entrust significant aspects of everyday life into the 'hands' of a machine?

The answer is a resounding: YES!

Once machines are working properly, people trust them more than they trust other people. While the technology can only guarantee up to 95% accuracy, we prefer it the other way around and people win. 95% reliability leads to too many frustrations. But once the machine reaches 99% accuracy, it is usually game over for people. Just think about the way sat-nav systems have developed. Ten years ago, a GPS system was only about 80% accurate. It would still occasionally lead you to the wrong destination or send you the wrong way down a one-way street. Today, the systems have achieved the crucial 99% threshold. So, ask yourself this question: if you are driving in an unfamiliar town and the sat-nav says "go straight on" but your map-reading partner says "no, you should turn left here", who are you going to believe? Today, most of us would go with the machine. Why? Because most people do not have anywhere near 99% accuracy when it comes to navigation. Once technology starts performing better than the average human being, we have more trust in the machine for that particular process than we do in our fellow man.

Of course, classic navigation systems can still sometimes fail to offer good alternative routes when there are traffic jams. On several occasions, my sat-nav has suggested alternatives that actually took longer to follow than if I had just waited until the jam cleared. Once this has happened a few times, you start to ignore the suggestions. However, Waze – Google's Israeli-developed navigation system – is able to succeed where others fail. After a couple of successful detours, Waze is now my primary navigation tool if there are ever problems on the road. Why? Because Waze is always right. We are entering an era when machines will compete increasingly against other machines. My classic sat-nav (a machine) has lost out to Waze (another machine). This battle between machines with the highest degree of accuracy is already raging in full fury.

Once an AI application is functioning as it should, it quickly becomes part of our lives. Andrew Ng is one of the world's top experts in artificial intelligence. His career so far has been impressive. He is a Stanford professor, founder of the online learning platform Coursera, founder of Google Brain and former chief scientist of the Chinese Baidu corporation. He says that NLP (Natural Language Processing) currently has an accuracy of 95%. This means that companies like Google can already understand 95% of what people are saying. 95% sounds a lot – but it isn't. People want 99% quality. A conversation with a computer that is only 95% accurate is like talking to an eight-year-old. It's not bad, but it's not exactly great either. You need 99% to have an acceptable level. Getting from 95% to 99% sounds like it shouldn't be too hard – but that last 4% contains the most complex parts. But as soon as NLP does become 99% accurate, people will find it perfectly natural to talk to computers and machines.[44]

As soon as technology works faultlessly, people trust the machine more than they trust other people. This is a hypothesis you can apply in almost every industry. Before too long, robot advisers will be playing a big role in the finance world. In the future, wealthy customers will choose to get their investment advice from a machine rather than from its human colleague. After all, the robot can store and process much more information in real time – and do it much better. The robot could be finished before the banker has even started.

Of course, for some people making investments is an emotional matter – but it shouldn't be. In essence, it is a rational process that lends itself perfectly to the use of machines. So, in the bank of the (near) future, a banker without a robot will be like a pub without beer: left high and dry. And the same will be true of a doctor without a smart computer at his/her side: they will soon lose the confidence of their patients.

The six fields where AI will offer added value in customer relations

So, in which phases of the customer journey can AI play a role for your company? This is a crucial strategic question that is central to any AI-first mindset.

Artificial intelligence has already been in our lives for several years. The Facebook timeline is a good example. Spotify rec-

ommendations are also supported by AI. Siri has been trying for quite some time to help us via our iPhone. Today (2017), we entrust all kinds of simple tasks to our virtual assistant, from setting our morning alarm call to timing how long it takes to boil an egg. Of course, in the big picture of AI this is little more than playing with simple ideas. Even so, it is the start of the evolution that will soon see companies offering significant added value to their customers through AI. This will happen in six steps, each of which will result in even greater AI impact.

The six steps in the AI customer relationship:

1. Curation of information
2. Provision of customized information
3. Recommendations
4. Predictions
5. Automation
6. Contextual analysis

1. Curation of information

The current Google interface was developed in the previous century. For each search task, we get dozens of pages of results with hundreds of links. Of course, nobody bothers to search through all those pages. We simply choose a link from the first three options and that's it.

This kind of information overload is something that we all try to avoid. True, in recent years a number of innovations have been introduced to improve the quality of search engine results. Google now corrects our spelling mistakes, and if we start typing in our search term it offers us a range of options after just the first few letters. In fact, it sometimes seems as though Google knows what we are looking for before we know it ourselves. Yet, for all these clever innovations, it is still essentially an old interface that gives its visitors far too much irrelevant information.

Artificial intelligence helps to curate content. Once again, Facebook is an excellent example. Instead of us making the choice, the computer determines what we get to see and what is blocked. For retail platforms, this is a major opportunity. On sites like Zalando you currently get offered page after page of clothes, most of which you wouldn't wear in a thousand years. A really good AI interface will only select clothes that it knows match your taste. With data being produced in ever-increasing quantities, information overload looks to be a problem for years to come. AI can help you to select the correct and most relevant content for your customers.

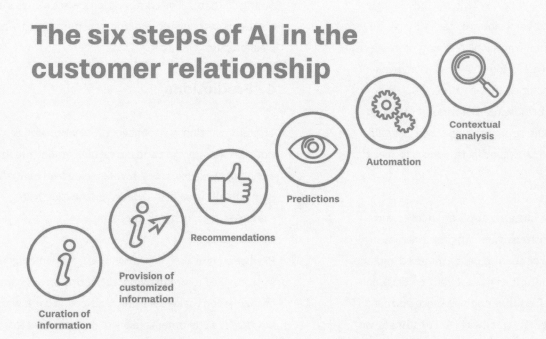

The six steps of AI in the customer relationship

Curation of information

Provision of customized information

Recommendations

Predictions

Automation

Contextual analysis

2. Provision of customized information

Imagine a smartphone that suddenly lets you know it's time to set off for your next meeting, taking into account the current state of the traffic on the roads. This is a good example of how AI can provide customized information. The computer combines different data sources to provide content that is tailored to your personal needs.

Concrete questions can now be answered almost instantly by smart interfaces. That's how Google Home works. Recently, my children asked me about the colours of the rainbow. In all honesty, I hadn't a clue. "Dad, you're useless! Google, what are the seven colours of the rainbow, please?" Within seconds, Google Home had the answer: "The seven colours of the rainbow are red, orange, yellow, green, blue, indigo and violet." Today, these kinds of relatively simple question are being answered with increasing frequency by talking machines. In the future, much more complex questions will also be possible. Before long, our virtual assistant will become our main source of help for all our daily queries and problems. AI provides specific responses to specific requests.

This has the potential to be a fantastic application for governments. Many thousands of citizens have concrete questions about taxes, subsidies, hours of opening, and a hundred and one other things every day. Wouldn't it be great if you could ask a concrete question to a central administrative service and get a concrete (and correct) answer straight away? As consumers, we would no longer need to waste time searching for the information we need – it will be handed to us on a plate, with minimal delay.

3. Recommendations

Recommending products has already become a familiar part of most e-commerce websites. In the coming years, the quality of these recommendations will improve. The more data that is available about an individual user, the more targeted the resulting recommendations will be. This is set to play a huge role in the financial sector. Blackrock is the largest asset management company in the world. Since March 2017, they have been getting recommendations from their AI interface about the buying and selling of shares. The computer processes all available data and comes up with well-founded suggestions about what the company should do.

4. Predictions

Content curation, customized information and recommendations are already part and parcel of everyday life for most of us, although the growth of AI will quickly lead to quality improvements in all these fields. However, the fourth step – predictions – is currently much less familiar.

Prediction is at the very heart of artificial intelligence. Self-driving cars need to predict what other drivers are going to do, so that they can make the right decisions. A bank wants to know in advance if a customer is likely to repay his/her loan. As the quality of AI predictions increase, the products that are dependent on the predictions will fall in price. The agricultural industry, transport and health care are three sectors that can benefit hugely in this manner from accurate predictions. Decisions will be taken more quickly with fewer mistakes being made, so the quality of the end product will improve correspondingly.

The same process will also be seen at an individual company level. Looking at the processes within your business that could benefit from more accurate predictions will become a standard part of most companies' AI strategy. Scriptbook is a Belgian company that works for several of the major studios in Hollywood. The studios send the first draft of a film script to Scriptbook. At the time, it is not yet known which actors and actresses will be playing the different roles. Even so, this input, a raw script, is enough for Scriptbook to predict the likely box office takings of the resulting film. True, it is not an exact science, but it helps the studios to better estimate their risks and therefore make better decisions. Every company has activities that can benefit from accurate predictions.

5. Automation

The next step leads us towards an automated world. In the first phase, many clearly defined steps in the customer journey will be mechanized. Chatbots can take over various aspects of customer service. Self-driving vehicles can take over numerous transport functions. The basic output of the accounts department, the writing of simple texts and instructions, the settlement of routine legal matters: these are all further examples of areas where automation can and will play a major role.

The second phase involves the full automation of many aspects of our daily lives. Our cars will drive us, instead of us driving them. Our basic daily necessities (washing powder, coffee, corn flakes, etc.) will be ordered and delivered automatically on the basis of input from a machine. Robots will help more around the house. They will also help in care homes and a thousand and one other places.

It is not yet clear when we will reach this phase. Pieter Abbeel, a Belgian professor at UC Berkeley, is one of the top five scientists in the field of artificial intelligence and robotics. Berkeley is also currently the best university in the world in this area of expertise. According to Pieter, the AI evolution will start slowly but then accelerate rapidly. "At a certain moment, we will suddenly be confronted with serious job losses in many sectors. It is difficult to say exactly when this critical point will arrive, but I believe it will be sooner than everyone thinks."

In an automated world, the sale of a product can happen completely autonomously. Based on its sensor data, your coffee machine will know when your supply of coffee is almost exhausted. Consequently, it will independently place an order with your local e-commerce supplier. In the supplier's warehouse, self-driving vehicles will prepare your order with the same level of independence. Then, it will be delivered to your home by a driverless lorry, where a small self-propelled robot will take the

Pieter Abbeel

delivery right to your front door – and, after that, the rest is up to you! It sounds futuristic? Possibly. But the building blocks are already in place to make this happen. Amazon is already working on sensors for household appliances, like your coffee machine, while Mercedes is developing self-driving lorries with drones and robots that can make deliveries. They both plan to launch their innovations by 2020...

6. Contextual analysis

In this final phase, AI will be able to perfectly understand the context of the consumer. When we reach that point, Netflix recommendations will be able to take the current mood of its viewers into account. If you are down in the dumps, it will suggest something to cheer you up. At the moment, it can only take account of your previous viewing preferences and that of similar customers. However, once the context can be analyzed properly, the level of the recommendations – and the level of automation – will improve dramatically.

Imagine you have just bought your dream house. You are probably in seventh heaven. At a moment like that, you want to listen to music that is different from what you usually listen to. Something special. Something celebratory. To make this possible, the AI interface will not only search for data in a well-defined silo, but will scan all available data. The complexity of such an analysis is huge. Today, an algorithm is asked to make recommendations on the basis of a well-defined task in a specific set of data. In the world of contextual analysis, the AI interface will need to trawl through all – I repeat, ALL – available data to reach its conclusion. The computing power that this requires is almost unimaginable.

The best comparison for this is the way that people converse with each other. At the moment, this is a form of empathy that is only possible between people. People have the ability to take all the different parameters into account when they talk to someone else. For example, they can see and hear whether you are feeling happy or feeling sad. The day that a computer or robot is capable of making the same analysis will be the day when one of the most important distinctions between humans and machines falls away.

AI = Data

The most important ingredient for AI evolution is data! Completing the six AI steps in the customer relationship requires masses of data. To start the introduction of AI applications in your company, you also need lots of data about all your repetitive processes. Once you have identified the phases of your business operations in which AI could add value, the next step is to collect as much data as you can about each phase. The computer will then analyze, imitate and optimize that data. Via repeated iteration, the computer is able to learn the process. But without data the computer can do nothing. Whatever kind of company you are, from now on you need to be a data company.

AI has a kind of virtuous circle of success. It begins with a successful product or application. This product attracts lots of users. These users generate data. Using this data, you can improve both the product and the customer experience. Good products that fail to collect data about their use are a missed opportunity.

The reason why we currently see so few robots in our daily lives is a lack of data. As a result, the virtuous circle cannot be initiated. A shortage of users means a shortage of data, which leads to the slower evolution of robots. Steven Miller is the founder of Fyusion. He is also a former student and associate of Pieter

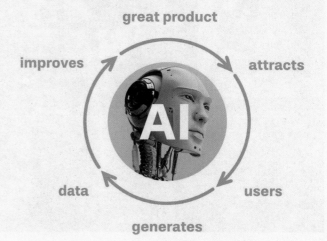

Virtuous circle of AI

great product

improves

attracts

AI

data

users

generates

Abbeel. Fyusion wants to solve the data problem for robots. Steven has developed an app that allows users to take 3D photos of their environment. By moving your smartphone around the object you are photographing, you get a really great 3D image. If you then move the smartphone while you are looking at the photograph, you can view it in 3D. The photos can also be used in augmented reality applications. For example, you can 'leave behind' a 3D photo at a particular physical place and everyone who views that place via augmented reality can also see the photo. Fyusion

has developed a network with millions of users who can share their 3D photos. In fact, the company has the largest 3D content database in the world. As a result, they are also best placed to map out the 3D environment. They can make a data analysis of almost every physical location. This data helps robots to visualize countless different environments and allows them to practice virtually at being in some of them. In this way, Fyusion has set the AI 'circle of life' in motion. They have built a good app. It has attracted millions of users. The users give them access to an ocean of data. The data is used to the benefit of robot development.

The logic of the virtuous circle of AI is difficult to beat. The players with the most data about the relationship with their customers will be the quickest to implement AI, and therefore the quickest to reap its many benefits. The resulting rapid learning curve will give them a lead that will be difficult, if not impossible, for competitors to overtake. Financial institutions that fail to collect data about credit applications; schools that fail to record their test results digitally; telecom companies that fail to keep all the data of their mobile customers: they are all missing out on a big opportunity.

Many other companies see big data as a way to earn additional income. I have lost count of the number of slides in presentations I have seen where big data is linked to a dollar sign. But big data is much more than just an opportunistic way to rake in some extra cash. Data is the fuel that makes the six AI steps in the customer journey possible. AI can only quench its insatiable thirst at the refreshing fountains of data.

From supervised learning to non-supervised learning

During the preparation stage of my book, I had the pleasure of interviewing Pieter Abbeel about the role of AI in customer service. You can view our full conversation on my YouTube channel (*www.youtube.com/stevenvanbelleghem*). Amongst other things, we discussed the current status and future of AI. I asked him about the biggest hypes of the moment in the world of AI and his answer was very clear: "Today, AI is very strong in the field of supervised learning, which is a well-defined task. Supervised learning means that a computer is given a clear task, a data set to help it complete that task and the necessary time to practice it."

Pieter became world-famous when he taught a robot to fold the washing. He gave the robot a task (folding the washing), he gave the robot a data set (examples of how to fold washing) and he gave the robot enough time to practice (x iterations before it was successful). The story of Google DeepMind and Go is similar. The computer was given the task of winning at Go, it was given the data of thousands and thousands of previous games, and was then allowed to practice. But both these tasks – folding the washing and winning at Go – are clearly defined and delineated.

Pieter published his research into the washing-folding robot in 2011. It was the result of two years of work. But if he wanted to programme his robot in the same way today, just six or seven years later, it would take him half an hour. The desired task is shown to the robot, the robot tries to copy it and after ten or so iterations it succeeds. What took two years in 2011 now takes less time than watching an episode of your favourite soap on TV. In other words, there has been tremendous progress in the field of supervised learning by computers.

This opens the door to the next step in AI evolution: unsupervised learning. With unsupervised learning, the computer successfully and independently analyzes huge quantities of data, but without a clear focus. The machine gets no training database and the outcome is not defined. If all the data that Google collects or all the data that Amazon collects via all Echo devices can be used for useful analyses, the possibilities for the future are almost limitless.

Unsupervised learning is currently the number one challenge for the big technology companies. Each tech-giant wants to be the first to automatically analyze huge quantities of data and provide the resulting added value to its customers. If or when unsupervised learning becomes achievable, AI will have an even greater impact on the customer relationship. AI will then evolve from being the performer of clearly delineated niche tasks to become an ever-present virtual assistant. Pieter Abbeel is reluctant to put a date on this evolution. Will it happen? No doubt about it, 100% certain. When will it happen? No idea.

The power of the six AI steps in the customer experience can only be realized in full in the world of unsupervised learning. Today, we are still in the improvement phase, where AI performs well-defined tasks for which people set the outcome in advance. This is great for increasing efficiency, but so much more is possible. The real disruption will come when the machine can deal with complex problems for customers without the need for human intervention. Above all, steps 4, 5 and 6 of the customer journey – prediction, automation and contextual analysis – need unsupervised learning. Using the huge range of data that is available for every customer, the computer will then be able to offer added value on a scale we have never seen before.

Weapons of mass influence

The ultimate objective of every business manager, marketeer and sales person is to turn the customer decision-making process in your favour. Every company does many different things in the hope that at the end of the chain, the customer will see enough positive arguments in their favour to choose them. The introduction of artificial intelligence into the customer decision-making process makes this persuasion game much more complex. Each of the six steps on the ladder of AI has a huge potential to influence people.

In this respect, the power of the major digital platforms cannot be overestimated. We all learned a lot about the Facebook filter following the election victory of President Trump. Half of the American population were shown messages and posts of people who were deeply unhappy with the new president. The other half – the Trump supporters – were shown only positive feedback. Facebook lets us see what we want to see. In the past, everyone read the same newspapers and our own brains were the filter. Today, the filter is an algorithm. There is a rumour that one day, Mark Zuckerberg intends to run for president. This probably shouldn't be allowed. With his Facebook platform, the man has such a huge weapon of mass influence at his disposal that his victory would almost be inevitable.

In the discussion of social and societal themes, this technology poses huge challenges and possible risks. It creates the impression that everyone has the same idea, whereas the reality is of course very different. As a result, each individual can potentially be given a distorted image of that reality.

From perception to real value

In the previous chapter we talked about changes in the customer journey. In the coming years, algorithms are going to play a more prominent role in the customer's purchasing decision. As AI continues to climb the six applications ladder, the quality of its recommendations will also improve. And the better the recommendations, the greater their impact on the purchasing decision. For social-economic themes, the masses will be increasingly influenced by algorithms. For personal purchases, the consumer will be increasingly influenced by a highly personalized form of recommendation – once again, created by algorithms.

It is also possible that some functional purchases will become fully automated. Once your washing machine is fitted with a sensor linked to an e-commerce platform, you, the consumer, no longer need to decide anything. The washing machine sees that your supply of washing power is running low and automatically orders some more. This change in the nature of decision-making will have a huge effect on marketing and communication. The greater the impact of algorithms, the lower the impact of classic marketing techniques.

You often hear it said that 'perception is reality'. It is not facts that are the deciding factor when people need to make a choice, but rather their perception of those facts. In recent decades, this perception has largely been constructed by the media and by marketing communication. Advertising has made Coca Cola a much-loved brand. But the naked facts about Coca Cola are not particularly positive. Sure, it's a refreshing and tasty drink, but it doesn't actually do your body an awful lot of good. Quite the reverse, in fact. Even so, Coca Cola continues to be a much-loved brand. The company has built this perception in the market – and they have done it brilliantly.

The moment that people feel able to trust the advice of machines, this marketing philosophy is dead and buried. A machine pays no attention to advertising when formulating its decisions; it relies exclusively on concrete data. When it books you a flight, it won't be dazzled by the flashy company logo on the plane's fuselage; it will just be looking at the price (and maybe the company's punctuality and safety records). If purchases are made on the basis of data analysis, 'real value' suddenly becomes more important than 'perceived value'. This means that marketing managers will need to have sufficient objective data about their products to post on the net – and hope that this is still enough to convince customers in their favour. From this point onwards, user feedback will become the most decisive factor in influencing the purchasing process.

In coming years, we are likely to see a division into two types of purchasing transaction. On the one hand, there will be functional transactions, like insurance, bank loans, telecom, energy, transport, etc. On the other hand, there will be transactions relating to products that help us to build up our own 'personal brand', such as clothes, shoes, jewellery, etc.

The classic marketing model will probably survive longer for this second category of purchase than for the more functional transactions. Functional purchases will be farmed out to computers. For purchases of this kind, the 'brand' plays a much less influential role. Instead, consumers are interested in quality and reliability at a good price. And in these circumstances, a computer can find a better deal – and find it more quickly and more easily – than a human. Once again, 'real value' becomes more important than 'perceived value'.

Initially, these developments will have less of an impact on products that support our personal image – although even here algorithms are likely to make themselves felt in the medium to long-term future. In mid-2017, Amazon launched Amazon Look. This is an Amazon Echo with a built-in camera. Its purpose is to give fashion advice to its users. After you have put on your outfit in the morning, you can ask Amazon to make a small video, so that you can see for yourself how you look. You can even ask Amazon what outfit best matches your hairstyle or is most suitable for the things you have planned for the day. And once the customer starts following Look's advice, its algorithms take this into account for future decisions relating to personal branding. The conversation will go something like this: "Yes, the outfit you have on is quite nice, but perhaps not formal enough for your meeting with the board of directors this afternoon. You haven't really got anything suitable in your wardrobe at the moment, but I can order something that's just right and have it delivered within the hour..." Amazon makes its recommendations on the basis of hair colour, type of appointment and all other available parameters.

"But surely," (I can hear you say) "this kind of thing won't happen with iconic brands like Coca Cola?" Perhaps not – at first. Initially, the role of algorithms will indeed be smaller with products of this kind. But once the health applications are working properly (with 99% accuracy), things will change dramatically for the food and drink manufacturers. If my smartphone evaluates my dietary consumption, it might recommend that it would be better for me not to drink cola for a day or two. Or maybe even a whole week. And as mentioned earlier, there are already sweet dispensers that only let customers buy a bar of chocolate if they have already taken their recommended daily number of steps. In every sector, the importance of real value will increase in inverse proportion to perceived value. Perception will no longer be reality. Instead, objective parameters will guide customers in their purchasing decisions. As a result, every industry will need to change and every product will become a commodity.

Of course, there will still be purchases where people make decisions the 'traditional' way. For purchases involving a high degree of emotional commitment, or products from a sector about which you are truly passionate, your decisions will still be based on gut feeling and not on algorithmic rationality. The product categories for this kind of decision will be different for each person, because we all have different passions. But the total number of product categories will be small in each case. For all the other categories – the huge majority – our emotional commitment is much lower, so that we will be more inclined to listen to the machines.

In other words, the AI-first mindset involves a dual approach. On the one hand, it is important to identify processes that are suitable for automation. On the other hand, it is equally important to investigate the likely impact of this automation on content marketing and online promotion in a world where consumers hand over (part of) their purchasing decisions to machines. As a result, studying how real value is built up can only increase in importance.

Too enthusiastic or too scared

On the BBC website there is a wonderful article about people's reaction to innovation throughout history.[45] The pattern is always the same. When something new appears, our first inclination is to focus on the potential dangers of the technology. When fire was discovered, people were afraid that the forests would burn down. When electricity was discovered, they were afraid that their homes would burn down. The car would kill millions on the roads. Planes would kill millions by dropping out of the sky. But my favourite technopanic relates to the written word. 400 years before the birth of Christ, people were afraid that writing would ultimately corrode the human memory. Why would people both-

er remembering things if everything could be written down...? After the event, we can only conclude that these fears were well founded. People do die in car accidents. Planes do occasionally crash. Electricity is sometimes the cause of domestic fires. However, we must also conclude that these disadvantages, tragic though they are, are insignificant in comparison to the advantages. Fire dramatically changed the evolution of mankind. Electricity not only helps to make our lives safer and more comfortable, but also keeps our economies turning. Roads may, sadly, claim a million victims each year, but they are also the arteries of our economic prosperity, which helps to save millions of lives each year. Likewise, plane crashes do sometimes cause loss of life, but they are still the safest form of travel and have opened a window on the world to all of us, as well as oiling the wheels (or should that be the wings?) of economic globalization. Every innovation has its downside. But the upside is often immeasurably greater.

There are currently similar discussions about AI. It is a subject on which people blow hot and cold. People like Elon Musk can see the end of the world approaching. People like Mark Zuckerberg see only the advantages of automating the routine (and sometimes not so routine) tasks in our everyday lives. Like every new technology, AI also has its pluses and minuses.

If we are too scared of AI, we will slow down its evolution. Of course, we have to accept that it will cost jobs in the years ahead. Everybody knows this. All the more reason why we need to conduct a debate about how best to deal with these social challenges now, rather than strangling AI at birth. Some jobs are inevitably

going to disappear, so we had better start getting used to the idea. Self-driving lorries will initially still need a human operator on board, because that is what the law currently demands. But it won't stay that way forever. At some point, the driver will become totally redundant: the trucks will drive themselves. But truck driver is one of the most common jobs in the United States. So what happens then? What are all these ex-drivers supposed to do? The potential social problems are real and there are no easy solutions. But there is no point burying our heads in the sand. We need to start discussing these things – and we need to do it now.

At the other end of the scale, if we are too enthusiastic about AI we are likely to be disappointed. As they work today, AI tools are far from perfect. It's a bit like we are currently in the MS-DOS phase of AI. Things have only just started. It will take another ten to twenty years before the real impact will be felt.

Too scared can lead to stagnation; too enthusiastic can lead to disillusion. It is crucial that we keep the balance somewhere in the middle. Identifying the processes where AI can play a role; collecting the data; launching the first applications: this is the right philosophy. In this way, your company will be able to evolve in the right direction in a realistic manner.

The most important thing, however, is to translate your AI-first mindset into consumer benefits. Because at the end of the day, it's not about the technology; it's about your customers. In the next chapter, I will be looking at precisely what benefits they can expect to enjoy in an AI world.

Jeremiah Owyang about the evolution towards automation

In recent years, I have collaborated on several occasions with Jeremiah Owyang. In the meantime, Jeremiah has become more than just a business partner; we have also built up a warm and friendly relationship. I have great respect for Jeremiah, both as a person and for his professional expertise. He was the first expert to map out the evolution of the collaborative economy. Nobody in the world has more knowledge and experience in this field than Jeremiah. His most recent research explores the impact of the third phase of digitalization: AI and automation. For this reason, I am delighted and grateful that Jeremiah is willing to share his thoughts on this third phase in my book. Thanks, Jeremiah!

Jeremiah is the CEO of Crowd Companies, a platform for innovation that teaches large companies how to deal with digital change. Jeremiah is one of the most appreciated analists of the digital world.

Collaborative Economy Business Models Set the Stage for Autonomous Innovation

In an Autonomous World, machines replace humans to deliver even greater convenience and efficiency. Today's Collaborative Economy, peer-to-peer business models, and on-demand expectations lay the necessary foundation for the Autonomous World to thrive tomorrow.

In the Collaborative Economy, humans get what they need from each other. In the next phase, the Autonomous World, robots will augment and replace humans, and they will serve humans. In some cases, robots will even serve other robots as technology advances.

The transition from traditional business models to the Collaborative Economy and ultimately to the Autonomous World is already creating ripples. We are in the midst of global disruption due to widespread mobile internet and cloud technology, vastly improved processing power of "big data," and the rise of the sharing economy and crowdsourcing, according to the *World Economic Forum*. These innovations are now spawning new energy supplies and technology, advanced Internet of Things use cases, and additive manufacturing and 3D printing — all of which are quickly altering expectations about the future.

Let's examine how this transition into an Autonomous World could look in varying business models in the coming years: How the Collaborative Economy will shift to Automation.

As shown in table 1, automation affects all industries and sectors, but the one area that will be most impacted will be the retail and logistics space. An estimate from the former White House administration forecasted the potential for an $82 billion American commercial drone industry with as many as 100,000 new jobs by the year 2025.

One example lies in Amazon's delivery drone that successfully *delivered its first order* of popcorn and a Fire TV stick to a rural customer near Cambridge, England, in December. The drone is designed to fly under 400 feet with packages that weigh 5 pounds or less within a 10-mile radius of a fulfilment center, enabling deliveries to be made in less than 30 minutes.

The collaborative economy shifts to the autonomous world

**Collaborative economy age
(now)**

**Autonomous world age
(tomorrow)**

TABLE 1. How the Collaborative Economy will shift to Automation

Category	Automation Phase	Examples	Impact
Ride Sharing (Uber, Lyft, Didi, Ola)	Self-driving cars are quickly emerging, most by 2021, from many car manufacturers	Uber has experimented with cars, Lyft's bold pronouncement, and Didi	Professional drivers will need to upskill and find a new career
Delivery (Postmates, Instacart)	Wheeled and flying drones will deliver packages, beyond humans	Starship, a six-wheeled drone, is delivering food, and Amazon's patents are inspiring	Postmates, Instacart and other human couriers will be displaced by robots
Home Sharing (Airbnb, VRBO, HomeAway)	Home automation will enable hosts to offer hospitality without being present	Airbnb could offer digital locks, Wi-Fi management, digitized home appliances, and more	Hosts can manage more properties, and guests get a personalized experience from digital hosts
Online Service Marketplaces (Upwork/ Freelancer)	Simple AI bots will complete rote tasks currently performed by online service providers	While a plethora of early-stage bots have emerged from M, Alex, and Watson, advanced AI to conduct intermediate tasks hasn't emerged	Online workers will need to specialize their skills for project or robot management, human-based design, community skills, and humanities
What's next?	Anywhere repetitive tasks exist but could be automated	Simple machines will replicate human behaviors	Jobs will be lost, so humans must upskill or specialize in humanities, or head to the beach

Traditional package players like UPS are also getting into the autonomous game though, driving to the forefront of the drone scene with its deployment of an electric delivery truck equipped with a drone dock on its roof (see image below). Its ubiquitous brown trucks have made news by teaming up with a CyPhy Works drone to make a package delivery to an island near Boston, and again partnering with HorseFly UAV *to lift off and deliver* a package in Florida. A lot is at stake for UPS; in addition to its standard-setting role in the delivery industry, the company projects that it could save as much as $50 million a year by shaving just one mile off each of its drivers' routes every day.

Beyond on-demand delivery, autonomous technology is already impacting other areas in the retail industry as well, like customer service (smart chatbots on websites and in Facebook messenger),

A lot is at stake for UPS; in addition to its standard-setting role in the delivery industry, the company projects that it could save as much as $50 million a year by shaving just one mile off each of its drivers' routes every day.

cashier-less brick-and-mortar stores enabled by sensored products (Amazon Go), and automation within warehouses to ensure greater efficiencies and safety in the back-of-house. With the addition of transparent data networks like blockchain, we'll see the supply chain further disrupted as tracking goods, origins, and vendor actions along a product's journey becomes automated via smart contracts self-executing on an immutable online ledger.

Jeremiah Owyang

CHAPTER 3

IT'S NOT THE TECHNOLOGY, IT'S THE CUSTOMER

It's not about the technology, it's about the customer

The Hidrate Spark smart water bottle lights up when you need to drink some more water. Thanks to this clever piece of technology, you will never again forget when you should top up on your water intake. Water under-consumption – or thirst, as it is generally known – is, seemingly, something reserved for past generations. The Kérastase hair coach is a smart hair brush. Amongst other things, the brush listens to your hair via a small microphone. In this way, you can be certain that you are not hurting your hair while you are brushing it. Apparently, being cruel to your hair in this barbarous manner is now also a thing of the past. The Griffin toaster sends you a message when your toast is ready. It seems that it is no longer possible to establish this with visual observation (i.e. by just looking at it).

The world is currently littered with this kind of useless innovation. We are in the middle of a kind of 'Internet of Things' hype, although it sometimes seems more like an 'Internet of Stupid Things' hype. A few years ago, there was a similar Uber-ization hype. Countless start-ups were determined to turn almost every aspect of life into an on-demand service. Today's start-ups want to equip every possible device in your home with a chip. This chip makes communication between the device and the home's occupants possible. The Uber-ization of society was not a huge success; only very few players were able to succeed in the mainstream market. And the prospects for the Internet of Things don't look any better.

Fortunately, some innovations do take a concrete need of the customer as their starting point. I am one of founders of Zembro, a manufacturer of a smart armband for senior citizens. When we started the company, our aim was to give greater peace of mind to the elderly and their relatives. The band makes it possible for older people to carry on living at home for longer, without their children needing to worry too much about them getting into difficulties without anyone knowing. For example, the armband can detect a fall, locate the position of the fallen person and pass on this information to a pre-specified list of people. We didn't start with the technology and then try to find a use for it. We started with a specific customer need and tried to find the technology to meet it. In fact, the idea was first floated after one of the initiators found his father-in-law lying in his garden after a fall. He had been there for hours, helpless and unable to contact the emergency services. Something similar happened to my own grandfather, who fell in his kitchen while putting on his pyjamas. He lost consciousness and was only found the next morning by a visiting family member. It

was this kind of harrowing and deeply emotional incident that inspired us to develop Zembro. We saw that there was a real problem – a market, if you like – and then went in search of the technology to solve it. Taking the customer as your starting point is not a guarantee of success, but it's a good start.

Car central or citizen central?

In recent years, we have often worked with Jonathan Reichental. Jonathan is the CIO of Palo Alto, one of the most digital cities in the United States, right in the heart of Silicon Valley. Jonathan was one of the people I interviewed as part of the preparation for my book. You can see the full interview on *www.youtube.com/ stevenvanbelleghem*.

Palo Alto is currently being made ready for the world of driverless cars. The cities of tomorrow will be built around the citizen. In the cities of today, technology, and in particular the motor car, occupies the central position. Everything revolves around the car and its need for parking. In America alone, there are more than one billion parking spaces, the majority of which are in use for less than 50% of the time. People always think that there is a shortage of parking space, but there isn't. There is actually way too much of it. At night, supermarket car parks are empty. The parking outside your local football stadium is used for just a few hours every 14 days. In the world of the self-driving car, the parking problem can be approached in a very different way. This will involve the car being dethroned from its current central position in future spatial planning for our cities. Instead, this central position will be allocated to the citizens, with the car and other technology merely playing a support role to help fulfil certain citizen needs.

In short, the cities of the future will no longer focus on the demands of technology, but on providing added value to the people who live there. This is the core challenge for artificial intelligence in every field: creating greater customer benefit. Some companies will continue to conduct the AI debate from a technological perspective. And there is nothing wrong with this, providing you are a leader in AI technology. Organizations like Microsoft, IBM, Facebook, Google, Tencent, Baidu and Amazon are perfectly capable of developing a powerful technological vision for artifi-

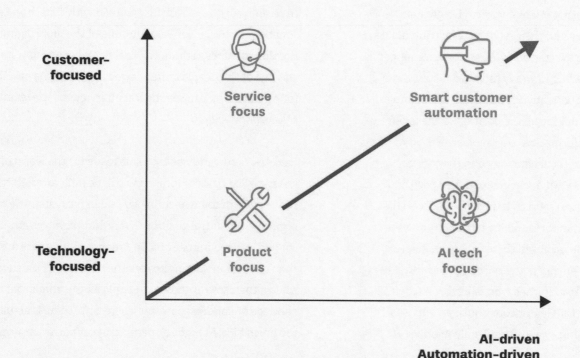

cial intelligence. But most companies are better advised to take the customer and customer needs as the ground zero for their discussion around AI.

The explosion of expectations

In my previous book, *When Digital Becomes Human*, I looked in detail at the case of Disney's magic bands. In Disneyworld, every hotel guest is issued with a magic band. This band does everything for you: it opens your room, it allows you to reserve attractions and restaurant tables in advance, it helps with park security, etc. Put simply, it is a fantastic tool. What's more, its users spend 30% more money in the park than non-users, according to Disney's own annual report, entitled: *The magic bands are magic money makers.*[46] The bands were a big success, but they needed to be: they were the most expensive IT project in the history of Disneyworld. However, there was no need to worry. The addition of a digital layer to an offline entertainment paradise was a touch of genius, never previously seen inside the sector or beyond. In short, the bands far exceeded the expectations of the market.

You probably think that an innovation of this kind gives a company a lead they can keep for years. But you would be wrong. At the start of 2017, Universal Studios opened a new theme park.

Vulcanic Bay is the newest water park belonging to the Universal group. In addition to dozens of cool attractions, one of the big pluses of the park is that it promises visitors a world without queuing. Universal uses smart technology to direct people to the right attraction at the right moment, the moment when they are least being used. As a result, waiting times have been slashed to almost nothing.[47] This is very clever. All theme park research comes to the same conclusion: people hate queuing. A few minutes is okay; but a couple of hours for an attraction that is over in

the blink of an eye? Nobody wants that. Even with magic bands, there are long queues in Disneyworld. So, Disney now has to play catch-up. But to make matters worse, the magic band team has been headhunted by Carnival, one of the largest cruise ship operators in Florida.[48] Carnival loves the idea of the magic band and thinks that the confined space of a cruise ship is a much better place to exploit its full potential. Disney also runs cruises, but so far without magic bands, except for children (for security reasons). As a result of these developments, Disney may soon find itself operating beneath customer expectations. Two years ago, its magic band was the most innovative project ever seen in the entertainment industry. Now, it's already yesterday's news.

A devilish dilemma

Many industries offer better levels of service than five years ago. But often, today's customers are less satisfied than they were back then. In the old days, a business won because it had a unique differentiator. For example, a local neighbourhood shop won because of its location. Customers accepted that the quality on offer was a bit on the low side, but this lower quality went hand in hand with lower price – and this low price was the deciding factor for the customer. For this type of business/shop, this

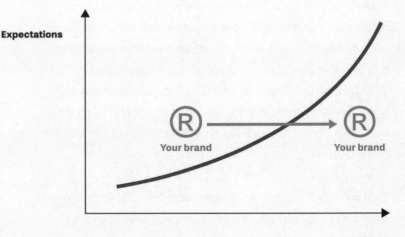

unique aspect is still a strength. But a differentiator of this kind on its own is no longer enough to win, because in many sectors the other less differentiating aspects have dramatically improved in quality in recent years. A good online shop has a wide offer, competitive prices and often an excellent service. Location and hours of opening no longer play a role. As a result, customers no longer wish to patronize businesses, some of whose elements are now below average. Today's customer wants it all and is not prepared to make compromises.

This reality leads to a devilish dilemma: as a company, do you invest more to improve those aspects that are now below par, or do you collaborate with companies that can make good your deficiencies? Both options cost the company money. Investing increases costs. Collaboration with existing platforms reduces margins.

This rat race will be seen in every sector. The possibilities offered by artificial intelligence and other technologies from the convergence point (the simultaneous maturing of different technologies) will improve customer service to a level never previously seen. Because most AI technology is invisible, the consumer will not immediately understand what is happening. Perhaps more important, many of your competitors will also not understand what is happening. This behind-the-scenes technology will, above all, make a difference in customer experience. In these circumstances, the answer to the devilish dilemma for most companies is simple: collaborating with an existing platform is the only way to survive. Investing on your own in the hope of continuing

to meet the ever-increasing expectations of customers costs an absolute fortune, with no guarantee of results. It's like committing financial suicide.

The real Customer of The Day After Tomorrow

If you want to understand The Customer of The Day After Tomorrow, it is necessary to try and assess the behaviour of the next generation of consumers. The people who are currently aged between 15 and 22 will be the next group of decision-makers for countless purchases. To gain a better insight into this group, I asked Joeri Van den Bergh to write a piece about them. Joeri was a former colleague at InSites Consulting. He is also one of the most knowledgeable experts in Europe when it comes to young people. His book *How Cool Brands Stay Hot* is a worldwide bestseller and won several prestigious awards. In preparation for my book I interviewed him about the impact of this new generation on marketing. Check out *www.youtube.com/stevenvanbelleghem* to view the full conversation.

An expert speaks: Joeri Van den Bergh

Is your customer approach NextGen proof?

The Customers The Day After Tomorrow? Yes, if you ask me, I think we already know what they look like. By 2020, the Millennial generation (born between 1980 and 1996 and now reaching young adulthood) will make up half the workforce. In the next five years, their spending worldwide will increase by 17%. This means they will equal the purchasing power of the entire baby-boom generation by 2018. Moreover, as brand-new parents, they are already giving birth to and raising the customers of The Day After Tomorrow. So it's high time to put our Millennial glass-

es on and think about the marketing challenges of the coming decades.

Millennials grew up in different times and were brought up in a different way. From their earliest years, they were taught that their own ideas and opinions are at least as important as anyone else's. Both at school and at home, they were integrally and inter-actively involved in decision-making and the learning process. So, it should come as no surprise that they have grown up to become an extrovert generation that knows what it wants. A generation that expects to be in control, both as customers and consumers.

The old marketing laws – segment the market, select target groups, position brands – won't work anymore with the Millennials. I like to call them Generation Flex. They are not easy to fit into a single pigeon hole. And it is precisely this unpredictable and constantly changing mix of completely different micro-passions, brands and styles that defines their identity. The same is true of their media use: nothing is linear and predictable. Everything is volatile.

Chatting is the new popcorn

If there is one certainty about the Millennials, it is that they're very social-orientated. They constantly want to give and receive feedback from their friends. And yes, they grew up with media and technology that makes this possible. From InSites Consulting's 'Who's up Next' research, we know that Millennials use up to five screens simultaneously to satisfy their insatiable desire to be

> **The old marketing laws – segment the market, select target groups, position brands – won't work anymore with the Millennials.**

connected. For them, the message streams in apps like Whatsapp, Facebook Messenger and Snapchat are proper conversations. And at work, Skype chats have replaced five minutes of gossip around the coffee machine. Audio, video, GIFs and emojis make these chats as interesting and as human as a normal face-to-face conversation, as well as being much faster and more efficient. It is no coincidence that the standalone Facebook Messenger is growing quicker than Facebook itself. At the end of last year, the cosmetics brand Cover Girl chose this kind of messenger to launch the chatbot version of the 16-year-old TV personality and influencer Kalani Hilliker. The bot generated 14 times more conversations than an average post from the real Kalani on social media. An average of 17 messages per conversation were exchanged and half of these led to the issuing a discount coupon.

IWWIWWIWI

The combination of all these micro-interests, a challenging job, children and the constant pressure to stay connected, as well as wanting to spend fantastic weekends, holidays and moments with family and friends, creates one massive scarcity among the Millennials: time. Consequently, as consumers they are also looking for ways to buy time, gain in efficiency and to farm out or automate non-essential repetitive processes. In October of last year, MasterCard introduced payment by selfie in 12 countries. It's a fast and easy way to round-off a purchase in (almost literally) the blink of an eye, using your smartphone. In London, Sainsbury's can deliver your groceries to your home within half an hour via the

Chop Chop App. The motto for this generation is: "I Want What I Want When I Want It" (IWWIWWIWI). They are not necessarily looking for a particular brand, but more for things that they immediately need. Again, it is no coincidence that Millennial-proof hotels like CitizenM, MamaShelter and Marriott's Moxy have replaced the traditional lobby restaurant, with fixed opening hours, with a grab&go that offers 24/7 availability for breakfast, snacks, lunch and drinks.

A study by Rocket Fuel revealed that 62% of 18 to 34-year-olds worldwide see artificial intelligence playing an important role in the specific recommendation of products and services. This is much higher than the percentage for the baby-boomers (just 44%). AI helps the Millennials to make the right choices faster in the maze of information clutter. Amazon's Echo Look – a voice controlled camera – not only takes 360° photos of your outfit that you can share and have assessed by your friends, but is also connected to the Style Checker, whose algorithms and fashion

> **Millennials are happy to give up a piece of their privacy in return for personalized advertising and recommendations.**

experts advise you on what outfits to wear. Millennials are already used to working every day with personal assistants like Siri on their smartphone and, with their hunger for innovation (for them, the coolest brands are Google, Facebook and Apple), are already convinced that AI gives them better service and better results than a human shop assistant. And they are right: the IKEA AssistBot knows the full IKEA catalogue far better than any flesh-and-blood assistant ever could.

Me, myself and AI

In the attention economy, the new currency – along with time – is relevance. Relevance is crucial. Millennials are happy to give up a piece of their privacy in return for personalized advertising and recommendations. Last summer in the United Kingdom, Renault introduced vehicle recognition technology to make its advertising posters for the new Megane more individually relevant for passing motorists. Even an iconic brand like Levi's has recruited qualified tailors for its flagship stores, so that Millennials can personalize their original Levi's 501 jeans to their own requirements. Millennials grew up with an e-commerce environment that made it possible to personalize their sneakers and with media like Netflix that offers them a permanent flow of new and 'made-to-measure' content. They now expect this same personal approach in every shop and service setting. Even traditional entertainment businesses like the cinema are starting to experiment with new formulas that can respond to the non-linear wishes of their younger customers. This year, the Vue cinema chain launched *Late Shift*, the first interactive film. There are 180 moments in the film when the viewers can choose how the storyline develops further, resulting ultimately in one of seven different endings. eBay's ShopBot on Facebook Messenger not only helps you via a natural virtual conversation to find what you are looking for amongst millions of listings, but also learns about your personal preferences through your Facebook profile, remembering the product choices you have previously made.

Be flexible

This rapidly changing environment comes with both choice-stress and endless possibilities. The new generation of consumers believes that technology can help to make their lives easier and save them time, which they can then spend on the things that really matter. Your real competitors in today's market, and in the markets of the future, are the ones who are faster than you are. There are plenty of them and they can pop up from anywhere – often from where you least expect it.

The best service level ever

For consumers, the AI-first world is going to be wonderful. We will discover new levels of service that we could have only dreamed of in the past. During my hundreds of visits to some of the most innovative companies in the United States, Europe, Africa and Asia, I drew up a list of benefits that we, as consumers, can expect to get from artificial intelligence. Three central aspects – three concrete advantages – keep on recurring, time after time.

1. *Faster than real-time customer service*: the aim is no longer to provide a faultless customer service, but to solve problems before they arise. Customer service is evolving away from being reactive towards being proactive.
2. *Hyper-personalization*: sales and marketing are no longer about the average customer, but about the needs of the individual customer. Joeri has rightly pointed out that relevance is one of the most crucial expectations of the next generation. Hyper-personalization will become the most relevant way to communicate with (and produce for) the customer.
3. *Unparalleled ease of use*: all of today's best interfaces are idiot-proof. There is no longer any need for an instruction manual or even a help function. This benefit seeks to cash in on what Joeri referred to as the greatest scarcity of future consumers: time.

1. Faster than real time: from reactive to proactive service

Until recently, the aim of most companies was to provide customers with a good after-sales service. This led to the setting up of well-functioning contact centres, with a team of efficient staff ready to help customers with any problems they might have. Some companies were better than others, but most of them managed to provide a service that was acceptable.

Anticipating problems and solving them before they affect the customer will become the new norm.

With the rise of social media, speed and availability were added as two important new elements to the service equation. People began to ask questions via Facebook and Twitter, and expected to get answers in almost real-time. In reality, service via social media has turned out to be a disappointment for both companies and consumers. The response times on social media are too long for most questions – an average of hours rather than minutes. In other words, the classic telephone call is still currently the best and fastest way to get the information you want. Okay, you may need to listen to muzak for twenty minutes or so, but it's still quicker than social media. But it won't stay that way for long. Automated interfaces will soon make real-time customer communication possible – but even this will not be enough in the years ahead. Anticipating problems and solving them before they affect the customer will become the new norm.

Sensors linked to automatic service provision facilities are the key to faster-than-real-time customer service. For example, modern central heating systems are already smart. The classic systems of the past can often break down without warning – which is a touch inconvenient if it happens to be the middle of winter. You arrive home after a hard day's work to find that your house has been turned into a fridge. This is where the problems start for you as a customer. You phone the service centre in the hope of getting help quickly. Will the call centre still be open? Can they send a technician this evening? Or will it be tomorrow? And does that mean you will have to take a day off work? Even if everything goes smoothly, customers don't like the uncertainty and they don't like having to invest their precious time in this kind of thing. In contrast, a smart central heating system will tell you a week in advance that a problem is going to happen. So, instead of arriving home to an ice-box, you arrive home to the following friendly message: "Hi Steven, this is your central heating speaking. I'm afraid I'm experiencing some problems at the moment and might break down shortly. If you press the 'okay' button now, someone will call around tomorrow to fix me – if that's convenient." It's almost as if the unit has come to life.

Products and services come to life

We have often had the pleasure of working with Mickey Mc-Manus. Mickey is a visiting research fellow at Autodesk. He is also chairman of Maya Design. A few years ago, he wrote the book *Trillions*.[49] His basic argument is that we are currently living

in a world of billions, but in the near future this will become a world of trillions. Today, we have x-billion smartphones. Tomorrow, we will have x-trillion devices connected to the web. According to Mickey, each of these

Smart Central Heating systems announce failures **before they occur**

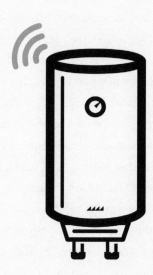

new devices will be capable of coming to life, which will open up whole new fields for applications. The explosion of data will have positive consequences for many different sectors. In factories, machines will decide when they need to be serviced. Sensors in furniture will adjust its shape to match individual users. For example, an armchair will be able to take account of the different physical characteristics of the husband, wife, children, etc. Once we have trillions of devices all linked to each other, the quantity of available data increases exponentially. As a result, the number of possibilities to improve service will also increase exponentially. There is a direct correlation.

The most important benefit of the trillions phenomenon will be faster-than-real-time customer service. Our smartphone alone contains something like ten sensors. If you combine the knowledge of these sensors with the other knowledge that the smartphone already possesses about our daily lives, the number of possible applications is almost limitless. In the near future, for example, airline companies will re-book your flight before you even know you are going to miss it. Your smartphone 'sees' that you are stuck in a traffic jam and relays this information automatically to the airport, where your booking is changed to the next available flight. As a result, your delay is kept to a minimum and the airline can re-sell your empty seat to another passenger. Win-win. In this way, it again seems as though your flight ticket has almost come to life, taking its own decisions to create the best outcome. I was able to interview Mickey McManus as part of my preparations for this book. Check out *www.youtube.com/stevenvanbelleghem* to view the full conversation.

The same evolution will be evident in business-to-business markets. In the near future, every machine, or part of the machine, will be able to come to life. The data these machines provide will again be the key to faster-than-real-time customer service. Spare parts will be delivered before the old parts have broken down. In fact, it will probably soon be possible to print new parts on site, cutting out the logistical link in the supply chain.

From sick care to health care

In the health sector, this new philosophy will lead to the complete change of the existing model. Today, we wait until someone gets sick and then hope that medical science has the answer to make this person better again. This is sick care – a reactive approach. In the future, care will become more pro-active. The new objective will be to ensure that people don't get sick in the first place. This is health care. Not only is this obviously better for the patient, but it is also the only way to keep medical care affordable in an era of growing and ageing populations.

Self-diagnosis and self-care will also increase. There is already a smartphone app that allows you to scan your skin for skin cancer, producing an analysis that is every bit as good as a dermatologist's. Another similar app is capable of locating eye cataracts at distance. Likewise, Google is working with Novartis to develop a smart contact lens that can measure a person's glucose level on the basis of their tears, so that diabetics can be given accurate information to adjust their medication, if necessary.

The smartphone will help both patients and doctors to make better diagnoses. This makes it much easier for people to monitor their own health. Proactive care of this kind also means that when problems do arise, they can be identified at an early stage, so that the chances of effective treatment are increased. It is not unrealistic to expect that before too long you may get a phone call to warn you of your impending heart attack! Like every other sector, medical care is also evolving towards the faster-than-real-time world.

In The Day After Tomorrow, every customer will be surrounded by sensors and smart technology that will turn the customer experience on its head. Reactive customer service will soon become a thing of the past. Solving problems before the customer discovers them is the new norm.

2. Hyper-personalization: from average to individual customer

Acustom Apparel is a great store in New York. If you look at the store window, it seems like a classic gentleman's outfitters. The window is full of elegant designer suits. In fact, Acustom Apparel specializes in personalized made-to-measure suits. Inside the store there is a scanner that scans two million data points on the body of each individual customer. This information serves as input to make the perfect suit. And once a customer's data is known and stored, he can order a new suit from anywhere in the world, delivered to his home in just a few weeks.

In 2017, the Adidas store in Berlin also started with the design and customization of personal sportswear. And Nike is also taking its first steps in this direction, offering the option of made-to-measure sport shoes to its customers. Many other brands in the fashion world are thinking about similar ways to personalize their products. The moment companies like Amazon and Zalando succeed in better personalizing their range in this way, the number of return deliveries will fall spectacularly – and so will the associated costs.

And it's not just products. In the future, services and communication will also be tailored more closely to the specific needs and context of the individual consumer. When people spoke about personalization in the past, all they meant was that a mail was introduced with a person's name ("Dear Steven...") rather than an anonymous greeting ("Dear Sir or Madam"). A few years ago, we saw the arrival of the first personalized brochures and magazines, where the cover was adjusted to match the profile of each reader. Digital printing has made more advanced forms of personalization possible, and companies like Nutella and Coca Cola have launched interesting campaigns where even the packaging is personalized to the name of the customer. The next step will be individual made-to-measure adverts and offers. The data and the algorithms know what the customers like and also the way they are feeling on any particular day. This will lead to a very specific and individualized form of advertising. In fact, it probably won't even seem like advertising. If your Google Assistant spontaneously makes a recommendation about some kind of relaxing activity for the weekend, the Google platform is taking account of your agenda, your mood, and the weather in the place where you live. This kind of advertising can actually sound more like a suggestion from a friend.

The segment of one

Hyper-personalization will become an important trend in the world of artificial intelligence. Once again, data is central to making this benefit possible. The more data there is available, the more relevant information and products become. This evolution means the end of the road for the old-style market philosophy of segmentation.

Segmentation divides the market into a number of groups with comparable needs. This allows the marketeer to match both communication and product characteristics to the needs of each different segment. Based on this philosophy, marketing people assume a high degree of homogeneity within segments and high level of heterogeneity between them. Segmentation still believes in the world of the average customer. If your market has four segments, this means you have just four types of customer. Each of these groups has its own persona and its own specific requirements. Imagine that your product is targeted at women between the ages of 35 and 40, with two children and a fulltime job. As an old-style marketeer, you will regard all these women as being more or less identical. But if you had the opportunity to see this group in real life, you would soon realize that they are far from identical!

Segmentation was a good halfway-house solution in a world where personal data was lacking. But this data is now available in abundance – and it shows that every consumer has a different personal context, which means that their consumption and communication needs are often fundamentally different. Segmentation still works, but only if the maximum size of the segment is one.

One of the major challenges in the telecoms market is to provide simple and effective support to customers when they want to change their provider. During a workshop at Telenet, one of the largest telecom players in Belgium, it soon became clear that this transfer process was something of a sore point. Many customers were not satisfied with the way the process was handled, even though Telenet had spent a lot of time and money writing out what it thought was a clear process. The problem was eventually solved when the people at Telenet finally realized that every transfer is different. As one of their managers put it: "We have made a standard process for the average customer, when we should be offering a personal service to individual customers." This is the segment of one in action.

A major transformation at McDonald's: Data and personalized service

McDonald's was founded in 1955. It is a classic company, active in a very competitive and price-conscious market that is complicated further still by the trend towards healthier eating. It is impressive how in recent years McDonald's has reinvented itself. Belgium is a test market for their restaurants of the future. The traditional system of queuing, ordering, waiting for your meal and then finding a table has been scrapped. A modern McDonald's restaurant has digital kiosks where the customers type in

The more data there is available, the more relevant information and products become.

their order and then go and sit down. Minutes later, the meal is brought to their table. Almost everything in the old philosophy has been thrown overboard and replaced by new ideas.

The next phase is even more radical: the transformation of McDonald's into a data company. The McDonald's app already helps the company to learn more about their customers. Sensors in the restaurants will soon be able to recognize customers as they enter. And not just the customers, but also those customers' individual needs. Imagine that a customer is allergic to cheese and taps this into the kiosk when making his/her order. The interface will store this information and, next time the customer

visits, the kiosk will proactively ask whether or not the customer would again like the cheese to be removed from the burger. If this request is confirmed on three separate visits, the cheese is thereafter removed automatically.

By using smartphones, sensors and data in this manner, McDonald's can go a long way towards personalizing its products, service and communication. The financial results from the first test restaurants are very encouraging. The majority of the restaurants have seen significant growth during the trial period with the new formula. For a company with its kind of historical background, operating in a hyper-competitive market, this is a remarkable transformation. As a result, in the first half of 2017 McDonald's share price rose by 26% to reach new record levels. There is talk that in the second half of 2017 a further 2,500 restaurants will be converted to this new approach.[50]

Personalized medicines

Today, medicines are developed for the average patient. We are, of course, very fortunate to have these medicines – they help a lot of people who are sick. However, the effect of an average medicine is often insufficient, and their average nature also leads to many different side-effects for different people. But now that the price for mapping the human genome has fallen from 100 million dollars (2001) to just 1,000 dollars (2015), we are standing on the threshold of personalized medication.[51] As soon as scientists are able to measure all the different elements of a person's body cheaply and effectively, there is no reason why medicines cannot be prepared to reflect the specific characteristics of those elements. This is the segment of one at work in health care.

Privacy?

Every consumer has a virtual footprint. Almost everything we do today leaves a trail of data. This information will be increasingly used to offer hyper-personalized service benefits to customers in a wide range of fields. However, this has led to discussions in some quarters about privacy. But not generally among consumers: the large majority are convinced of the potential benefits. A recent study showed that 71% of the respondents wanted to receive personalized communication and services.[52] Consumers want fast and relevant products and services. If this means sharing some of their data, it is a price they are willing to pay.

Too many companies see AI as a direct means to earn more money. You can almost see the dollar signs lighting up in their eyes whenever they hear the words 'big data'. However, the impact of AI and data are indirect. By offering customers extra relevance and personalization, you make those customers more satisfied. And if they are more satisfied, this will have an indirect influence on their future purchasing decisions. This is where you reap your financial reward: in the mid-to-long-term, not the short term.

3. Unparalleled ease of use ('convenience'): a world without a manual

Ready for a short test?

Do you ever use Booking.com?

If you do, please name five positive things about the site in the next 30 seconds.

Super, thank you.

Third question: are you (secretly) a little bit in love with the brand Booking.com? Are you a big fan?

During the last 12 months, I have done this little experiment as part of keynote speeches in just about every country in Europe. These are my findings (the target group is, of course, a business public):

There is roughly 90% market penetration for Booking.com in the business community.

The most common answers shouted out in the allotted 30 seconds include: fast, personal, the app, easy cancellation, no advance payments, the reviews, the photos, the maps, easy, the point scores and the huge range on offer.

Only 1% is a real fan of the Booking.com brand.

To me, this is amazing. Almost everyone uses the platform. Everyone is very positive about it. But almost no-one is a fan. For classic marketing profiles, this is a remarkable paradox. But in the new marketing world, this is the new normal. People don't fall in love with the brand, but with the brand's interface. If a new platform is launched tomorrow that is faster, easier and cheaper, they'll drop Booking.com like a stone. What's more, they will probably actively promote the new site to their friends.

The interface is increasingly becoming the key determining factor for brand positioning. Consider, for example, your bank. The most crucial interface for a bank, the one that can make or break it as a brand, is the mobile banking app. Why? Because people use it dozens of times each week. The impact of this app is much greater than anything that marketing and advertising can ever hope to achieve. The user interface determines market perception.

'Convenience is the new loyalty' is one of my mantras. In an impressive recent study, Byron Sharp came to the conclusion that classic loyalty programmes no longer work. These systems are based more on a reduction in the financial margin than on an actual increase in customer loyalty.[53] People are less faithful to their brand than to their favourite interface.

Another recent research project[54] into search behaviour on Amazon revealed that consumers today search much less on brand names than they did 10 years ago. If someone wants to buy shoes on Amazon, they are five to six times more likely to search by category name than by brand name. Once this has been done, they generally follow the recommendations suggested by the Amazon algorithms. The same is true to a lesser extent for people wanting to buy accessories. Here they only search three times more by category than by brand. One of the few exceptions is certain types of beauty products, where the category is 'only' 30% ahead of the brand. But in every category the same general conclusion holds true: generic searching is more important than brand searching. Loyalty to a brand has been transformed into loyalty to the most user-friendly interface.

Platforms are eating the world

We are now living in a world where individual market sectors are increasingly dominated by a small group of very big players. In the West, companies like Google, Amazon, Facebook, Uber and Airbnb have taken over their specific sectors. And it's the same story in the East, with the evolution of giants like Tencent and Alibaba. Google and Facebook have a duopoly in the field of online advertising, with everyone else pushed to the margin. Amazon and Alibaba tower above the rest of the online retail players, with the third placed company lightyears behind. Uber has conquered the on-demand mobility sector. In Asia, Tencent has a stranglehold on digital transactions and communication. What all these companies have in common are a gigantic customer base, an internationally dominant position and a huge lead in the technology stakes.

Voices in society sometimes express concern about the concentration of power in just a handful of mega-companies in the platform industry. Viewed from a social perspective, some of these arguments perhaps hold water. But the majority of consumers aren't really bothered: all they see is the benefits. Today's dominant tech- platforms are experts in offering faster-than-real-time service, hyper-personalization and unparalleled ease of use, supported by the very smartest state-of-the-art technology. For consumers, this is fantastic; for other smaller companies wanting a little piece of the action, it's a nightmare. The major technology players set the bar, and that bar is very high. 80% of the time spent by consumers on their smartphones is on one of these major platforms. Half is spent on Facebook and the rest is shared between YouTube, Google, Amazon, Netflix, etc. They determine the standards in service, interface and personalization, not their direct competitors. And the only way for the rest to survive is to try and follow – if they can.

In every industry, platforms will appear on the scene that rapidly accelerate the market dynamic. The more users they have, the greater the power of these platforms becomes. Nowadays, you have little choice other than to join in this platform economy.

There are two strategic options. The first is to build your own platform. This is what BMW decided to do: it built its own mobility platform. They want to make BMWs available in the world's major cities to provide a ride-sharing service à la Uber. Today, a BMW is sold once for 30,000 euros; in The Day After Tomorrow, a thousand BMWs will each be sold for 30 euros. In this way, BMW hopes to evolve as a car manufacturer with a mobility platform.

Unfortunately, for many of these new platforms it is already too late to make a difference. Once a leader has established its position, it is extremely difficult to overthrow them. Even a quality brand like BMW can already see the writing on the wall and has conceded that it will never be the biggest fish in the pond. Tony Douglas, their director of strategy, has even said so explicitly: "BMW won't be the biggest player in this field, but we hope to be the coolest."[55] The strategic choice to build your own platform certainly sends out a powerful signal, but it is difficult to do and costs a fortune.

The second strategic option is to hang on to coattails of an existing platform. In this way, for example, Walmart has chosen to collaborate with Uber's logistic network for its e-commerce deliveries.[56] Walmart's much bigger rival, Amazon, has already developed a gigantic logistic network of its own. It would take Walmart far too long to build something similar, even if they had the financial resources to do it. Making use of existing platforms is therefore the smart choice for the vast majority of companies.

Volvo also works with Uber. Uber doesn't make cars, but needs lots of them if they want to maintain their dominance in the world mobility market. Closing a big deal with an existing platform giant can often kickstart accelerated growth. And Volvo is not alone in this approach. Many other companies, often major players in their own right, use Amazon or Alibaba as their most important distribution channel. In all honesty, they don't really have much choice – because there is no viable alternative option.

Some companies try to avoid collaborating with the giants, for fear of making them even more powerful. This is nice in principle, but near suicidal in practice. These companies either eventually see sense, or else they go to the wall. If option 1 is not feasible – and 999 times out of a thousand it isn't – then option 2 is all that's left. The only way out of the devilish dilemma is to accept the rule of the strongest – and seek their co-operation.

WeChat: The operating system of China

The most influential platform in the world is undoubtedly WeChat. WeChat is part of the Chinese company Tencent. Some people call WeChat the Facebook and/or Whatsapp of the East. But that's not strictly true. WeChat has a totally different business model from Facebook. And it is lightyears ahead in its development.

At the time of writing (mid-2017), WeChat has some 938 million users.[57] Most of them, as you might expect, are in China. Internationally, it scores best where there are large Chinese communities – or so say some of the more mischievous commentators.

In reality, WeChat can be best described as the operating system of China. Almost every business transaction in the country takes place through WeChat. People buy flowers via the platform. They book restaurants and taxis. They even manage their finances through it, rather than via their bank app. The Chinese government is also happy to make use of the platform's immense power. For example, Chinese citizens can download and keep their identity cards and driving licenses on it, while all the administration linked to hospital visits are processed and stored in its data banks. The largest part (66%) of WeChat's turnover comes from these 'value added services'. The company receives a micro-payment for every transaction consumers, companies and organizations carry out. In the western world, if Facebook failed to work for a day it would be headline news, but the world would keep on turning. If WeChat failed to work for a day in China, the whole nation would grind to a halt.

The platform is the primary communication channel for the business community in China. Email is only used to communicate with foreigners. If you meet a new business contact, you show him/her your WeChat QR code. He/she scans the code and communication can begin. The WeChat QR code is also given a prominent place on Chinese business cards.

QR codes are very important for WeChat. In China they are often referred to as the gate between the digital and analogue worlds. Almost every payment is made by scanning a QR code in the We-

Chat application. 15% of WeChat's revenue comes from financial transactions, a functionality it only made available some three years ago. Before then, AliPay (the Alibaba mobile payment app) had a 100% monopoly. In just a few years, WeChat has already clawed back 50% of the market. During our innovation tour in China, it was noticeable how people gave you a strange look if you wanted to pay with a credit card, almost as though it was something from the Middle Ages!

Equally noticeable was just how proud the Chinese are of their super-app. In the western world, some people are critical of the power of Facebook. Nobody in China would ever dream of criticizing WeChat. In part, that's because the benefits to the Chinese people are huge.

- *Faster-than-real-time customer service*: the data held by WeChat is phenomenally impressive. They know everything: every transaction, every hospital visit, where people spend their money, what restaurants they eat in, what cars they drive, etc. They use this mine of information to anticipate behaviour in fields as diverse as mobility, healthcare and security. For example, their analyses of financial transactions can already help to identify and stop certain criminal activities.
- *Hyper-personalization*: everyone uses WeChat in his or her own specific way. People choose their own value-added services and therefore organize their lives the way they want, quickly and efficiently.
- *Convenience*: if you can do everything (business communication, purchases, payments, reservations, administrative mat-

ters, etc.) on a single platform, it is difficult to imagine anything that could be more convenient for the user.

WeChat is such a powerful platform that Chinese people, companies and organizations have no option but to use it. There is no Plan B. All you can do is accept its benevolent dominance and make best use of its many powerful facilities to extract the maximum amount of benefit.

Amazon Prime is the modern Trojan horse

Over the past 20 years, Amazon has evolved from a small online bookseller into the most powerful retail platform in the world. The Amazon share was launched on the stock market in 1997 at a price of 18 dollars. After various stock splits, this 18 dollars actually had a real value of just 2 dollars. Twenty years after the IPO, on 30 May 2017, the share finally passed the magical landmark of 1,000 dollars per share. In other words, if you bought 5,000 dollars of Amazon shares at the time of the stock market launch, in 2017 these shares would now be worth around 2,500,000 dollars.

In recent times, the company has undergone a remarkable metamorphosis. Not only have we seen the evolution from an internet bookseller to an online store where you can buy almost anything, but alongside their retail activities they have also been developing a cloud hosting service known as the Amazon Web Services. This cloud service has been amazingly successful and in 2016 had a turnover of more than 12 billion dollars.[58] Not bad for something that stated as a side-line. In June 2017, Amazon bought Whole Foods to enhance its footprint in the physical world. The company has also started to make its own hardware, with the Amazon Echo as its most successful product. It is a story of non-stop progress and success. But the most brilliant innovation of all is the introduction of Amazon Prime.

Prime was developed after Jeff Bezos gave a group of high potential professionals the task to design a business model that could break the Amazon empire. After a period of intense brainstorming, the group came up with the Prime concept. Jeff Bezos thought that it was such a good idea that he decided to implement it himself. In that way, he could beat the competition to the punch. And so Prime was born.

Prime is a modern loyalty programme. But it doesn't work like the classic loyalty card, where you need to buy ten loaves before you get an eleventh loaf for free. The Prime model works the other way around. You first pay an annual fee to be recognized as a loyal customer. But once you are an Amazon Prime member, you can enjoy many different kinds of benefits, such as the faster and cheaper delivery of the products you order.

Prime has been yet another bullseye shot for the company. In mid-2017 some 64% of American families have an Amazon Prime subscription.[59] The secret of the system's success lies in its psychology. Once people have paid for the extra service, they want to make sure that they get the most out of it. Human self-interest and greed does the rest. The more you buy from Amazon, the

Jeff Bezos

lower the Prime fee per transaction becomes. The annual fee for Amazon Prime is 99 dollars. So, if you buy something from the platform 99 times that year, the Prime subscription cost is just 1 dollar per transaction. But if you only buy something 10 times, the cost of Prime rises to 9.90 dollars per transaction. In other words, the more you buy, the cheaper it gets – or that's what the customer thinks.

Amazon continues to invest in new interfaces that make it even easier to buy things via Prime. We have already mentioned Amazon Echo, an interface already used by 30% of its owners to order products from Amazon by voice command, which is faster (and more fun) than via a number of mouse clicks on the website or in the app. Amazon has also invented the Dash button. These are little re-ordering buttons that you can put in convenient places, like next to your coffee machine. Once you run out of coffee, you just press the button and within an hour Amazon has delivered a new supply of your favourite brand.

The next step will be an interface that the customer doesn't even have to press. When Amazon starts working with the manufacturers of household devices, it will install smart sensors in every conceivable domestic appliance. These sensors will be able to measure the objective consumption of, say, your coffee percolator or washing machine. Before the customer even knows it, Amazon will deliver a new supply of washing powder or coffee beans before the old supply has been used up. Once Amazon succeeds in doing this, it will have built the biggest Trojan horse the business world has ever seen.

The result will be to strengthen Amazon's already huge dominance, based on satisfied and loyal Amazon Prime customers. Why? Because Amazon scores well on the three core benefits from the third phase of digitalization.

- *Faster-than-real-time customer service*: thanks to their data analysis, Amazon can already predict with reasonable accuracy when someone needs to buy something. In the near future, it will have even more information about its customers via interfaces like Amazon Echo and sensors in domestic appliances. This will mean that consumers no longer have to think about routine purchases. Amazon will deliver the necessary products before the customers even know they need them.
- *Hyper-personalisation*: Amazon's recommendation engine is world-famous. From day one, Amazon has been focused on personalization. Thanks to the Prime system, Amazon will get even greater insight into the needs and preferences of its individual customers, so that the personalization of recommendations, communication and deliveries will become even better than it already is.
- *Convenience*: struggling to carry heavy bags from your car to your house will become a thing of the past. Visiting your local supermarket will no longer be necessary. Amazon will allow you to order everything you need, quickly and easily, and will deliver it to your front door. And the quicker and easier it becomes, the more people will buy.

Jeff Bezos says in almost every interview: "Amazon has a laser focus on customers." At Amazon meetings, there is always an empty chair at the table – the customer's chair. The reflex to ask "what will the customer think?" is built into the company's culture. Amazon has become what it is today because they understand the needs and frustrations of customers in retail. Jeff Bezos is clear on this point. "Ideas are worthless. It's execution that determines what the customers get out of the deal."

"Start with the customer experience and work backwards"

There are lots of legendary videos with Steve Jobs. In my field of expertise, the most classic video of them all dates back to 1997. During an Apple developers' congress, a member of the audience asked an aggressive question. This man was disappointed that Apple was planning to scale back its OpenDoc platform. So disappointed, in fact, that he insulted Jobs by telling him that he didn't know what he was doing. When you read Steve Jobs' biography, you might expect him to hit back hard at this kind of attack. But precisely the opposite happened. He said that the man was right on some points. After this, he launched my favourite Steve Jobs quote: "You have to start with the customer experience and work backwards." This quote dates from before the mega-success of the iPod, iPhone and iPad. But it was at the heart of the vision that Steve Jobs wanted to develop for Apple. The customer experience has to come first, not the technology. If you start with the perfect customer experience, you will always end up with a positive result. If you start with the technology, the chance of ultimate disappointment is much greater.

Steve Jobs

AI is capable of helping customers in a faster, more personalized and more user-friendly manner. To determine your first AI applications, it is necessary to first think about the biggest frustrations of your customers. Make a list of the things about your company that you know are inconvenient or even irritating for them. Then search for ways to automate the processes involved. This is the way to achieve AI success.

Good for the customer! Good for society?

Good times are coming for customers. Service levels will be quicker, easier and more personal. The effort needed to buy things – personally or professionally – will diminish. We will all get used to the new AI world pretty fast. But there is another side to this story. A question I often hear during my presentations is this: "Fine, Steven, we can all see the benefits for the individual customer, but is this a good thing for society as a whole?"

Everyone knows that I am a positive person. The purpose of my books is to make people enthusiastic for the future. I hope that my ideas and opinions encourage entrepreneurs to take action that will make their customers happier. And so yes, I have a positive view of AI as well.

The evolution towards artificial intelligence also offers many benefits to society. A number of major societal problems will be solved, thanks to the power of automation. Driverless cars are probably the best example. Once the majority of cars are self-driving, the problem with traffic jams will disappear. According to the World Health Organization, more than 1.2 million people die each year from traffic-related causes. This figure will fall dramatically. Parents will be less worried if their kids ride to school each day on their bike or take the car at weekends to visit their friends. At the same time, we won't need as much space for car parking, so that more green zones can be introduced back into our towns and cities, improving both air quality and general public health.

In fact, AI is expected to help solve a number of crucial medical problems. A cure for cancer and several other currently fatal conditions is not beyond the bounds of possibility and it is certain that diagnosis and treatment of these conditions will significantly improve, increasing average life expectancy as a result. Even the major technology giants are enthusiastic about playing the health card. Microsoft, for example, has the ambition to eradicate cancer by 2027.[60] They want to fight the disease in the same way they fight computer viruses. If they are successful, a longer and healthier life is a clear positive result for society.

The potential benefits of AI are huge and the leaders of the major industrial players are anxious to use their 'new power' for the good of the planet. In a conversation with the *MIT Technology Review*,[61] Demis Hassabis, CEO of Google DeepMind, outlined his company's main objectives. He wants to use DeepMind to tackle the world's great problems, starting with climate change and the global food shortage. In the same interview, Mike Schroepfer, the Chief Technology Officer of Facebook, expressed similar ambitions. "The real power of AI is it scalability for dealing with big problems. The things that we are carrying out today on a small scale, we will soon be able to carry out on a large scale." Yes, there are reasons to be positive.

At the same time, it would be naive to pretend that there is no potential downside. Even the greatest optimists can see possible dangers and major challenges in the years ahead. At the end of his second term of office, President Obama gave a frank interview to *Wired Magazine*.[62] Obama demonstrated a good knowledge of the world of technology, and in general, he supports the current evolution of AI. According to the former president: "History shows that new technology leads to new jobs and improves people's standard of living." But he also sounded a note of warning, pointing to a number of possible threats that we need to think about seriously. "Imagine that someone develops an AI that can crack the codes for nuclear rockets, so that they can programme them to launch. If that happens, we've got a real problem."

However, the biggest problem is not likely to be military, but socio-economic. AI will lead to sudden and unexpected unemployment in a wide variety of sectors. "Highly educated people will no doubt be able to reap the rewards of the new developments. But for blue collar workers and for people who do work that is today important but repetitive, AI will probably make their jobs redundant," says Obama. AI expert Pieter Abbeel also talks of "sudden and large-scale unemployment" as a result of artificial intelligence. The possibility that we will create a 'useless class' is real.

The most serious threat posed by AI is not a Terminator scenario, where machines take over the world, but rather its potential to undermine the foundations of our social system. For this reason, conducting a debate about the possible impact of automation must be high on the agenda of all the world's leaders. It is a global problem that needs to be solved at a global level. Local solutions will not be enough.

In this book's final chapter, I will look more closely at these problems and the ethical debate related to the evolution of artificial intelligence. For now, it suffices to say that the years ahead promise us mixed fortunes and a bumpy ride. The world is standing on the eve of radical change. Some of these changes will be highly positive for the individual and for society. Sadly, some of them will be highly negative for the individual and society.

> **The world is standing on the eve of radical change. Some of these changes will be highly positive for the individual and for society. Sadly, some of them will be highly negative for the individual and society.**

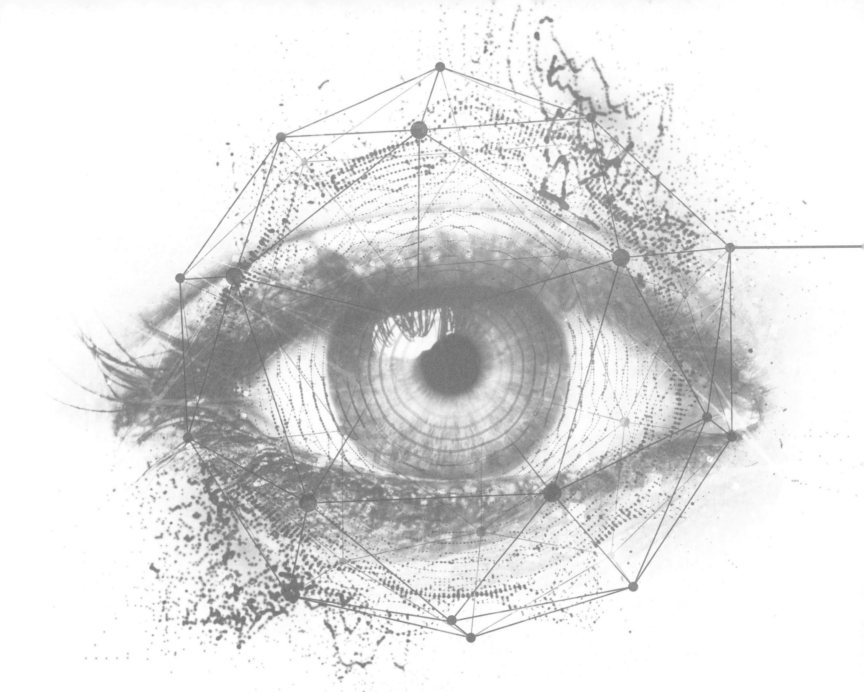

CHAPTER 4

THE DAY AFTER TOMORROW MODEL

The Azure Window

One of the top tourist attractions in Malta is the Azure Window, the most photographed rock on the island. Or rather, I should write that the Azure Window *was* the most photographed rock, because it no longer exists.[63]

The Azure Window owes its fame to its unique and beautiful shape. It is a gigantic rock formation attached to the coastline, with an arch through its middle, so that it looks like a natural bridge between the land and the sea. At high tide, boats can sail under the arch and it is a perfect place for really great photos. Or it was. Between 1980 and 2000, the forces of erosion began to do their silent but deadly work. The base of the arch became wider and wider. In 2012 and 2013, a number of large pieces broke off and fell into the sea, making the gap yet wider still. Tourists were no longer allowed to walk across the bridge. Boats were no longer allowed to sail under it.

At twenty to ten on the morning of 8 March 2017, the inevitable finally happened. The magnificent rock collapsed into the sea. One minute it was there; the next it was gone. There had been several severe storms in the weeks before 8 March, fatally weakening the rock's stability. Its foundations lost their strength and the rock tumbled into the waves. The Maltese government is currently

thinking about what to do next. One idea is to recover the shattered fragments of rocks from the sea floor, so that tourists can at least be photographed with the ruins of the Azure Window. Another option is to create an augmented reality application, so that tourists can see exactly where the rock once stood via the screen of their smartphones. One thing, however, is certain. The original rock is gone, and gone for good. Suddenly, just like that. First light erosion, then a more serious undermining of its foundations, and finally, the big crash.

This is a fantastic metaphor for the business world. The story of the Azure Window is the story of Nokia, Kodak and Blockbuster. It is also the story of tens of thousands of other smaller companies, whose names we have long since forgotten. We don't really miss these companies. Like the rock, they simply disappeared. Suddenly. Taken by surprise. Not that there were no warnings. On the contrary, there were clear signals that problems were on the way. First a little light erosion, with perhaps a decline in market share. Then a more and more serious undermining in consumer satisfaction, fatally weakening the stability of the business model. Finally, the mass defection of once loyal customers and the inevitable collapse into bankruptcy.

This metaphor is a challenge for every company. The third phase of digitalization will create new patterns of consumer behaviour. Many of them will only be observable in the market gradually over time. But once the tipping point is reached, the new behaviour will be adopted by the majority almost overnight. If you wait for that moment before you take action, you risk being swept away in the storm. It is not the new technology that causes the disruption; it is the changing behaviour of consumers. In most cases, you can see these changes coming, if you are alert. But if you do nothing in response, you will have no cause for complaint when your rock tumbles and falls.

The Day After Tomorrow

In mid-2017, a book entitled *The Day After Tomorrow* was published. It was written by Peter Hinssen,[64] a good friend and my business partner at nexxworks. Peter is both a technologist and an entrepreneur. No-one is better suited to describe how new technology is likely to impact on business. In his book, Peter outlines a new management model that we have devised and developed at nexxworks. It is our own Day After Tomorrow model and it is almost certainly the simplest management model in the world. Yet notwithstanding its simplicity, it creates the necessary degree of sharpness. It stimulates a different kind of debate. It promotes better understanding between the innovative and conservative forces that are present in every company. It helps business leaders to think in concrete terms about the future.

The model has three dimensions: Today, Tomorrow and The Day After Tomorrow.

Investing in Today results in value creation in the present. Investing in Tomorrow will result in value creation in the near future. Investing in The Day After Tomorrow will result in long-term value.

It is not the purpose of our model to convince companies to commit all their energy and resources to this third option. Far from it. Investing in Today is also necessary if you want to pay your bills. Your existing way of working ensures that you have cash in the bank, without which, you won't survive until Tomorrow, let alone The Day After. Having said that, if you do no more than invest in your current operations, at some point their value will inevitably start to decline. The trick is to keep your current situation profitable, while at the same time preparing for the future. There can be no future value without current value, but also no future without a viable scenario for The Day After Tomorrow.

When we first proposed this model to a client in the car sector, he was quick to offer us some concrete feedback. "Your model is incomplete," said the CEO. We didn't immediately understand what he meant. After all, our model is the simplest model ever!

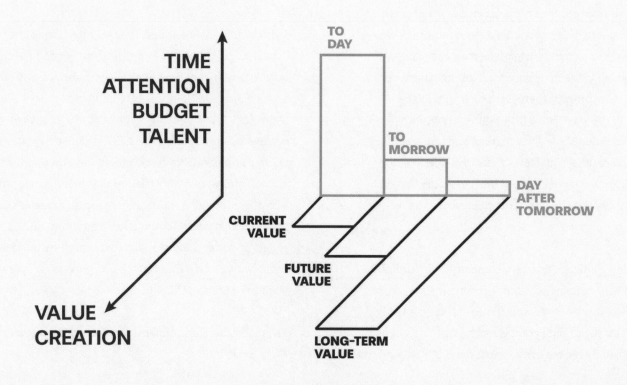

What more do you need than Today, Tomorrow and The Day After Tomorrow? "What you need," he explained, "is a dimension that you have completely overlooked: the Shit of Yesterday. We have dozens of old processes and procedures that are hopelessly out of date. There is no way that they can be of any use to us in The Day After Tomorrow."

This was good feedback. 'Shit of yesterday (SOY)' creates negative value for a company. We now realize that this aspect is very recognizable for most company leaders. You can't deny the existence of the shit of yesterday. Nor is it easy to avoid, in the sense that it is impossible to remove it surgically from your organization. All you can do is nurse it as best you can, while making the necessary preparations for The Day After Tomorrow. If you are too busy with the problems of the present, so that you fail to devote sufficient time and resources to the future, you will soon find yourself in a Malta scenario.

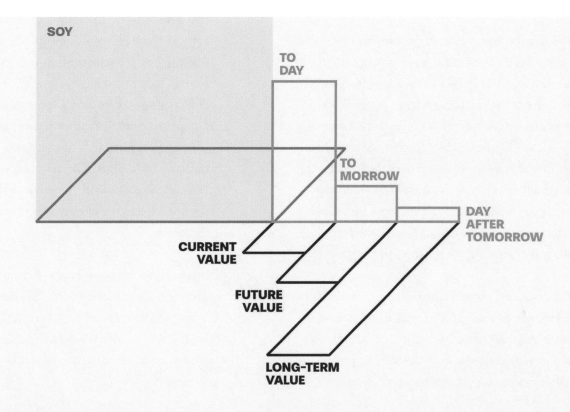

Towards the new customer relationship in The Day After Tomorrow

As a company, there are two ways you can get ready for the customer relationship of the future. You can take your current situation as your starting point and elaborate different scenarios to give a possible shape to the years ahead. In other words, you look at the present and work forwards, although there is a good chance that this will lead to careful, classic patterns of thought. Alternatively, you can take The Day After Tomorrow as your starting point and elaborate different scenarios to make this vision happen. In other words, you look at the future and work backwards, which is more likely to lead to more ambitious plans and certainly to different kinds of decisions, both in the short and long term.

Preparing for the customer relationship of The Day After Tomorrow is different for every company. Each sector has its own specific characteristics and challenges. Even so, it is possible to see a number of common patterns. There are three starting points that determine to a large extent how your change process will run:

1. *Companies with an analogue DNA*: these companies have often been in business for decades. They were set up long before there was any talk about online and digitalization. Most of them have grown on the basis of a good product, good service or a good sales organization, or in many cases perhaps, even a combination of all three. Introducing digital into these companies is difficult, both technically and in human terms. There is often quite a lot of shit of yesterday that needs to be cleaned up.

2. *Companies started in the first or second phase of digitalization*: these companies already have a digital DNA, but a DNA that is still stuck in the early days of the digital revolution. Many of these companies are now 20 years old, or even more. Recently, I even heard someone at Google complain – off the record – about their legacy systems. Their search engine was built in 1998. In other words, it comes from a different century.

3. *Companies started in the third phase of digitalization*: this is the youngest generation of companies, created in response to the latest technological developments. As a result, their digital DNA is fully up-to-date. They have very little shit of yesterday. In fact, they are already almost living in The Day After Tomorrow.

In their different ways, each type of company needs to think carefully about the challenges of The Day After Tomorrow. The last group will have fewest problems with the accumulations of the past, and so, with the right minimal adjustments, they should be able to adapt fairly easily to the new environment of the future.

The second group often includes some pretty large companies, maybe even one or two giants. These companies developed during the first phase of e-commerce, so it is open to question whether or not their systems are already adjusted to meet the needs of automation and the world of AI.

This will certainly not be the case with the first group of companies, the ones without a digital DNA. In many cases, the complexity of these organizations leads to slowness in response and a lack of flexibility. Three totally different starting points, but the challenge remains the same: avoid being surprised by the Malta scenario, so that you are ready for The Day After Tomorrow.

Customer 2020 at the KBC

The Belgian bank KBC is a typical example of a company setting off on its AI journey from the first starting point. The bank has been in business for decades and has an analogue DNA. Even so, it manages to approach its customers in a modern manner. The management team, under the leadership of CEO Johan Thijs, has made a clear choice to invest heavily in digital and in particular in improved customer experience. This brave and decisive approach, quickly taken, has put the bank in a strong position against its rivals in the battle to retain customers in the challenging world of

The Day After Tomorrow. It also prompted the *Harvard Business Review* to select Johan Thijs as the 19th best-performing CEO in the world.[65] KBC also won the 2017 award for the best bank transformation in the world.[66] No mean achievement for a Belgian bank.

Erik Luts, a member of the senior management team, is responsible for managing the customer of the future in KBC. Erik told me: "Large companies shouldn't complain about the speed at which they need to change their approach to customers. You can see most of these changes coming a mile off. There is time and money enough to adjust. The only thing you need to watch out for is that you don't waste too much time at top level in endless discussions about "the future"." KBC's flagship transformation project is the Customer 2020 initiative. You might also call it the bank's Day After Tomorrow project. The people who work in the Customer 2020 team are giving shape to the future of customer relations in the mid-to-long term.

Customer 2020 is an ambitious and wide-ranging project. Its aim is to give the bank a significant lead over its local competitors in the world of mobile banking. To make this possible, the IT department was completely revamped. CIO Rudy Peeters had the bright idea to let his IT team operate as a network. This resulted in greater speed and flexibility in the implementation of IT projects. When KBC Touch was launched in 2015, it was clear that the team was working well and reaching its objectives. This mobile and online application was built at lightning speed, but the quality of the interface is still top-notch.

What's more, the Customer 2020 team has a list of other projects in the pipeline, all intended to dramatically improve the experience of their customers. This list is based on input from three sources: first, an examination of existing customer frustrations and potential solutions; second, a list of specific questions answered by customers; and third, ideas originating from within the bank itself. The ideas on the list are then put into concrete practice by a team that now has more than 250 members. One wall in the Customer 2020 headquarters is covered with stars. Each star represents a project that has significantly improved customer experience in one way or another. There are already more than a hundred stars.

Of course, the vast majority of KBC employees continue to work, for the time being, with their familiar 'old' procedures. After all, the bank still needs to meet its current financial targets. But the sizeable group of Day After Tomorrow trailblazers are already making things better for their customers in the here and now, and are also sending an important signal to their colleagues for the future. Customer 2020 shows that KBC wants to be a company that can rise to the challenges of the years ahead – and it is impressive just how many Day After Tomorrow ideas they have already brought to fruition.

The next phase for Booking.com

A company like Booking.com is a good example of the second of our three starting points. It is a typical company from the first phase of e-commerce. They have a platform that works well. The customers are satisfied. The results are good. The scalability of the model is impressive. So much for the past and the present. What about the future? During a visit I made to Booking.com it immediately became clear to me that they see their current success as just a first step in a long process. The company is still fiercely ambitious. In fact, in terms of ambition, culture and general positive atmosphere, it is one of the most impressive companies I have ever visited. Today, Booking.com has a highly transactional process that allows customers to book a hotel room in a quick and easy way. If something goes wrong, there are 7,500 staff on hand to sort out the customer's problem proactively. But is their approach, service provision and technology already prepared to meet the challenges of The Day After Tomorrow?

Well, not really. Their Day After Tomorrow will look very different from their current situation. Booking.com dreams of even greater levels of personalization and ease of use. In fact, they want to become a one-stop-shop for holidays. If people can arrange all aspects of their entire holiday via Booking.com in the simplest yet still highly personal manner, the potential for a further increase in their business opportunities is huge. They can already see a trend towards bigger, better and faster platforms that help customers like they have never been helped before. This is the new wave they want to surf. They don't just want people to book a room with them, but also excursions, concerts, restaurants, etc. Perhaps there will even be Booking.com buses driving around at popular holiday destinations. The evolution from a booking site to a travel and holiday platform is their particular journey on the way to The Day After Tomorrow.

Lemonade, a very tasty insurer

Finally, you have a company like Lemonade. Lemonade is not in the soft drinks business, but is a new player in the insurance world. It was set up in September 2016 by people with no previous insurance experience. By June 2017, just nine months later, it already had more than 14,000 customers.[67] The company is one of the most exciting new arrivals to the insurance market for many years. During their first round of investment, the founders managed to secure no less than 13 million dollars of capital. This made them the company with the world's largest first investment round in 2015. The well-known investment corporation Sequoia Capital led the way with their largest seed investment ever. During the second capital round, it was Google that set the pace. These are impressive references for a young and previously unknown company, and it testifies to the strength of their business model.

Their focus is on the insurance of houses and their contents – a traditional insurance product – but their approach is fully geared towards The Day After Tomorrow. To begin with, they are 100% transparent about their business model. "Classic insurers seek to maximize their profit. By definition, that's bad for the customers," say the founders of Lemonade. Lemonade wants to keep a margin of 20%, but no more. If there is extra profit, the customer can choose to which good cause it should be donated. In addition, their pricing strategy is very simple. There is a fixed cost each month and no small print. Concluding a contract with Lemonade lasts on average about 90 seconds. If you have a claim against your policy, you don't talk to a person, but to a Lemonade chatbot. They have made a deliberate choice to automate all their service procedures. In other words, artificial intelligence is central to their thinking. This means that for customers everything is remarkably quick and easy in comparison with the rest of the insurance sector. Once you have submitted your claim to the chatbot, it takes an average of three minutes before the compensation payment is in your bank account. Of course, like every bot, the Lemonade bot still has a lot to learn. Until then, it will still occasionally be assisted by human personnel. But that's just a temporary measure. In the short term, the aim is to handle 90% of all claims using artificial intelligence bots.[68] In the medium term, the aim is 100%.

This is a terrific example of a company that already has one foot in The Day After Tomorrow. They have no problems whatsoever with shit of yesterday. They can build everything from scratch with the focus exclusively on the needs of the consumer of the future.

Knab moves into the insurance world

Knab is the online bank of financial player Aegon. The name is actually 'bank' spelt backwards – symbolism that is important to Aegon, who founded the new bank in 2012 with the aim of turning the traditional banking world on its head (or at least back to front). It is an interesting story. Aegon is unquestionably a company in the first of our three starting positions: it is a large corporation with a rigidly analogue DNA. But Knab is clearly an example of the third position. This is a deliberate strategy by Aegon. To prepare themselves for The Day After Tomorrow, they have set up this separate company. In this way, they hope to make the AI transformation more quickly, without being held back by the mother company's accumulation of shit of yesterday.

The online bank had a difficult start, but is now a big success. One of their most lucrative products is a mortgage targeted particularly at business customers, introduced online in November 2015. The bank's total number of customers grew rapidly in 2016, from 81,000 at the end of 2015 to 121,000 just 12 months later, of which 52,000 were business customers.[69] Their next planned step is to break into the insurance market. Their service provision will be organized with more than one eye on The Day After Tomorrow. Like Lemonade, they will publish transparent prices and deal with claims through automated systems. In one sense, it is fascinating to watch how a classic player like Aegon is attempting to adapt to the revolutionary Lemonade model, notwithstanding its old and complex structure. The solution they have developed works for Aegon, but there are other organizational models that companies can use to prepare for the future. In chapter 9, guest author Peter Hinssen describes these alternative models, which will help you to survive and thrive in The Day After Tomorrow.

Three starting points, one philosophy

There may well be three different starting points (analogue DNA, digital DNA from phases 1 and 2, or digital DNA from phase 3), but The Day After Tomorrow philosophy remains the same in all three cases. No matter where you start from, you need to think up scenarios to meet the changing future needs of your customers. Every company must address the crucial task of allocating its resources of time, money and talent to projects that will ensure stable progress not only Today, but also Tomorrow and The Day After Tomorrow.

Solutions to get around The Day After Tomorrow stalemate

Most company leaders and managers are enthusiastic when you talk with them about the future. Yet strangely enough, very few of them do much to prepare for that future with the necessary speed and urgency. This difference between 'talking the talk' and 'walking the walk' often lies in a stalemate inherent in planning for The Day After Tomorrow.

Consider the following situation, which will be familiar to many of you. Imagine that you are wildly enthusiastic about a new product that will take your customer relations to the next level. You present the idea with passion to your various teams. Their initial response is also positive, but there always comes a point when someone says: "Yes, that's a great idea but... perhaps it's a little too early to invest in it just yet. Our present operations are still far from perfect. Shouldn't we get that sorted out first before we start on a new adventure for the future?"

This is the most irritating thing that can happen to anyone who wants to put forward a new idea. The initial enthusiasm fades

away and before you know it the meeting is locked in a stalemate situation. Some people want to push ahead; others want to keep their hand on the brake. In the following months, nothing much happens, apart from an occasional update of progress (or the lack of it) on some PowerPoint slides. The innovators lose patience with the conservatives, who are more concerned with jam today rather than jam tomorrow. In turn, these more cautious souls cannot understand the frustration of the futurists. Yet the truth is very simple: both sides are 100% correct. It is crucial to invest in the present, but at the same time it is equally crucial to invest in the future. It is not an 'either... or' discussion. It is an 'and... and' discussion. However, agreeing in advance whether the meeting is about Today, Tomorrow or The Day After Tomorrow can make things a lot clearer for all concerned.

It is crucial to invest in the present, but at the same time it is equally crucial to invest in the future.

The expectation of Today versus The Day After Tomorrow

As a company, it is important that you specify your expectations for each different project. During an interactive workshop, I once listened to a manager in a large banking organization talk enthusiastically about a project with IBM Watson in his bank. He was pleased that the organization was experimenting with new technology. His only fear was that the evaluation would be negative. The project was turning out to be more expensive than originally anticipated and the results were also less than had been hoped. It turned out that the Watson project was set up to simulate the introduction of new savings product. The expectations and evaluation parameters were exactly the same for The Day After Tomorrow project as for a routine Today project. This is always doomed to fail.

In Today's world, investment is relatively straightforward. You invest in your present model and you expect an immediate return. Every dollar you put into Today has to make money. Using the same philosophy for Day After Tomorrow projects is a big mistake. Day After Tomorrow projects are subject to different criteria for success and failure. And it has to be accepted that failure is much more common. Today is about making money. The Day After Tomorrow is about preserving customer relevance. For this reason, every company would be well advised to define these different parameters clearly and keep them apart.

Typical parameters for Day After Tomorrow projects are:
- Potential for *upscaling*: if you try something new and it turns out only to be relevant for a handful of your customers, you are clearly on the wrong path. Scalability for the majority of your customers is crucial.
- *Potential for increased efficiency*: what is the likelihood of significant savings in the long term? Starting with small-scale automated applications is a good learning school for larger-scale automation projects later on.

The expectations and evaluation parameters were exactly the same for The Day After Tomorrow project as for a routine Today project. This is always doomed to fail.

- *Potential for reaching new customer groups*: will the project attract new customers and, if so, which ones and how many?
- *Potential for improving the Customer Effort Score*: will the project reduce the effort customers need to make? The lower the Customer Effort Score, the higher the level of convenience, which is better for all concerned.

In short, Day After Tomorrow experiments are about the long-term potential of the project. Today experiments are – quite rightly – about assessing short-term potential, something for which most evaluation parameters are perfectly suited. Business case templates are designed for the Today business. But it is a mistake to judge Day After Tomorrow projects on the basis of short-term parameters.

Play offensively

Digitalization puts pressure on the turnover and profit figures of companies. As a result, company leaders are still too cautious about investing in digitalization, according to a wide-ranging report by McKinsey.[70] This is short-sighted, because the same report also concludes that the more aggressively a company invests in digital applications, the more positive its business results become. There is one exception. If a company launches an attack on one of the major digital super-platforms, it is doomed to fail. Trying to fight superheroes is never a good idea. Collaborating with them is much smarter. Making use of their immense scale works well in combination with serious investment in your own possibilities.[71]

Excessive caution and a too limited focus on The Day After Tomorrow will restrict your growth. For some managers, this sounds counterintuitive: investing more in uncertain applications increases the company's overall cost structure, which (theoretically) will slow down profit growth further still. Once again, the McKinsey results prove the opposite. By investing more in an uncertain future, you help to give that future shape and form. You are not chasing the game; you are making the game. So, focus on your offence, not your defence. It pays!

Customers The Day After Tomorrow in Efteling

Efteling is one of the most visited theme parks and holiday destinations in Europe. In 2017, it was chosen as the best amusement park in the world.[72] Located in the Dutch province of North Brabant, it is famous for its nostalgic enchanted forest, its state-of-the-art attractions and its friendly atmosphere. 2017 marked the park's 65th anniversary, and its history makes interesting reading. It was started in 1952 by a group of monks who wanted to give local children somewhere fun to play. Originally, the idea was to create a set of fairy tale scenes in a piece of woodland owned by the local authority. But the burgomaster, or mayor, was an ambitious man with an ambitious plan. He chose Anton Piek, a well-known artist, to designs the scenes and the results were so magical that people not only came from the surrounding villages, but from all over the Netherlands to see them.

Today, Efteling is still owned by a foundation; nobody makes any money from the park. All the profits are split between reinvestment in the park, nature preservation projects and donations to good causes. In theory, everything that Efteling does is meant to be lasting, or 'forever', as they say. Quality and history mean more than short-term financial gain. For example, there is a rule that no more than 11% of the park can be devoted to buildings; the rest must remain natural. This is the kind of decision that typifies Efteling.

 In February 2017, I had the pleasure of accompanying the management and a group of enthusiastic staff from Efteling on a visit to Silicon Valley. My task was to draw up a programme that would teach them more about the future of customer-orientation and marketing. It was a fantastic week, during which we talked to more than 20 of the Valley's experts. The topics we discussed had nothing to do directly with amusement parks, but were focused on likely changes in consumer behaviour in the years ahead. These insights had a

major impact on Efteling's development of their own Day After Tomorrow strategy.

For my new book, I interviewed Fons Jurgens, CEO of Efteling. Once again, the full interview can be seen on *www.youtube.com/ stevenvanbelleghem*. Fons and his team have tried to map out what the customer journey will be like in 2030. In other words, they are already starting with The Day After Tomorrow. Efteling has a clearly defined area, where the opportunities for using sensors in combination with smartphones are almost limitless. With this in mind, the Efteling team began to dream about the possible future for their park. Wouldn't it be great, for example, if people didn't have to queue at the ticket office when they arrived? In this way, physically checking the tickets could also be eliminated. People would buy their tickets in advance and just stroll into the park past sensors that would decide whether they had the right to be there or not. Instead of being welcomed by turnstiles and security monitors, they would be welcomed by fantasy figures. Investing in new parking areas will probably also be unnecessary in 2030, given the advent of self-driving cars. If you know that Efteling invests in 'forever', then you can understand

that for them further investment in parking space is something they would rather not do. Perhaps more in-keeping with their philosophy is the idea to construct huge roundabouts to allow people to get out of their cars at the entrance of the park, before the vehicles self-drive themselves to the nearby holiday homes that their owners have booked for later that evening. Once inside the park, your personal AI assistant will help you work out your programme for the day, as well as buying your food, which can be delivered to the picnic area of your choice at the hour you stip-ulate. Once again, no queuing, no wasted time and no splitting up of families during lunchtime. Are some attractions more or less accessible today? Your AI assistant will tell you... These are the kind of scenarios that the Efteling team are already working out in detail. And so, the world of 2030 slowly takes concrete form.

Efteling in 2030 will not only be a fun attraction park; it will be a world of perfect customer experience. An experience tailor-made to meet guests' requirements, using technology to eliminate all

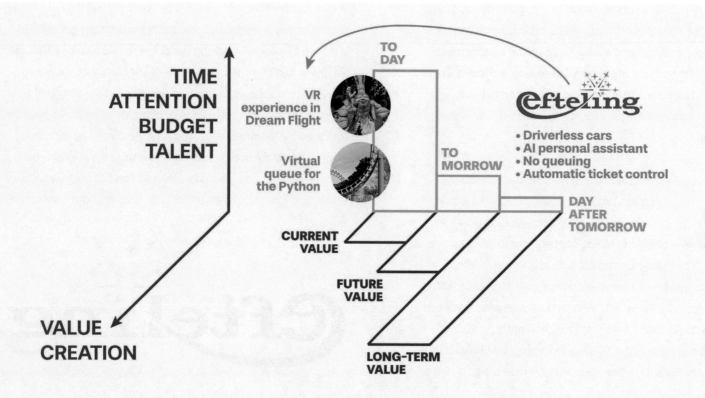

the things that customers currently find tiresome. But at the same time, it is also important for Efteling to maintain its identity. Good, honest human fun is the park's DNA. This will not be lost. Technology will just make things run even more smoothly, allowing Efteling more room to take its human interaction to a higher level. The 'when digital becomes human' philosophy remains central.

That is how the world will be in 2030. That is how the Efteling experience will be in The Day After Tomorrow. Dreaming about these fantastic scenarios is a wonderful starting point. From there, the Efteling team can work back towards the present. This brings the future very close. Of course, not everything will work out the way it is envisaged in the scenarios, but they are a good basis for making the right strategic choices. What's more, Efteling is already investigating how some elements of this future can be realized today. In fact, two such elements have already been implemented in practice.

A first benefit relates to the Dream Flight, one of the park's top attractions. Dream Flight has one major disadvantage: for safety reasons, it cannot be used by people with certain disabilities. To overcome this, a VR application has been developed to replicate the flight. That way, everyone can share in the experience. So even if a family needs to be separated (some go on the real ride, some follow the VR version), they can still talk about it afterwards. One of the main problems with VR is that it is usually a highly individual experience – but not in this case. From the start of 2018, this particular dream will become a reality.

Efteling has also started with its first virtual queue. Starting from September 2017, the Python roller-coaster ride no longer has long lines of waiting people. A reservation system in the Efteling app allows visitors to choose and book their own ride time. Efteling guarantees that no-one will ever need to wait for more than 15 minutes. This is long enough for the pre-ride tension to build up, but gone are the days of waiting times of up to 90 minutes or more.

The way in which Efteling is preparing for the future is the ideal approach to bring The Day After Tomorrow to life. You start by looking far into the future. You write scenarios to match that future. You then work backwards, gradually developing projects to make your dreams happen in the real world as soon as possible, sometimes even in the relatively short term. Does it always work out as planned? Maybe, maybe not. But one thing is certain: the choices you make would never be the same if you tried to start this process from the situation as it exists today.

The way in which Efteling is preparing for the future is the ideal approach to bring The Day After Tomorrow to life.

Four axes of investment on the road to The Day After Tomorrow

Gaining insight into The Day After Tomorrow is not easy. The secret is to write scenarios for the future and use them as your starting point. If you try to extrapolate from the present situation, the results will never be up to scratch. Your aim is to bring to life the customer benefits described in chapter 3. How can you offer faster-than-real-time service? What must you do to make that service hyper-personal? How can you make your interfaces as user-friendly as possible? These are the crucial questions on the road to The Day After Tomorrow.

In the next four chapters I will describe four investments that can bring you closer to your goal. Each one will help you and your company to transform your customer relations.

1. The data lever

How much data does your company have about your customers? Even more importantly: to what extent do you manage to use that data as a lever? In the years ahead, there will be major budget shifts in most companies. The budget for classic marketing will be reduced in favour of data management. The marketing of The Day After Tomorrow will be less about creativity and more about scientific analysis, with data as the central element of strategy.

2. New user interfaces

The world of AI will generate countless new interfaces. We will see more and more chatbots, smart speakers and self-driving cars. The new interfaces will make new customer benefits tangible. Ease of use will become the biggest driver of loyalty. The purpose of AI is not to eliminate every single fault; its purpose is to reduce user effort to a minimum. If user effort increases, user loyalty falls. Having the right interfaces – fully automated, real-time, 24/7 availability – means this won't happen to you.

3. Fighting the commodity magnet

Digital increases the likelihood of commodity forming. Information and pricing will be transparent. The difference between products will shrink. The power of the great digital platforms will reduce most brands to a lower status. What was once an A-brand will become a B-brand. The new A-brands are the digital platforms themselves. The new reasoning says: "I trust Amazon because they give me good recommendations". So, Amazon becomes the A-brand and you are reduced to the B-levels. There's not much you can do to fight the immense power of the digital giants, but you must do everything possible to resist the strong pull of the digital commodity magnet – and your investments must reflect this.

4. Intelligence augmented

Technology helps people to perform at a higher level. Just as our physical limitations were overcome by the machines of the Industrial Revolution, AI will help us to overcome our mental limitations. When farmers first started using machines in their fields hundreds of years ago, people looked at them as though they had gone mad. Were these strange contraptions really necessary? But it soon became clear that the innovators had the best crop yield and earned the most money. As a result, others soon followed. And it will be the same in the future. If companies invest in AI software to improve the performance of their people in customer service, better results will be achieved. Technology always enhances the quality of human output. Computer power boosts existing levels of intelligence, so you can't afford for your company to be left behind.

The data lever

Fighting the commodity magnet

New user interfaces

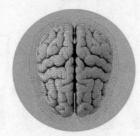

Intelligence Augmented

THE
DAY
AFTER
TOMORROW
INVESTMENT AXES

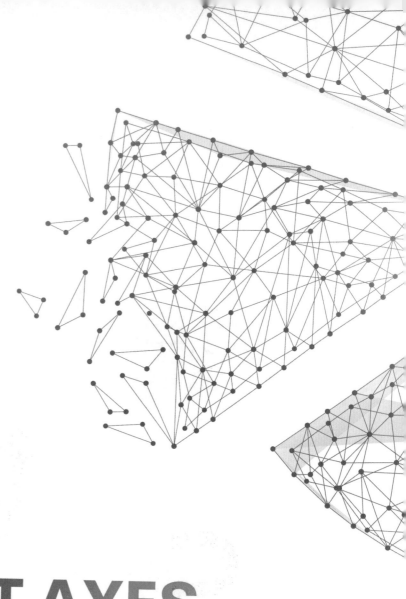

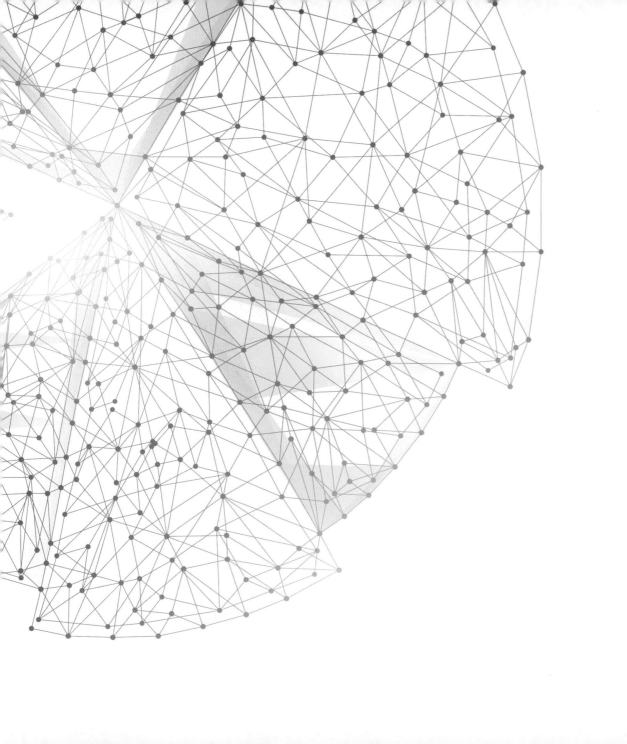

CHAPTER 5

THE DATA LEVER

The limitations of segmentation

Segmentation is a concept from classic marketing science. But segmentation will no longer be sufficient to achieve the three key customer benefits in the third phase of digitalization. Why? Because segmentation makes two wrong assumptions. First, it assumes that everyone within the same segment has the same needs. As a result, it works with the average customer instead of the individual customer. The average customer was a good proxy to work with in a world without personal data. But not anymore.

Second, it assumes that the needs of a segment remain identical at each moment in time, whereas customers can actually have different needs, depending on their context. A businessman with a tight schedule might decide to fly business class to save time. But if his schedule is more flexible, he may decide to fly economy

The average customer was a good proxy to work with in a world without personal data.

class to save money. And if he decides to fly with his family, the context changes again. Similarly, some people may want the luxury of a 5-star hotel in the Seychelles for this year's holiday, but may be content to go back-packing in the Himalayas next year. Or what about the VIP guests who are offered business seats at football matches, but prefer to stand in the crowd behind the goal for the atmosphere?

Segmentation almost becomes ludicrous if it is applied too rigidly. A friend of mine once sold his company for a tidy sum of money and so became a private banking client at his bank. From that moment on, he started to receive a very different kind of hospitality invitation from his local branch. All of a sudden, he was invited to attend high-class luxury events. There was just one problem: he wasn't interested. Puzzled, his bank asked him what kind of invitation he really wanted. He answered: "Before I was a private banking customer, you used to send me invitations to music festivals. I enjoyed that. It would be great if you could start that again." To which his bank manager replied with embarrassment: "I'm terribly sorry but I'm afraid that's not possible. Those kind of invitations are not available for our private banking customers..." In other words, once you have a couple of million in your bank account, you are expected to attend a different type of social and cultural function! Segmentation in its most distorted form.

Since the arrival of the smartphone, we all leave a huge trail of data behind, wherever we go and whatever we do. As soon as a child opens its first account on Snapchat or Playstation, the trail begins. And it only ends when we are old and grey. All this information makes it possible for companies to hyper-personalize their products, services and communication. And the more extensively this data is used, the more personal the approach to the individual customer becomes. Managing this lever is an important investment axis for The Day After Tomorrow.

The power of context

Marketeers are in urgent need of a crucial new skill: contextual awareness. Understanding the customer's personal context is the only way to effectively realize the three key customer benefits of the future. Fortunately, technology will soon offer us increasing possibilities to map out the constantly changing contexts of customers and their associated needs. At its current stage of development, AI is not yet powerful enough to do this adequately. It is only when the breakthrough to unsupervised learning is made that machines will be able to automatically monitor and plot the customer's context. And once the context is known, machines can respond to it with a high degree of personalization. For example, the Spotify algorithm currently recommends songs we might like to hear on the basis of our past listening behaviour. This is fine, but it takes no account of context. Even if your grandmother has just died, Spotify will keep on recommending happy tunes, whether you like it or not. But in the world of unsupervised learning, Spotify will be fed with data from multiple

sources that will allow it to assess your mood and adjust its recommendations accordingly. You can almost regard it as a kind of artificial empathy.

In other words, your action for today is to think about ways to install more data points that can gather the information you need to understand the contexts of your individual customers. The present generation of machines is not yet capable of drawing the right conclusions, but people are. So, give your people all the different data at your disposal and let them get started. Work out what influences the context of your customers and build up a data plan to reflect your findings.

Who is reading who?

Gathering knowledge about your customers and their contexts will be a fundamental principle of marketing in The Day After Tomorrow. Every company will need a data plan. How can the data be collected? What tools should be used to interpret that data, so that the context of individual customers can be better understood? How can this information be used to achieve better results?

Consider for a moment the evolution of books. I am delighted that you are currently reading this book of mine. But if you read the book in hard copy, I can learn nothing about your reading behaviour. True, I get a report from my publisher each quarter about the number of copies sold, and that's fine . But again, it doesn't tell me much about my reading public. Are the books actually being read, or are they just put on a shelf and forgotten?

In the world of e-books, however, things are very different. If people buy books digitally, the author knows whether they are being read or not. In fact, such is the range of data provided that he even knows which chapters are being skipped, which ones are being re-read and whether or not the reader fell asleep before getting to the end. In this world, the reading of a book changes into a process of data provision and analysis. If you read a book on an e-reader, you can reasonably ask yourself who is really reading who? And the answer is clear: the e-reader is learning much more about you than the other way around!

From security to knowledge

Until recently, security was the main purpose of the many closed-circuit camera systems in the world. Think, for example, of the hundreds of cameras in Las Vegas casinos. These cameras once had just a single purpose: to keep a watchful eye on the gambling public. They can spot potential cheats or people getting progressively agitated ad aggressive as they lose more and more money. But during the past few years the main function of such cameras has been slowly changing from security to knowledge. The casinos now study how the players handle their cards or bet on the roulette wheel. They watch for signs and learn techniques that will keep people at the gaming tables for longer. The better the casino understands the contexts of its punters, the more money it will be able to extract from them. The camera no longer just keeps an eye on the players, but also on the setting in which they operate.[73]

The Dutch company Big Brother has been analyzing the data from video recordings in petrol stations for years. The main reason is to track down non-payers. The camera scans the car number plate. If the car then drives off without paying, the garage can easily set the police onto them and recover their money. Yet here, too, the main aim of the video analysis is slowly changing. The focus is switching from security to knowledge to automatic service provision. The smart cameras not only identify bad customers but also loyal customers. If you link this information to an app, a whole new range of services suddenly become possible. Big Brother recently launched their 'my order' service, which allows people to fill up with petrol on the basis of number plate recognition. The camera recognizes the car. The driver starts refuelling. Payment takes place automatically through the app. And you can take things much further than that. For example, you can allow your customers to order and pay for food and drink from the service station shop through the app. This is a typical example of where data leverage works well. Initially, the

data was only put to limited use. But once the data is exploited to understand the customer and the context better, the lever comes into action. This results in automated services that improve the customer's experience. Which ultimately leads to better results for the petrol station.

Google retail lab

In the previous two examples, the offline environment goes to a lot of effort to digitalize their world. They collect data and then use that data as a lever to provide modern services. In the first phase of digitalization only the digital world was digital. A few years ago, both of these examples would have been more difficult and more expensive to achieve technically.

Today, the offline world is also digital. In the past, Amazon had a huge advantage over offline stores: data. Amazon had masses of data about everything their customers did and bought. In comparison, the classic department stores had only limited data about their customers. But this is now changing – on the condition that the analogue world is willing to invest sufficiently in data build-up.

During a recent visit to a Google research centre, we were shown a number of their trials. One involves experimenting with some of the tech-elements of self-driving cars in a retail environment. More specifically, they are making use of the 360 degree laser scan-

Once the data is exploited to understand the customer and the context better, the lever comes into action.

ner in the roof of the car. Through this scanner, the car 'sees' what is happening around it. The resulting data then serves as input for the car's next movement. This same technology is now being tested in the Google gift shop on the Google Campus in Mountain View. As output, the shop receives a detailed summary about how people are moving through the store. There is even a kind of laser analysis that indicates which individual items they are looking at. In effect, this tool translates the offline environment into data. The analysis of this data provides offline stores plenty of information to better understand consumer behaviour. At last, it gives them the same weapons as the pure digital players like Amazon.

Ali-ID: the power of Youku Tudou and Alibaba

Collecting data and gaining insights is just the first step in using the data lever. The next step is to extract effective commercial value from it. The combination of Youku Tudou and Alibaba is unquestionably one of the most powerful examples of how data can be used as a lever for further growth.

Youku Tudou is one of China's largest video companies. If you can imagine an Oriental cross between YouTube and Netflix, you begin to get some idea of its scale. Youku Tudou makes its own content productions and also allows user-generated content. The company is the result of a merger between Youku and Tudou in 2012, a merger that immediately boosted them into the position of market leader in the online video sector. In April 2016, the company was sold to Alibaba for an estimated 4 billion dollars.[74] Alibaba (China) is the largest e-commerce marketplace in the world. For many observers, this acquisition was difficult to understand. Why would an e-commerce giant want to buy a media giant? The answer is to be found in a single word: data! Imagine the possibilities that open up if you can link the database of the world's largest e-commerce platform to the database of one of the world's largest media players. Providing you can develop the technology to hyper-personalize the use of this mountain of data, you effectively have a licence to print money.

Over the last two years I have visited Youku Tudou twice. The first time was a week before the takeover by Alibaba, and the atmosphere was clearly positive. The second time was some 18

months later, but you could immediately feel that the merger had created a degree of tension on both sides. However, these are just teething troubles. The pieces of the puzzle will soon fall into place, so that the data lever can do its magical work to the benefit of all concerned.

All Alibaba customers have a unique Ali-ID. This ID is used on various Alibaba sites and is now also used by Youku Tudou. In other words, Youku Tudou knows who is watching what content. Of course, Netflix knows that as well, but the big difference is the link to a company like Alibaba. This link connects the public's viewing behaviour with the public's shopping behaviour – and this is something that Netflix can't currently do. It would only be possible in the West if, for example, Netflix joined forces with Amazon. This would create a combined data source of immense potential. And this is what their Chinese counterparts already have. As a result, Youku Tudou can personalize advertisements for its programmes on the basis of the individual consumer's purchasing behaviour. Imagine that you watch *The Voice* on Youku Tudou and that your favourite drink is Cola. Your best friend also watches *The Voice* and her favourite drink is Cola Zero. Well, in the version of the programme you watch all the coaches will drink Cola; and in the version of the programme she watches all the coaches will drink Cola Zero. Before too long, you will also be able to click on the cans to order a new supply, which will be delivered to your home an hour later by an electric Alibaba scooter. Likewise, in the near future actors will be using phones that Alibaba thinks you might like to buy; again, you will be able to click on the phone to order it, with delivery taking place before the end of the programme. In the next episode, the same actor will be using a different phone, with the aim of attracting different customers with different tastes! The possibilities are endless.

In these examples, the Ali-ID is the unique interface that brings the different data sources together. This ID, combined with the technological ability to personalize consumer content, is an impressive and powerful tool. The value for the consumer is a higher relevance via personalized messages. The value for the company is in the bottom line.

One Football: Youku Tudou on a smaller scale

When they read about examples like Youku Tudou and Alibaba, many smaller companies start to doubt whether the data lever could ever work for them. But it can. Big is beautiful, but small can be beautiful as well. Consider the case of One Football. With more than 24 million users, One Football is the most popular football app in the world.[75] It was started by a German company in 2008 as a text service, which made it possible for football fans to follow the results in 16 countries via sms. A short time later, One Football became one of the first sport apps in the app store. The headquarters of One Football are great. The office looks exactly like a football stadium. The floor is made of artificial grass. There are goal posts. The meeting areas are like the terraces and stands that you see in a real football ground. Not surprisingly, the atmosphere is fun and friendly.

One Football is proof that small companies can also succeed in the digital world. But to do it, you need to make maximum use of the data lever. When I visited the company, it soon became clear that they apply the same philosophy as Youku Tudou, but on a smaller scale. When downloading the app, the company asks its users one crucial question: what is your favourite football team?

It sounds like nothing, but just this single data point opens up a whole range of possibilities.

My favourite football team is Club Brugge. I downloaded the app at the start of 2016. It was 11 years since Club had last won the title, but this time things were looking promising. The crunch game was played in May 2016 against our biggest rivals, Anderlecht. If Club won, they would be champions for the first time in more than a decade. In other words, a match of life-or-death importance! As soon as One Football knows that Club Brugge is my favourite team, all this information (not champion for more than

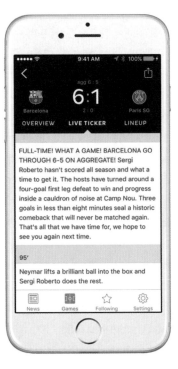

10 years, arch rival, crucial match, etc.) becomes readily available to them, because it is already in the public domain. The app takes account of this data and makes personalized suggestions based on it. When Club took a 1-0 lead in the game against Anderlecht, I was immediately offered the opportunity to buy the shirt of the player who had just scored! This is a great example of a data lever. One Football is like an eagle that circles above its prey. Once the right moment arrives to use its data, it swoops!

The company has also become skilled in developing relevant partnerships. Their deal with Heineken is a case in point. Heineken is one of the main sponsors of the Champions League, probably the most watched football competition in the world. If the users of the app in Berlin are viewing a Champions League game involving their favourite team, the One Football app offers them an extra option. They can order a free six-pack of Heineken lager and have it delivered to their home in just 20 minutes. Using the data provided by One Football, Heineken will be able to know with 100% certainty whether or not consumers are drinking their beer during the football matches they sponsor. At the same time, they perhaps secretly hope that some of the supporters will share the free beers with friends via Facebook or Instagram, giving them a little free advertising in return.

This partnership is a modern form of sampling. The brand knows perfectly that its product is reaching the right target group at the right moment. And once again, it is data – data about the team, the timing and the location – that plays a vital role in setting up this successful commercial action.

"Our gut feeling is worthless": marketing has become a science

The Industries of the Future by Alec Ross[16] is an impressive book. Ross is one of America's leading innovation experts. For four years, he worked together with Hillary Clinton, who was then the US Secretary of State for Foreign Affairs. During this period, he visited more than 40 countries and was given not only the opportunity to study many new innovations, but also to discuss them with world leaders. His book, as the title makes clear, describes what industries will look like in the years ahead. And he sees a prominent role for data.

One of the things he does to explain his ideas is to give an analysis of Barack Obama's campaign strategy in the US presidential election of 2012. Data was the driving force behind the collection of funds to finance the campaign. Obama had put together a team of hundreds of data analysts. Their task was to collect money with maximum efficiency and advertise with maximum efficiency, so that the campaign as a whole could be run with maximum efficiency. The data analysis made it possible to take decisions in quasi real-time. Within the team there was a sub-group responsible for the email campaigns. For each campaign, different types of emails were tested, and there were often as many as 18 different variants of the same one. The reactions of the trial public eventually decided which version would be used for mass circulation. The difference in impact between the different emails was astounding. The key was in the right choice of words for the message title. Ross describes how the least successful email title – 'The one thing the polls got right' – brought in just 403,603 dollars, while the most successful title – 'I will be outspent' – grossed 2,673,278 dollars. In total, the Obama team collected 1.1 billion dollars of campaign donations – four times more than the Republican candidate, Mitt Romney.

The most crucial piece of feedback from the Obama team was the admission that: "Our gut feeling was worthless". This has huge implications for the future of marketing. Today, marketing

In The Day After Tomorrow, this balance will change. Data analysis will be at the heart of marketing strategy.

is a creative profession. Creativity carries more weight than data analysis. In The Day After Tomorrow, this balance will change. Data analysis will be at the heart of marketing strategy. Creativity can still help, but will be limited in impact unless built on a serious foundation of data. Marketing is becoming a science – and this poses a problem for the classic advertising agencies. Their greatest strength is currently their creative genius. Their creative communication can improve company results. But it is already becoming clear that even the very best creativity is no longer enough by itself to ensure success. It needs help from the data lever.

Imagine that Facebook will one day have the technology to generate automated advertising messages tailored to each individual user. To do this, Facebook will first call up all the data it holds about a particular user. After that, a computer will automatically compare this data with millions of successful advertising messages from the past, before eventually picking and amending the one that gives the best match. In other words, the computer will take on the creative role. What is creativity, anyway? It is trying something a million times until you find the combination that works best. Computers can do this more easily and more efficiently than people. In the future, many aspects of marketing will be automated and personalized in this way, using data as the basis. The value of marketing 'gut feeling' will grow smaller and smaller each day. And the value of scientific analysis will grow bigger and bigger.

A fundamental shift in value creation

In 2018, the brand is still important, but only half as important as fifteen years ago.

There is currently a furious debate about the role of brands in the digital world. Ever since the advent of digital, one group of commentators has been arguing that classic branding will become less relevant. Because potential customers can find all available information about a brand online, they claim that the consumer decision-making process will become more rational. As a result, the emotional power of brands will decline. I made more or less the same argument in my second chapter, where I explained how algorithms will enhance real value at the expense of perceived value. However, there is a different group of experts who contest this point. They believe that brands will retain their emotional value for the market. And to be honest, a case can be made for both sides.

Christof Binder, CEO of Trademark Comparables, and Dominique Hanssens, Professor of Marketing at the UCLA Anderson School of Management, are both fascinated by this discussion. Consequently, they decided to set up a large-scale study to investigate its scientific bases. They examined the financial details of 6,000 mergers and acquisitions between 2003 and 2013. Their use of acquisition values meant that it was possible to have a high degree of certainty about the value of the company at that particular moment in time. The researchers then looked at what percentage of the value could be attributed to the strength of the company's brand and what percentage to the strength of the company's customer relations.

Their findings were published in the *Harvard Business Review* in April 2015.[77] The title of their article was: 'Why strong customer relations trump over powerful brands'. The results were crystal clear. In 2003, the brand was the most important driver for value creation. In 2013, the brand was still important, but only half as important as ten years previously. During that period, the share of the brand in value creation fell from 18% to 10%. The role of customer relations during the same period doubled from 9% to 18%. All other factors were more limited in impact and remained stable throughout the period.

The conclusions allow for no other interpretation. The role of brands is declining versus the role of customer relations.

This graphic similarly explains why radio stations are losing out to Spotify. Spotify focuses 100% on its customer interface, data and customer relations, whereas most radio stations persist in sticking to their brand, which means they market themselves as though it is still 2003. Industries that grew big on the back of classic advertising sometimes find it hard to let the past go. Which likewise explains why Netflix is winning more and more viewers from the traditional TV stations: it is another example of classic branding versus interfaces, data and customer relations. Netflix invests everything in up-and-coming lines; the TV stations still invest too much in classic marketing. And it's the

same story with Booking.com versus the hotel industry. Hotel managers cling to the belief that customers still find the brand of the hotel as important as they once did. Booking.com invests everything it's got in improved customer relations.

Traditional players over-invest in classic branding and under-invest structurally in the digital customer relationship. If value accumulation continues to develop as it has in recent years (and there is no reason to assume it won't), company budgets will need to correct this situation – and correct it quickly. Blind faith in yesterday's philosophy is the wrong choice.

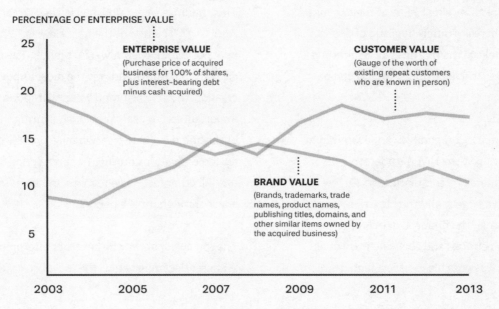

The declining value of brands (and the rise of customer relationships)

PERCENTAGE OF ENTERPRISE VALUE

ENTERPRISE VALUE
(Purchase price of acquired business for 100% of shares, plus interest–bearing debt minus cash acquired)

CUSTOMER VALUE
(Gauge of the worth of existing repeat customers who are known in person)

BRAND VALUE
(Brands, trademarks, trade names, product names, publishing titles, domains, and other similar items owned by the acquired business)

25
20
15
10
5

2003   2005   2007   2009   2011   2013

Netflix as the king of consumer science

The growth of Netflix has been impressive. At the start of 2016, the streaming service had 72 million active users. By the start of 2017, this had increased to 98 million.[78]

One of the most important success factors in the Netflix story is their absolute belief in data and science. Almost every decision is taken on the basis of data. When the company started making its own content, *House of Cards* was their first big programme. They picked Kevin Spacey as lead actor on the basis of an analysis of their streaming data. They could have just asked their customers to name their favourite actor, but they didn't. People might have replied 'Tom Cruise' out of nostalgia for *Top Gun* or 'Leonardo DiCaprio' for his looks. Instead, they decided to look at their customers' behaviour. The actor with the highest loyalty rating among the Netflix viewing public was Kevin Spacey, and so they chose him for the role of Frank Underwood.[79] The rest, as they say, is history. The company still uses data as the input for decisions on every content production.

And not just for content productions. Netflix tries to base as many of its decisions as possible on data. From the quality of the streaming with a slow Wi-Fi connection to the design of the user interface, everything is subjected to an A/B test.[80] For example, via an A/B test Netflix looks at the behaviour of customers using an unchanged interface (scenario A) and then compares this with their behaviour using a new trial interface (scenario B). The customers don't realize they are being used as guinea pigs in a test. In fact, all 98 million customers take part, divided between different test cells. Often, they take part in more than one A/B test at the same time, as long as they don't conflict with each other. The purpose of all these tests for the Netflix team is simple: to make sure that the streaming time per customer increases, because there is a massive correlation between streaming time and loyalty to the platform.

During a visit to Netflix, we were told about an interesting case study. It was about the procedure to become a Netflix customer. Before you subscribe to Netflix, you get a free months' trial, so that you can see what you think of it. Even though this first month is free, Netflix immediately asks for your credit card details. From the start of the second month, your card is automatically debited for a subscription, after you have first received a clear notification that you can stop now, if you want to. The CEO of Netflix wasn't really happy with this procedure. "If we're giving the customer something for free, we shouldn't be asking for credit card details straight away. Let's just give them the free month without asking for any additional info. Once they decide to become a customer in their second month, we can ask them anything we need to know then. Otherwise, we're building in a financial threshold to membership." It sounds a reasonable argument, don't you think? In many companies, this suggestion would be implemented immediately, because it came directly from the CEO. But not at Netflix: they decided to conduct an experiment. It doesn't matter where the idea originates. All ideas are potentially good ideas, but it's the data that decides whether the idea gets implemented or not. That's the Netflix way.

The experiment was started a few days later. For the largest group of customers, the procedure remained unchanged (scenario A): a free first month after providing credit card details. For a more limited group of just a few thousand, the new procedure was introduced (scenario B): a free first month and no credit card details until the start of the second month. Which scenario would you prefer? Keep things the way they are or go with the CEO's new proposal? When I ask this question in seminars, opinion is usually divided about 50/50.

But the data doesn't lie and it was immediately clear to Netflix what they had to do – or not do. If they had followed the CEO's idea, the membership conversion rate would have dropped by 40%. As a result, the registration procedure today is still the same as it has always been. The data decided.

New members	Random sample	Test behavior	Analyze results
	A	[credit card 1234 567 890]	Control
	B	[credit card 1234 567 890 crossed out]	Signups up a bit Conversion to paid down 40%

"In God we trust; all others bring data"

William Edwards Deming was one of the 20th century's most influential statisticians. He worked for many years in Japan, where he lectured on the principles of statistical process control. His most famous oneliner is: "In God we trust, all others bring data".

It's a quote you often hear in the Netflix offices. Reed Hastings, the CEO of Netflix, swears by it. "If someone discusses something with me on the basis of opinions, my opinion will win. That's why I prefer people to argue with me on the basis of data, because then the data will win." The company's extreme focus on a scientific approach to data when making decisions has two concrete benefits. The first benefit is obviously for the customer. They get to decide for themselves (even though they don't often realize it) what kind of interface they will use. In this way, the system gradually evolves towards becoming the perfect user interface. The second benefit is for the company, because it completely undermines the basis for the traditional method of hierarchical decision-making. At Netflix, it doesn't matter if the idea comes from the CEO or from the office cleaner. Hierarchical position means nothing; the data decides. There is no discussion about the quality of the idea. It is simply tested and the resulting data is analyzed. This analysis is the most important driver for every Netflix decision.

"In God we trust, all others bring data."

At Netflix, it doesn't matter if an idea comes from the CEO or from the office cleaner. Hierarchical position means nothing; every idea is tested, and the data decides.

Planet Labs turns insurance into a science

Planet Labs was founded in 2010 by three former NASA scientists. Their idea originated from their belief that the process for making a NASA satellite had outlived its usefulness. NASA invests a huge budget in each satellite. But the long construction process means that by the time the satellite is actually launched, the technology has often already been superseded. The three scientists wanted to build a satellite based on the technology in a smartphone. Seven years later, Planet Labs has more than 100 satellites orbiting the earth at a height of roughly 400 kilometres. Most of them are about the size of a shoe box and weigh less than five kilograms. Each one is equipped with a high-grade camera, which takes photographs of our planet and sends them

back to a control centre. Thanks to the high resolution, the earth can be viewed up to an accuracy level of 3 to 5 metres.

During our visit to Planet Labs in the centre of San Francisco, the added value of their brilliant idea quickly became evident. The Planet Labs satellites make a scan of the planet each day. Every

square metre is photographed. It is not hard to imagine that this information might be useful to an awful lot of people. Not surprisingly, the US Ministry of Defence is a customer. Every time a potential enemy moves a tank, Planet Labs has a photo of it. But other government departments also find the Planet Labs data of immense value, in matters ranging from climate control to the monitoring of certain types of natural disasters.

One of their biggest markets is the agricultural industry. In the United States, some farms are so huge that you literally need to fly over them to check on their condition. Or you used to. Farmers can now monitor their crops more quickly, cheaply and easily using Planet Labs photos. The photos are also particularly useful when it comes to assessing damage. If a tornado races over a farm, there is bound to be damage. In the past, a human assessor from the insurance company had to visit the farm to quantify this damage. But not anymore. This can now be done at a distance and also more objectively using Planet Labs images. The insurers and the farmer both look at the same photo taken

Thanks to data from their first products, they have been able to penetrate a completely new market.

the day before and the day after the storm. There is no discussion necessary. The damage is plain for all to see and can easily be measured. In this way, damage assessment for insurance claims has been turned into an exact science.

Ant Financial Services: the data lever in a classic industry

The biggest financial 'starter' in the world is Ant Financial Services. It was previously known as Alipay, a subsidiary of Alibaba, but changed its name in 2014. They now run the largest platform in the world for mobile payments and also manage Yu'e Bao, the largest money market in the world, as well as being in charge of Zhima Credit, the group's credit rating system.[81]

Ant Financial Services has turned the credit market upside down by its clever use of data. Between 2014 and 2016 the company lent more than 100 billion dollars of credit to small Chinese entrepreneurs and other consumers who were not deemed creditworthy by the classic financial world. Its working methods are similar to those of the Grameen Bank, which since its foundation in Bangladesh in 1976 has lent 17 billion dollars to similar 'poor' borrowers without the need for security. Ant Financial Services applies the same philosophy but has simply upped the scale.

In China, almost everyone pays by mobile. Alipay built up this market and consequently has at its disposal a treasure trove of data about the financial situation of a very large group of Chinese companies and consumers. They now use this data in real-time to assess whether a loan applicant will be able to make the necessary repayments. It is their own credit score that decides whether the applicant gets the loan, not the classic sources of credit rating.

Thanks to data from their first products, they have been able to penetrate a completely new market. In the meantime, their credit line has grown to become one of the largest credit providers in China.

Investing in the data lever

"Our gut feeling is useless." This quote says it all. For decades, marketing has been a profession governed by instinct and creativity. In The Day After Tomorrow, the 'Mad Men' will be replaced by the 'maths men'. The *Harvard Business Review* was predicting it as early as 2012: data analyst is set to become the sexiest job in the 21st century.[82]

The first axis of investment to secure the key customer benefits in The Day After Tomorrow is the data lever. Artificial intelligence needs data. So much is obvious. But investing in data is more than just investing in the raw material for AI. It is also investing in a lever that can have a positive impact on your customer relations.

- *Faster-than-real-time*: sensors detect data that allow problems to be identified before they arise. In other words, data serves as input for new levels of service provision that will solve problems before customers are even aware of them.
- *Hyper-personalisation*: understanding the context of the individual customer is the new core competence in marketing. Data makes it possible to better assess how a customer is feeling and behaving at any given moment. Analysing this data is the most important source of input for taking personalization to a higher level.
- *Convenience*: the automation of key customer processes is only possible if you have the right data. Interfaces adjust themselves to customer behaviour, using smart A/B tests. This also takes ease of use to a higher level.

Better understanding your customers and using this knowledge to adjust your own actions will be the foundation of customer experience in The Day After Tomorrow. Data works as a lever on all other investments in customer relations. In The Day After Tomorrow, every organization will be a data organization. Whenever you are developing a new product, your first question must be: "Where can we find the data that tells us what we need to know about this product?" Why does Tesla install hardware for self-driving cars years before the cars themselves will ever be allowed on our road? Because it already wants to collect data to learn about the future. Why does Google invest in Planet Labs? Because it can provide real-time data about the evolutions of our planet that Google currently does not possess. So, make a data plan and make the right investments to support it. This is fundamental to success in The Day After Tomorrow.

The effects of the data lever become tangible if you compare the performance of a classic sat-nav with a product like Waze. Waze is an Israeli company that was recently bought by Google and its navigation system is unquestionably the best in the world. A classic sat-nav uses data from maps to suggest the most efficient route to your destination. A smarter system will receive data input from traffic control centres about possible road works and jams. Waze uses both these sources, but supplements it with data provided by the user. Like all of us, there is a chance that a Waze user will run into trouble en route. Based on data from the customer's other devices, Waze can assess the context, identify the problem and plot the best solution, far better than any other GPS system. With classic systems, you are always taking something of a risk when you follow their suggested alternative route. You may end up where you want to go, but not always and often only after a detour taking hours. But you can rely on Waze routes every time. Why? Because the company thought carefully about their data strategy and used it as a lever to provide the three core Day After Tomorrow customer benefits.

CHAPTER 6

NEW
USER
INTERFACES

A virtual assistant for students

Ashok Goel is one of the world's top professors in the computer sciences. He has been lecturing for many years at Georgia Tech. His subjects are so specialized that he usually only has 20 or so students in his class. But his online course is very popular and attracts about 400 students each year. This group is highly international and eager to learn. In fact, they ask so many questions that it is no longer feasible for Professor Goel and his team of assistants to answer them properly.

And then came Jill Watson!

Jill is a bot. Jill is a computer programme with the clear task of helping students (customers) in a quick and efficient manner. Jill must answer the routine questions of students so that the workload of the human teaching team is reduced.

Every bot first needs training. The first time that Jill was tested, it was not a great success. The bot not only gave wrong answers, but also quite a lot of strange ones that had nothing to do with the question asked. Naturally, the teaching team wanted to avoid potential confusion and so Jill was tested for a further number of months in a closed environment. The students' questions were put to Jill, but initially the students weren't shown the resulting answers. In this sense, educating a bot is a bit like educating a child. The bot tries to answer the questions independently and is corrected by its human 'parents' when it gets something wrong. This way, the bot gradually becomes smarter, until it reaches such a high level that it can be let loose on its own – in Jill's case, to actively answer student questions in a live environment.

Jill has evolved into a kind of personal assistant. She responds objectively to the students' simpler questions. She answers queries about data use, about the office opening hours, about different types of files, etc. The more complex questions are still dealt with by the human teaching team.

As an interesting twist, at first the team didn't tell the students that Jill Watson is a machine; they only revealed her 'secret' at the end of term. The students were amazed; not one of them had guessed.[83]

Social media are too slow!

In my first management book, *The Conversation Manager* (2010), one of the things I discussed was the use of social media in customer service provision. At that time, people still needed a lot of convincing about the possibilities offered by 'new' platforms like Facebook and Twitter. In subsequent years, most major companies invested heavily in developing their service offer through these new channels. Even so, seven years on we must now conclude that social media can still only answer a fraction of the questions asked by customers. Social media are much better suited as content channels than as service channels. The expected huge shift from dealing with customer queries by telephone to dealing with them via social media never happened. The telephone is still far and away the most important channel for customer contact.

The explanation for this is the relative slowness of social media. KLM is generally regarded as one of the best examples of providing service through social media. And rightly so! The company answers questions 24/7 within 30 minutes. Which is excellent – except for passengers who have an urgent question about a flight that leaves in less than 30 minutes... In some circumstances, 30 minutes can seem like an eternity.

The expected huge shift from dealing with customer queries by telephone to dealing with them via social media never happened.

Originally, we thought that speed would be the big advantage of these channels, but that's not the way it turned out. Customers are still helped quicker by telephone than by Facebook. Even if you need to listen to on-hold music for a quarter of an hour, you still get your answer faster than you would with social media. What's more, the level of service provided by most telephone call centres is generally good or even very good. In other words, social media are too slow and too limited in quality for most customers.

Real-time is the new minimum

The success of messaging apps like Facebook Messenger, WeChat and Whatsapp has catapulted us into the real-time world. And the symbol of this new age is the dancing dots. If you send a message to someone, you hope that you will be rewarded with three dancing dots on your screen, which indicate that the person has received your message and is already typing a reply. The dots are also a good symbol for our increased expectations, because the longer the dots dance, the longer the reply you will receive. If after 30 seconds you only get a bland 'OK' as your answer, it is often the biggest disappointment of your day!

We live in a real-time world. If you search for a shop in Google, you not only get all the content information you need, but can also see how busy the shop is at that particular moment. If you use Waze as your navigation tool, you not only get a 100% reliable route but also lots of extra and equally reliable real-time information about that route. If Waze tells you that there is a car broken down on the hard shoulder 600 metres ahead, that is exactly where the car will be. Real-time information is becoming increasingly available and increasingly accurate.

Jill Watson gives feedback in real-time. Communicating with a bot is fun, because the dots always begin to dance straight away. The bot is always awake and always ready for action. If the student asks a question, even in the middle of the night, the dancing dots work their magic and, hey presto, within seconds, the answer arrives. Real-time is becoming the new minimum for routine questions in customer service. And since the vast majority of customer questions tend to be routine, this means that the vast majority of customers can be helped with little or no delay. But if you want to keep your customers happy in this way, it will be impossible without the help of automated interfaces.

Blue is my favourite colour as well!

Many of today's bots work with a pre-programmed tree structure. In other words, the programmers design dozens of different possible conversation flows. These multiple scenarios form the basic structure for the machine's interaction with the human customer. Effectively, modern customer service bots are a more sophisticated version of the 'frequently asked questions' page in a website. A kind of automated search function.

This summer I needed a new raincoat. During my online search, I came across the website for The North Face, where I was helped quickly and efficiently by an extremely friendly bot. Our conversation went something like this:

Steven: I'd like to buy a coat.

Bot: Super! And what would you like to do in your coat?

Steven: Go walking in Yosemite.

Bot: Cool, Yosemite. In what season are you going?

Steven: During the summer.

Bot: Got it. What's important for you when choosing your coat?

Steven: It needs to protect me against an unexpected shower.

Bot: Perfect. Anything else specific I need to know about your coat?

Steven: Yes, I'd like a blue one, please.

Bot: Super, blue. That's my favourite colour as well! So, here's what we've got for you...

As you can see, I had a really great conversation with the bot. And it seems we even have the same good taste! This is top-class customer service: fun, user-friendly, instant, and available 24 hours a day. With each answered question, the bot's filters were able to narrow down the selection for my coat. Wonderful! And both the conversation and the product selection happened in real-time.

Compare this with buying a coat from Zalando. Zalando has a range of 3,573 men's coats, covering 48 pages of their website. Zalando expects the customer to set the necessary selection filters. In other words, all the effort comes from the customer side. With The North Face, the selection is made automatically. In other words, all the effort comes from the company side, which gives the customer a really great feeling. In the years ahead, bots will develop at an astonishing pace, so that they are soon destined to become our daily conversation partners for the answering of basic service questions in a whole variety of settings.

Solving the shortage of doctors

The World Health Organization estimates that in the coming decades, there will be a worldwide shortage of some 13 million doctors and other medical personnel.[84] As is so often the case, Asia and Africa seem likely to be hardest hit, with serious health consequences for their populations. Moreover, the effects of this shortage are already making themselves felt. Doctors in China are currently expected to see something like 80 to 100 patients a day. As a result, the doctors often have too little time per patient to make a proper diagnosis.

The Chinese Baidu company wants to solve this problem with artificial intelligence. With this in mind, Baidu has launched Melody, a medical bot. Melody asks patients questions about their symptoms. If the patient complains of headaches, Melody asks further targeted questions to better understand the nature and origin of the headaches. How long have you had the headaches? Is the pain constant or does it come and go? These are the questions a doctor would also ask during a face-to-face consultation, but the doctor now gets this information without the need for the patient to make a time-consuming visit to his/her surgery.

The purpose of this bot is not to replace doctors. Its purpose is to help doctors, by giving them better information about the patient before they actually see them. In this way, the doctor's limited consultation time is put to best use: for making accurate diagnoses and suggesting the right treatment.

A world full of micro-bots

Melody is an example of a micro-bot. A micro-bot is a computer programme. It automates clearly defined aspects of the customer relationship. In the near future, customer service will be a combination of micro-bots and people.

Booking.com is already developing this combination. They want to make their service provision as proactive as possible. If a problem with a hotel booking is identified, the team will proactively phone the customer to suggest a solution. Of course, this part of the proactive service is performed by people. But Booking.com also gets thousands of other, more routine questions each day. At the moment, they have a team of some 7,500 employees to deal with these routine matters. 7,500 sounds like quite a lot, but most of the time they are struggling to cope with the workload. And as Booking.com continues to grow, the situation is only going to get worse. This is where bots come in. By programming bots to deal with simple queries, human staff will have more time available to deal with the more complex problems.

But the combination of humans and bots goes much further than just after-sales service. Imagine the following scenario, if you want to change your telecom provider. The customer contacts the bot of the telecom company of his/her choice. The bot asks a number of questions to assess which package is most appropriate for the customer. If it is a standard package, the bot can complete the transaction. The customer is helped in real-time and can start using the new subscription immediately. This is super-efficient, both for the customer and the company. However, if the customer's requirements are more complex, the bot transfers the call to a human advisor. The advisor listens to the problem and discusses the various options with the customer, before arriving at the perfect subscription formula. To activate the subscription, the advisor passes the call on to another bot for the completion of the necessary routine administrative matters. In other words, you have an integrated sales system involving the use of two bots (pre-sales and administration) and one human (customer advice).

In customer service management, it is an interesting exercise to see which aspects of your customer conversations can best be dealt with by bots, and which aspects are better suited to human interaction.

The end of 'search'?

Bots can help in many different areas of the customer relationship. For instance, in the above telecom example the first bot effectively takes over the salesperson's role. The bot helps, advises and recommends, just like a real salesman or woman. This type of smart interface is destined to change the way customers buy products.

In addition to micro-bots, virtual personal assistants will also play an important role. Just look at the huge investments already made in virtual assistants by Apple (Siri), Microsoft (Cortana), Google (Google Assistant) and Amazon (Alexa). People are finding it increasingly normal to talk to these personal assistants. Only 2% of iPhone users never talk to Siri. 70% say that they use their digital assistant 'regularly'.[85] Just like it took us a while to get used to the idea of people using their phones on the street and in trains, we are now in the phase of adjusting to the daily need to converse with smart digital interfaces. This will happen faster than we think. Talking to technology is already becoming mainstream. Gartner expects that by 2019 20% of your interactions with your smartphone will be by voice.

Once voice interfaces have been perfected, people will use them for almost everything. One in three users of the Amazon Echo are already ordering products from Amazon by voice command.[86]

Google is rightly concerned about the success and impact of Alexa, the Echo's virtual assistant. If people start buying things directly from Amazon by voice, the search phase of the customer journey will disappear completely.

For this reason, it is no surprise that Google – the search experts – are ploughing billions into the development of their Google Assistant. They see the Assistant as their best chance to preserve their dominant position in the search market. The current Google search engine was built as long ago as 1998. Of course, the quality of the interface has been upgraded regularly ever since, but even Google admits that it is no longer optimal. When people search for something, they get countless pages of output and only bother to look at the first three links. Google Assistant works differently. You ask a specific question and immediately get a specific answer. You can even develop a kind of conversation by asking further questions. Imagine that you ask:

If people start buying things directly from Amazon by voice, the search phase of the customer journey will disappear completely.

"OK Google, who is the king of Belgium?" Google answers: "Filip is the king of Belgium." You can then ask: "And who is his wife?" Back comes the Assistant: "Queen Mathilda is his wife." You can carry on like this for quite a while. It may sound fairly simple and logical, but this is actually quite an advanced conversation for a computer. Until recently, the second question had to be asked in a much more convoluted form: "OK Google, who is the wife of King Filip of Belgium?" The conversation is now more 'normal' – but the technological difficulty of making it so is huge.

In fact, in terms of conversational skills, Google Assistant now scores much better than Amazon's Alexa. Researchers asked 3,000 questions to both systems. Google answered 72% correctly, Alexa just 13%.[87]

Google sees these smart interfaces as the future of the search phase. Users ask questions and machines try to answer them as accurately as possible. For future purchases, virtual assistants will take over from the classic search processes of the past. Imagine in ten – or maybe even five – years' time that you want to book a flight to Barcelona. You can ask your Google bot: "OK Google, can you book me a flight to Barcelona for next week? And can you take into account the things I already have planned in my agenda?" Google will talk with the bots of the different airlines, and the bots of the airlines will talk with the bots of the hotels. Once the information has been collated, Google will get back to you, the customer, with a number of options. You then simply pick the option that best suits you and the confirmation is posted to your mailbox in real-time. The whole process will only take a matter of minutes. But how long would it take you today?

The evolution of interfaces

The way in which new interfaces are playing an increasing role in pre-sales, sales and after sales processes is impressive. This evolution is moving fast. It is evolving from complex to simple and from automated to augmented. The major technology platforms are experts in developing modern interfaces. They succeed in making the lives of consumers as easy as possible. This is probably the biggest challenge for companies that don't have a digital DNA: making interfaces of the same quality and with the same benefits as the major platforms.

Complex

Simple

Automated

Augmented

From complex to simple

In the past, all interfaces were complex. Some people say that they are still too difficult from a technological perspective. But that's not true. It was only really difficult back in the 1980s and 1990s. To work with MS-DOS, you needed to be a half-nerd. Today, technology has never been simpler. The iPhone was the first technology product without a help function and an inch-thick instruction manual. Since then, the world has been treated to a wave of new interfaces that are getting less and less complicated all the time. They have to. If something is too complex for the consumer to use it easily, it simply won't be used. End of story. Consumers usually give a new app 30 seconds to prove itself. If they don't understand it within those 30 seconds, it will be ditched. That's how quickly customers make judgements nowadays.

In recent years, we have seen the arrival of the one-button interface. Apps that allow you to order a pizza with just a single press of a button. Apps that allow you to order a car with just a single press of a button. Amazon Dash buttons work the same way: just hit the button to buy a new supply of coffee, washing powder, etc. When the Tesla 3 was launched, the Tesla website also had a single button with a single capitalized word: BUY.

Simplicity has become the new norm in the second phase of digitalization. Like most norms, it can sometimes be taken to extremes, so that you occasionally see 'one-button' interfaces in almost ludicrous situations. In Singapore there is a 'dispenser' where you can buy a luxury car. It looks a bit like a bread machine, but is the size of a small apartment building and instead of being filled with fresh loaves, it is filled with Porsches, Ferraris and Lamborghinis. At the bottom, there is a single button. You press it, pay a few hundred thousand dollars with your credit card, and out pops your brand new car.[88] What could be simpler?

Customer-friendly mobile interfaces push satisfaction and conversion at Belfius

In March 2012, the Belgian bank Dexia changed its name to Belfius. The new brand's new start was not an easy one. The recent financial crisis meant that confidence in the brand was low. Over the past five years, the bank has had to work hard to rebuild consumer trust.

Their mobile-first strategy was an important element in this process. While the majority still had their doubts about the bank, the first users of the Belfius mobile app soon became its most satisfied customers. This strengthened the resolve of the Belfius management to play the mobile-first card 100%. It was a focus that produced excellent results. The Belfius app now has the largest number of satisfied users in the Belgian market. A benchmark report by McKinsey[89] concluded that in 2016 Belfius was the fastest growing player in the world in terms of mobile banking for its customers. With its wide range of mobile functions and progressive mobile sales, McKinsey ranks Belfius among the other digital leaders in the banking world.

"Within our mobile-first strategy, the customer experience is the most important guide for determining our priorities. New features must work perfectly and are tested to extreme levels with customers, until they give a 99% satisfaction rating. The crucial thing is to ensure a perfect redesign of the end-to-end user mobile experience," says Geert Van Mol, Chief Digital Officer at Belfius. "The simpler the interface, the more satisfied the customer. But it also means a higher rate of conversion for our services, with customers coming back more frequently, simply because of the ease of use. Today, we have an average of 26 visits a month by the customers who use our mobile app. In this way, digital contact with the brand is increased bit by bit."

The different options available for the Belfius credit card are a good example of their strategy. You can apply for a credit card through the mobile app, have your card activated abroad and alter your credit limit, all with just a single click. This increased ease of use has led to a significant growth in both the direct and mobile sale of Belfius credit cards. One out of every three new credit cards is now sold through the mobile channel. And the same strong results were also seen following the launch of a new mobile pension savings fund via the smartphone in 2015. Customers can join the fund with just two clicks – a simplicity that has again resulted in impressive growth. By the end of 2015, Belfius had secured 2,700 new pension contracts. By the end of 2016, this had grown to 8,800 contracts, 36% of which were set-up via the app. The message is clear: mobile simplicity and real-time solutions lead to high levels of satisfaction and conversion.

From simple to automated

The next step is even more interesting. This is the evolution from the 'one-button' to the 'zero-button' interface. When this happens, customers will no longer need to do anything at all, not even press a button. Everything will be fully automatic. Earlier in the book, we have already mentioned smart central heating systems and the automatic rebooking of missed air flights. These are both good examples of 'zero-button' applications. So too is the new Starbucks App, which allows customers to give their orders verbally. The bot sends the order to the relevant shop, so that the coffee is ready when the customer walks through the door. Payment is also made automatically via a mobile app. All hands-free. Not a single click involved. Without the need to wait a single second, the customer has completed a perfect transaction with Starbucks. And this is what today's consumers expect. In a world where time is the consumer's scarcest resource, every second counts – which makes this kind of interface worth its weight in gold.

Amazon Go is an offline retail experiment. Amazon has opened a test store in Seattle where everything works via automatic interfaces. The customer scans his Amazon app when he/she enters the store. He/she then selects the goods he/she wants from the shelves, puts them into his/her bag and leaves. The products are not physically scanned and there is no cash desk. You just walk in, take what you want, and walk back out again. At first, it almost seems like shoplifting, but payment is fully automatic. Amazon has not yet revealed how this system works, but experts think it must be based on data analysis from the combined input of sensors and camera images.[90] But the technology is not the most important thing. The impact on the customer is what really matters. And that impact is huge!

Amazon Go has removed all the aspects that people don't like about shopping. Queuing, putting your purchases on the conveyor belt, paying, putting everything away in carrier bags: this has all been eliminated from the process. The focus is just on one thing: shopping. Imagine what it would be like if airports adopted a similar approach! Let's assume it is possible for the airport to link your boarding pass to your credit card. As soon as you have scanned in your boarding pass as you enter the airport, the shopping can begin. You fancy a sandwich and a beer? No problem! Just take them and go. No queuing. No paying. Something to read on the plane? Same story. Something from duty free to take home for your partner? Ditto! You don't need to be a management genius to work out what this will do for the total turnover of the airport's retailers. If a passenger has little time before his flight for a sandwich and is faced by a queue of a dozen people, he will buy nothing. With the Amazon Go model, there is no queuing – so the passenger will almost certainly buy something. And something is always better than nothing.

Buy the best cakes in San Francisco – automatically

Vive la Tarte is my favourite bakery in San Francisco. They've got the best cakes in town. But that's hardly a coincidence: the business was started by a Belgian couple – and we all know that the Belgians make the best cakes in the world! Joking aside, Arnaud Goethals and Julie Vandermeersch's story is a remarkable one. In 2010, Arnaud and Julie were both successful management

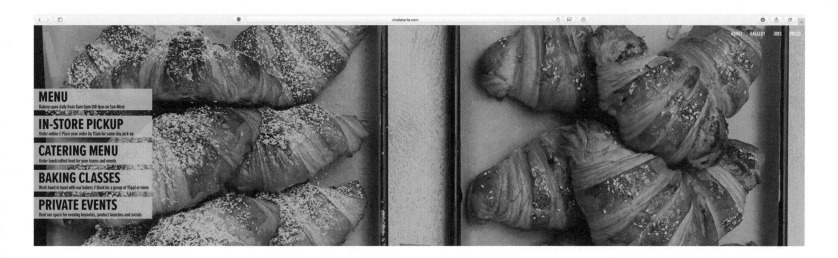

consultants in Belgium. But their holiday to the west coast of America was so fantastic that they decided to give up their jobs at home and relocate to San Francisco, where they hoped to start a business. But doing what? What were they good at apart from management consultancy? They soon hit on the answer: baking cakes – and so Vive la Tarte was born.

That was back in 2011. In the meantime, they have developed a highly successful bakery and are one of the preferred caterers for events organized by the Googles and Facebooks of this world. They are now thinking about opening at a second location and eventually hope to have a string of their unique bakeries from coast to coast.

Even though their business is small-scale and essentially traditional, they still work with automatic interfaces for their loyal customers. Vive la Tarte uses the existing technology of Square to automate payments in the bakery. This makes it possible for even a small enterprise like Vive la Tarte to offer the same levels of service as major players like Starbucks and Amazon.

Blockchain has even been called 'the internet of contracts'.

Smart contracts using Blockchain

Automation will find its way into all phases and facets of the customer journey. Thanks to Blockchain technology, it is now even possible to implement contracts automatically. Blockchain can best be compared with a digital ledger.[91] Ledgers form the basis for the confidence and trust we have in important transactions. Financial transactions are recorded in a ledger. The buying and selling of land is also recorded in a ledger. The ledger is a way for both parties to express and record their confidence in each other in an official and analogue manner. Ledgers are usually held at a central location (a bank, a solicitor's office, etc.) and are effectively closed databases. The market has faith in the holder of these central databases.

Blockchain is a digital alternative for these ledgers. Blockchain has even been called 'the internet of contracts'. Blockchain is decentralized and open. Like the internet, Blockchain has no owner. Like the internet, everyone can use Blockchain as a basis for building further applications. Its decentralized nature means that it is impossible to defraud people using data from the ledger. If someone changes something in the ledger, all the other users can see it, so that irregularities can never pass undetected. It is a network in which all the participants in the network share the ledger. It's a bit like having a shared document in Microsoft Excel. Everyone sees every transaction in the database. If someone adds a new line to a spreadsheet, all the other users can read it instantly. The difference in Blockchain is that you can never alter a transaction once it has been made. You can only add new lines. As a result, existing transactions are permanent, as if they had been engraved in stone.

Blockchain technology first became widely known from its use as the basis for the crypto currency, Bitcoin. But Bitcoin was just the tip of the iceberg: the possibilities of Blockchain are endless. In particular, it is now being increasingly used to explore the automation of contracts. Smart contracts are essentially lines of computer script, which describe a particular scenario. Once the scenario becomes reality, the terms of the relevant contract are automatically and immediately implemented by Blockchain. In this way, for example, insurance companies can tailor certain forms of micro-insurance contracts to the specific needs of the customer. Imagine you have planned a flight to meet an important business contact. If your flight is cancelled or delayed, you might miss the meeting and lose the business deal you were hoping to win as a result. In the future, you will be able to take out micro-insurance to cover this situation. Micro-insurance involves a smart contract between the insurance company and the customer. The script of the contract can be extremely simple.

'If flight X leaves on time, customer Y will pay us Z euros.'
'If flight X does not leave on time, we will pay customer Y Z euros.'

The most important parameter in the contract is the flight departure time. This information can be established objective-ly by Blockchain from online data. The system can also check automatically which of the two scenarios actually transpires in reality and therefore make the necessary payment as soon as the departure time has passed.

A robot as financial adviser

Robot advice in financial markets is a hot topic. In the United States, more and more wealthy people are turning to robots for recommendations before deciding where to invest part of their fortune. By 2017, 11% of America's wealthiest citizens had bought investment products from a virtual banker.[92] *Business Insider* estimates that by 2022 robot advisers will be managing portfolios worth 4.6 trillion dollars.

Robot advisors can deal with different types of investment products. Some of these products are already fully automated: the product proposal, the preparation of the contract, the monitoring of performance, the calculation of expected growth, etc. But there are also hybrid products, where an algorithm initially puts together a possible investment portfolio, which a human adviser then discusses further with the customer.

Robot advisers make it possible for asset managers to provide a better service at a lower cost in comparison with the use of human advisers. The majority of wealthy investors have no problem with robot advice, but still prefer it to be combined with a degree of human interaction.[93]

Vanguard grows thanks to robot advice

Vanguard is the world leader in robotic financial advice. This might make you think that Vanguard is some kind of hip start-up – but you would be wrong. The company was founded back in 1976 and manages around 4 trillion dollars. In May 2015, the company began with its first robot-advice product. The minimum investment was 50,000 dollars, with a service cost of 0.3%. The aim was to tap a new market in the hope of attracting financially promising but not-yet-fantastically wealthy clients in a highly efficient manner. At the time of writing in mid-2017, the Vanguard robot now manages 65 billion dollars.[94] Its nearest rival, the Charles Schwab robot, manages 'just' 16 billion dollars.

Vanguard's plan was to trawl a new and, above all, younger market of moderately wealthy customers. In reality, two out of every three of its robo-customers are retired and already very wealthy.[95] These customers are enthusiastic about the fast, simple and cheap solution the product offers. What's more, in view of the fi-

nancial assets available to this group as a whole, the total amount of invested capital is increasing rapidly. When I interviewed Joeri Van den Bergh about the future generation, he talked about what he calls 'the flat generation'. The behaviour of the new generation is increasingly being copied by the older generation. Why? Because older people need to evolve along the same lines as the youngsters if they want to be able to communicate with them. As a result, the differences between the generations are getting smaller – hence the term 'flat'. Robot financial advice sounds more like something for the millennials, but new digital products have the potential to be popular with every generation, if they are done correctly. New and improved automated interfaces are crucial for every type of customer in every market.

From automated to augmented

Interfaces are evolving from complex to simple and from simple to automated. It will soon be possible to automate every aspect of the customer relationship. The next evolutionary development will see interfaces make the step to augmented reality. Augmented reality (AR) adds a digital component to the real world. Google was one of the pioneers in this area with Google Glass, but the product was a flop because of its lack of useful applications for ordinary consumers. A more well-known and certainly more successful example of augmented reality is Pokémon Go. These virtual creatures were scattered into the real world and millions of people went in search of them in what was the hit summer craze of 2016. But Pokémon Go hardly scratched the surface of what will soon be possible with AR.

The coming years will see a huge growth in augmented reality applications. It is estimated that the market size will amount to 108 billion dollars in 2021.[96] The possibilities offered by AR in improving customer experience are much greater than those of VR (virtual reality). Virtual reality can be fun for specific applications, like buying a house, booking a hotel or enjoying a top entertainment event. But VR is essentially an individual experience.

AR can be more widely experienced by more people at the same time. However, the real breakthrough in the market will take a little longer, because the current technical complexity of AR is too great. We also need faster processors to allow AR to work optimally.

Even so, there are already a number of fun AR applications in commercial use. IKEA has an AR app that allows you to see how the furniture you are planning to buy will look in your house, using the screen of your smartphone. And the New York metro has an AR application that helps you to find the nearest station, again via the screen of your phone.

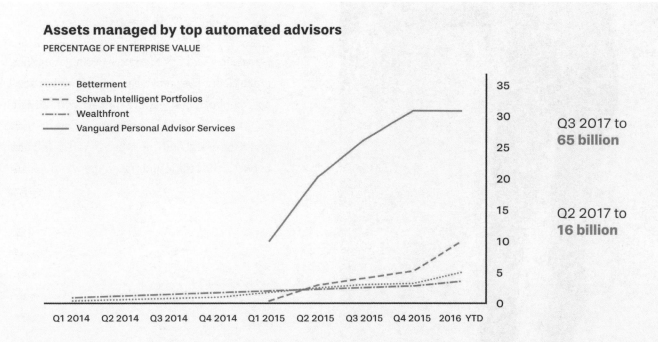

Assets managed by top automated advisors
PERCENTAGE OF ENTERPRISE VALUE

········· Betterment
– – – Schwab Intelligent Portfolios
–·–·– Wealthfront
——— Vanguard Personal Advisor Services

Q3 2017 to **65 billion**

Q2 2017 to **16 billion**

Q1 2014 Q2 2014 Q3 2014 Q4 2014 Q1 2015 Q2 2015 Q3 2015 Q4 2015 2016 YTD

Sundar Pichai
CEO Google

Google Lens!

Google Lens wants to bring your smartphone camera to life. When you point the camera at something, Google will give you extra information about that item. Imagine that you are walking through a forest and suddenly see a beautiful flower. If you look at the flower through Google Lens, Google will immediately identify what it is and tell you something about it. If you are later walking past a restaurant that looks a good place to eat, point Google Lens at it and you will immediately get an evaluation score, as well as offering you a list of the house specialities and the option to book a table! There's a poster for a concert on the wall next to the restaurant? Point Google Lens at it and you can make a booking for that as well!

Google foresees a whole range of similar applications that will make all our lives much easier. And they don't all need to be spectacular. If you want to connect with Wi-Fi, all you need to do is turn Google Lens towards the code on the modem. In this and a thousand and one other ways, AR will blur the difference between the offline and the online world.

A world without screens

Today, the smartphone is the most important distribution channel for AR. AR uses the camera and the screen of your smartphone to operate its applications. But an increasing number of observers already believe that the breakthrough of AR will eventually lead to the disappearance of the smartphone. They claim that within the next five to ten years a completely new set of interfaces will be developed specifically based on the many possibilities offered by AR.

At the present time, Microsoft Hololens and Meta Vision glasses are the two most well-known examples of augmented reality hardware solutions. Both systems make use of a large pair of goggles or spectacles to observe the digital layer superimposed on reality. This kind of technology is mainly used in B2B applications, but there are also a number of potential uses in the medical world. For example, the Hololens is used during complex operations to give the surgeon additional information about the patient. Another important but very different market is gaming. How cool is it to blow away your enemies while you are using a pair of AR glasses! It really looks as though the bad guys are everywhere in your home, sometimes quite literally coming out of the walls and ceilings to attack you. The intensity of these games cannot be compared with the games you play on a 2D screen.

The AR vision of Meta goes a very long way. As humans, we have two eyes, through which we see everything in three dimensions. But when we look at a screen, we only see things in two dimensions. In other words, we are under-using the full potential of our eyes. Meta therefore wants to create a world without screens, a world full of holograms. Imagine that your favourite football team is playing away from home in the Champions League. Wouldn't it be great if fans, instead of travelling abroad, could go to their home stadium and watch the same game being played by live hologram projections? It could also raise extra revenue for the club. Win-win. Or what about an AR home shopping experience? Instead of popping down to your local branch of H&M, their range of clothes could be projected into your living room. Look down and you will see your new shoes on your feet. Look at your arm and you will see the wrist watch you have always wanted. The possibilities in a world without screens are truly limitless.

Towards augmented customer experience

The added value of automation for customers is obvious. Automation provides faster, more personal and more user-friendly transactions. To see the added value of augmented reality at this stage requires a little more creative imagination. Above all, it will change the customer experience in the online world, by making it more personal and more digital.

Just imagine what the advertisements of the future will be like. Once we all view the world from an AR perspective, advertising will be different for each of us. In much the same way that advertising can now be personalized in the online world, AR will be able to personalize it in the offline world. Billboards will become blank spaces, onto which different images are projected for different people, depending on your personal AR interface. Advertising games can also be given a new dimension, by leaving digital objects in the real world. For example, the first person to find the hidden digital 'treasure' gets a big reduction on their next purchase of product X, Y or Z. And instead of hunting Pokémons, consumers can hunt for discount vouchers and other benefits.

The offline retail experience will also become more digital. For example, an AR app could show the locations of all your favourite shops and brands within a shopping centre. You quite like a particular blouse but wonder what it would look like in a different colour and size? AR can show you that as well, and it can also tell you if it is still available or where it can be ordered. In an amusement park, AR could guide you to all the best attractions, as well as giving details of the current waiting times.

In a different field, augmented reality will scale up the knowledge of experts. If a company only has one technical expert who needs to physically travel to different locations to inspect and solve complex customer problems, this is clearly a limitation in term of scale. In The Day After Tomorrow, this expert will stay at the company headquarters (or perhaps even at home). From there, he will be able to use AR applications to view the problems at a distance and give advice to his less technically skilled colleagues who are actually on site. In the past, it may have been possible for the expert to visit 10 customers a day, with most of his time wasted on travelling. Using AR and the help of less expert technicians, his specialist knowledge can now be made available to 100 customers a day. In other words, his impact is increased by a factor of ten! The waiting time for customers is reduced and the costs for the company fall.

These are just a few of the examples of how augmented reality can have a beneficial effect on your customer relations. What's more, it must be remembered that these examples are based on our current – and very limited – knowledge about AR. As this knowledge increases in the years ahead, new applications will be developed that for now we can only dream of. But ten years ago, this was equally true for the mobile revolution. Which of us could ever have imagined the huge impact that smartphones and apps would have on our daily lives? And just as we now find it impossible to imagine how we ever lived without this technology, in ten years' time, we will wonder how we ever managed to get by in the world before AR.

An automated world with perfect timing

The evolution in interfaces is remarkable, and will continue. The speed, personalization and user-friendliness of customer transactions in The Day After Tomorrow will be taken to new and previously unseen levels of excellence. Every form of delay or complexity in the transaction is a source of irritation for a customer. State-of-the-art interfaces will remove these irritations and lead us to a fully automated world with perfect timing.

Investing in new user interfaces is the second axis of investment if you want to secure the key customer benefits in The Day After Tomorrow.

- *Faster-than-real-time*: bots help customers with their questions, needs and problems in real-time. More advanced personal assistants like Google Assistant will be able, for example, to take into account the customer's agenda and proactively offer help to make the customer's progress through the day as smooth and as effortless as possible.
- *Hyper-personalization*: will be taken to an even higher level as a result of the full personalization of advertising based on each person's individual profile. Since the arrival of the iPhone, people have become used to personalizing their own interface. As

a result, no two smartphones in the world are the same. This process of interface personalization will be intensified.
- *Convenience*: the effort that customers need to make will reduce day by day. The purpose of the new user interfaces is to allow every transaction between a company and its customers to run as smoothly and as painlessly as possible.

After reading this chapter, I have an important task for you. Take your smartphone and send yourself an email with a list of the five interactions between your company and your customers that are most likely to cause customer frustration because of the lack of good interfaces. Commit yourself to tackling at least one of these interactions during the coming week. In that way, your change process will already be under way! Remember it is crucial to ensure that your new interfaces meet customer needs and provide customer benefits in the best possible way.

The speed, personalization and user-friendliness of customer transactions in The Day After Tomorrow will be taken to new and previously unseen levels of excellence.

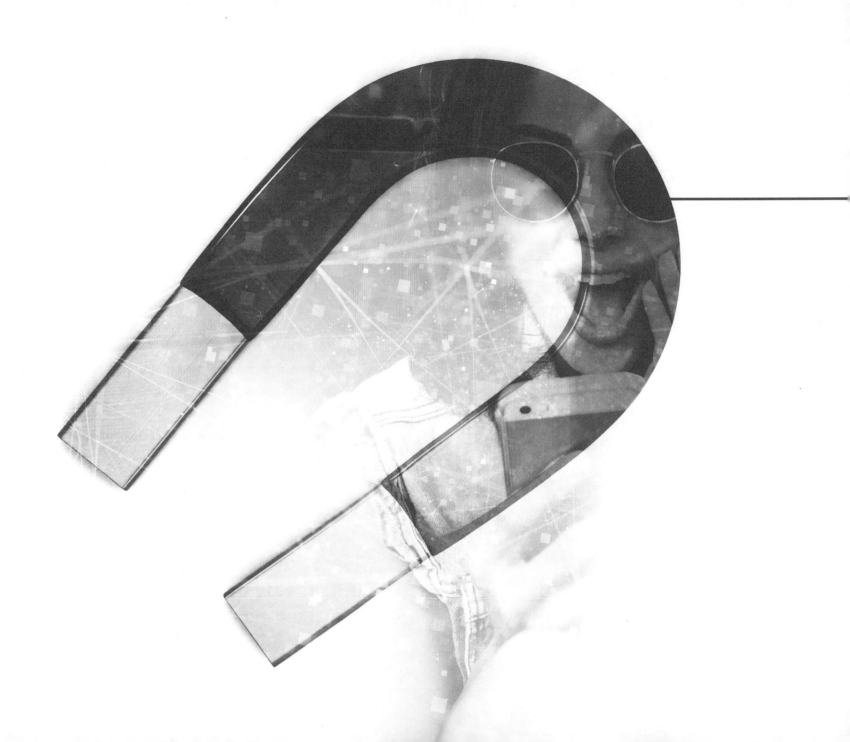

CHAPTER 7

FIGHTING THE COMMODITY MAGNET

The platform as a marker of trust

If a businessman needs to book a plane ticket to Barcelona, today he can arrange it himself in a few different ways:

- The customer goes directly to the website of an airline and books the flight on this site. In this case, the customer deliberately chooses to fly with his airline of preference. This preference can be based on past experience, force of habit, the airline's loyalty scheme, etc. In other words, the airline's brand is the key determinant.
- The customer goes to an umbrella website, where the flights of different airlines are on offer. In this case, the customer knows where he wants to go – Barcelona – and isn't too concerned about which airline flies him there. In this case, the best price, best time, best connection, etc. will be the factors for his final decision. In other words, choice is the key determinant.
- The customer makes use of a travel agency to find the right flight. In this case, the customer relies on the expertise of the agency to find him the best deal. In other words, the advice of the travel agent is the key determinant.

Each of these three purchasing models requires a degree of effort on the part of the customer. He needs to surf to a website, make a choice, contact a travel agent, etc. But if our businessman has a virtual personal assistant in his life, things would be very different. He could just ask Google to buy a ticket for him, and that would be that. This requires much less effort than any of the three scenarios above.

From the moment a virtual assistant is given responsibility for buying a plane ticket for a customer, there is a fundamental change in the hierarchy between brands. The customer will now have most confidence in the brand marketing the virtual assistant (Google, Apple, Amazon, Microsoft), rather than the airline or travel agency brand. The greater the trust a consumer places in the brand of the technology platform, the less relevant the power of other brands becomes. The reasoning is: "If Amazon says that brand X is best for me, then it must be so". Because of their outstanding performance and customer service, in recent years the major technology platforms have all built up a high degree of trust in the market. If something goes wrong with Amazon, there is never any discussion. The problem is solved quickly and correctly, in a manner that asks as little effort as possible from the customer. Similarly, Google is getting better every day. And the iPhone is the most successful product in history. Once the tech giants start helping consumers with their daily purchases – whether it is an airline ticket or a tin of beans – the technology platforms will become the gatekeepers for all other brands.

Of course, if someone is a big fan of a particular airline and instructs Google to book a flight with that company, the virtual assistant will do it efficiently. However, in all other cases the customer simply wants to get from point A to point B at the right time and for the best price. This type of 'non-brand-loyal' consumer leaves the choice to the technology platform.

> **This evolution is first and foremost a threat for sectors that sell functional products; products where the actual brand is not so important for the consumer.**

This evolution is first and foremost a threat for sectors that sell functional products; products where the actual brand is not so important for the consumer. This includes sectors like insurance, telecom providers, energy, business travel, etc. In these sectors, billions have been spent over the years on marketing, in the hope that creative communication would make the difference. And it often did – in the past. But in the world of virtual assistants this strategy will be less successful. The virtual assistant only looks at objective value and makes a suggestion to the consumer on this basis. When this happens (as we have already mentioned), perceived value will fall and real value will rise. The impact of marketing communication will decrease and the impact of the algorithms installed in the personal virtual assistants will increase.

Products that have a strong influence on the 'personal brand' of the consumer will be hit less hard by this development. For this kind of product, consumers usually stick consciously to their favourite brands, the brands that help to define who they are. But even here, the available data suggests that the technology platforms are climbing steadily up the brand hierarchy. Of all the people who buy shoes from Amazon, only 6% ask for a specific brand. The remaining 94% let Amazon make the choice.[97] It seems as though 'shopping', as we know it today, will cease to exist in its current form. Giving verbal instructions to a machine is in no way comparable with today's purchasing models.

It is highly likely that the impact of the technology platforms will increase further still in the years ahead. They will use their accumulated trust to become more closely involved in the purchasing behaviour of consumers. As far as Amazon's strategy is concerned, this is a logical move, given the nature of their business. The easier Amazon makes it for people to buy products from them, the stronger their growth will be. This is the company's core focus. But because Amazon's strategy threatens to make the classic search process redundant, Google has little option but to follow in Amazon's footsteps. In 2014, 55% of consumers began their search for a new product by using a search engine. In 2017, this has fallen to just 26%. During that same period, the number of people who began their search on Amazon has risen from 38% to 52%.[98] And if this trend results in Google also developing its own high-performance virtual assistant, this in turn forms a threat for the Apple ecosystem, bringing a third giant onto the playing field. The resulting rivalry will lead to the rapid evolution of new and improved services that can only work to the benefit of every consumer. The same rule applies to all the players: the better your service provision becomes, the more dominant your brand will be. In this way, the technology giants will rise to the top of the brand hierarchy. All other brands will operate at a lower level, where they risk becoming the football in the game of the Amazons, Apples and Googles of the world.

The commodity magnet

The concept of the commodity magnet was first introduced in the *Harvard Business Review* in June 1994 by Professors Kasturi Rangan and George Bowman.[99] The commodity magnet is a danger for any new product introduction. In their article, the professors outlined the cycle that products go through, on the basis of two dimensions:

- The cost to serve: how much money does it cost to reach the customer and to provide your service successfully?
- Relative price: how much does the customer pay for the product?

When a new product is introduced, the price and the cost to serve are usually both high. The innovation and marketing cost for a new introduction is significant, which companies seek to counterbalance (if they can) by initially charging a premium price for their newest brainchild. At this point, the number of users will start to grow, and the cost per user therefore falls, but because the product still retains its newness and uniqueness at this stage, the price remains high. This is the phase when the innovation yields its highest return. Of course, in the meantime competitors will have started to appear. They copy (part of) the innovation and launch a comparable product, which may have a lower price that allows it to quickly capture part of the market. The result is not difficult to predict: a price war breaks out. Both products become cheaper, but fortunately the costs remain low. This is the moment when customers become aware of fierce competition in the market place. As a result, their expectations rise. To meet these expectations, service costs increase, although the price has to remain the same for competitive reasons. The product eventually finds itself in an impossible situation where costs are high but the price is low. Companies are sucked into this untenable position by market dynamics. This is the power of the commodity magnet.

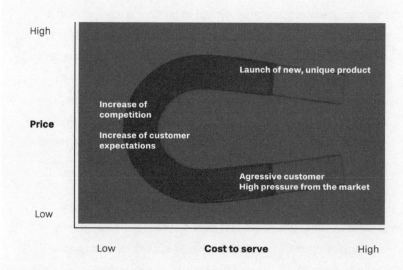

The strongest commodity magnet ever

Automation creates the ability to offer some services free of charge. This is not a tactic in a price war. It is simply an expression of the potential to offer interesting services for no return in the world of AI. In 2015, the British entrepreneur Joshua Browder launched DoNotPay, a website that helps people to contest parking fines. It is a very simple and completely free system. The consumer talks to the DoNotPay chatbot. The bot asks a number of questions and on the basis of the answers writes a letter that the consumer can use to contest his/her parking fine. The letter looks highly professional. In fact, it seems like it has been written by an expensive lawyer. In reality, it has been written by the bot. The success of this service is phenomenal. In a period of just two years, the bot has successfully contested more than 375,000 parking fines at a success rate of 64%! In total, 9.3 million dollars of fines have not been paid as a result of this automated service. On the back of this success, Browder decided to add roughly a thousand different categories to the service range. Customers can now demand money back from airlines and the makers of defective products, or even insist on things like the right to paternity leave from their employers.[100]

During the third phase of digitalization, the effect of the commodity magnet will become a harsh reality for many businesses. Digital forces not only put prices under pressure, but also increase the expectations of customers, so that costs rise. Seeking legal assistance used to be an expensive business. But now you can get good quality legal help free of charge, with 24/7 availability and no need to visit a lawyer's office! This is the digital commodity magnet at its strongest. Sectors that work with low margins today will be most vulnerable to the effects of the commodity magnet in years to come. The retail industry is a good example. Costs are already high and the price pressure is enormous. New competitors like Amazon, Alibaba and Zalando compete in a totally different way with a totally new philosophy. These new players have given a huge boost to customer expectation. As a result, most retailers have been sucked into the bottom right quadrant of the commodity magnet.

Sectors that work with low margins today will be most vulnerable to the effects of the commodity magnet in years to come.

The theory behind the commodity magnet is more relevant than ever. When the idea was first aired in 1994, the magnet was mainly activated by a (direct) competitor who introduced a comparable product to the market. In this scenario, it was only at the end of the product cycle that the customer became more demanding. But times have changed. Today, the main drivers for commodity forming are much more varied and more powerful than twenty years ago:

- *The large digital platforms*: Amazon, Google and Apple are actively involved in the purchasing decisions of customers. They influence the choice process from the front line. Products are given less chance to differentiate themselves, because there is an intermediary filter. Just as Facebook decides what news you get to see based on what they already know about you, Amazon, Google and Apple are building filters that do the same for the type of products you can buy. As a brand, it is becoming increasingly difficult to influence customers directly.

- *Global forces*: competition is more global than ever. For just a few euros, you can have products sent from China to Europe. Price pressure is fiercer and more international than it has ever been. Consumers are placing ever more trust in online players – even in companies they have never heard of. Their general (and generally positive) experience of online shopping is already so large that they are prepared to take the risk. In this way, convenient location and familiarity are no longer effective as weapons against commodity forming. What's more, the service provision of the vast majority of e-commerce players is excellent, so that pressure is exerted not only on prices but also on service levels, which increases costs.

- *Automation*: consumers want things to be as easy as possible. Technologically supported purchases make the fewest demands for effort from the consumer. What they buy and who they buy it from are less relevant than the time and energy it takes. If a company wants to improve ease of use for its customers, it first needs to invest in new interfaces. Initially, this will increase costs, particularly in companies with an analogue DNA.

- *Transparency*: full information about most products is readily available online and the web makes it easy to compare this information. When this comparison task is delegated to a digital assistant, the customer will be less involved in the purchasing process. As a result, perfect transparency in price and quality will make it difficult to differentiate on the basis of classic marketing techniques.

- *The demanding customer*: In the past, companies were able to differentiate themselves by being outstanding in a specific aspect of the market. They were either the cheapest; or they offered the best service; or they had the newest product. You could make the difference through excellence in just one of these aspects. But not any more. Today's customers want top service *and* competitive prices. Being good at just one thing is no longer enough. Today, expectations for your non-differentiating aspects are also high. This means that the cost of serving the customer will increase, often without the possibility for any compensatory increase in price.

Marketing: influencing the consumer *and* influencing the algorithm

As a business leader, you need to allow for the fact that your products are likely to be pulled with considerable force towards the commodity magnet. Once the magnet starts to do its work, your company will be in a difficult position. And if you ever allow yourself to get pulled to the bottom right quadrant of the magnet, your battle for survival is almost certain to become a losing one. In The Day After Tomorrow, you must do everything you can to resist these destructive forces.

You can only fight against the powerful commodity magnet if you are willing to move away from the classic philosophy of marketing and sales. For many years, the task of the marketing and sales departments has been clear. Their aim is to influence the purchasing process of the customer by all legal means, so that he/she buys your product or service. Marketing experts use all the tactical elements from the marketing mix to achieve this: product, price, place and promotion. The company with the smartest and most effective influencing strategy ends up as the winner in the marketplace. Having a strong brand helps customers to deal with purchasing stress, since the brand serves as a marker for trust in an overcrowded market. Or that, at least, is the way it used to be.

Don't misunderstand me – influencing the purchasing processes of potential customers will continue to be an essential part of marketing in the future. The purpose of marketing will always be to manoeuvre consumer choice in the direction of a particular product or service. However, new technology now has the poten-

Marketing for machines will become an essential part of every marketing strategy.

tial to soothe away consumer stress in a highly personalized and user-friendly manner. In the markets of the future, simply trying to influence people alone will not be enough to keep you out of the grips of the commodity magnet. You also need to influence the algorithms on which the new technology is based. Marketing for machines will become an essential part of every marketing strategy.

Preparing marketing teams to meet the challenges of The Day After Tomorrow involves developing these dual competencies: the ability to influence both people and machines. Today's marketing teams still rely too much on classic marketing skills. Many companies are already feeling the pull of the commodity magnet, but try to resist it with classic marketing budgets (= marketing communication) as a way to increase their influence

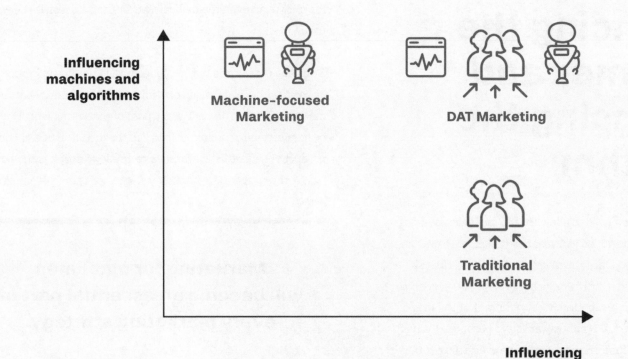

on consumers. However, there eventually comes a point when further investment in marketing communication starts to yield diminishing returns. Attracting the consumers' attention costs more and more.[101] Buying the public's attention on TV is expensive. Buying their attention on Facebook or Google is becoming expensive. There is a ceiling to these forms of influencing.

If you want to win in The Day After Tomorrow, it is crucial to add data and AI expertise to your marketing team. Currently, the budgets allocated to influencing people are often huge, whereas the budget to influence algorithms is small or non-existent. This needs to change.

> **If you want to win in The Day After Tomorrow, it is crucial to add data and AI expertise to your marketing team.**

The marketing department for The Day After Tomorrow

For many companies, it will be a real challenge to get this new expertise on board. Top data and AI talent is scarce. These talents often work for the tech-giants or else have started their own company. If you don't feel confident about attracting these whizz-kids to your company, it may be a good idea to set up your marketing department as a network. Via a network it is often easier to gain access to the knowledge and skills you need.

This is the key. You don't need to have the expertise on the payroll, but you do need to know where you can find it when you need it. Today, there are lots of interesting little niche companies that are open to AI collaboration. This can give you the knowledge and skills access you need. What's more, this approach is also highly flexible. Skillsets are changing so quickly that having an 'expert' on the payroll may eventually become a limiting factor for your flexibility. Working with different niche companies allows you to switch between skillsets as and when the need arises.

Of course, you always need some degree of in-house expertise. So, what are the foundations for the marketing departments of the future? It can be summed up in a single word: strategy! You must decide in which direction your ship is travelling. Making the right strategic choices will become the core task of your permanent marketing team. This also involves choosing the right project managers to work with your external network partners. It is this network model that will give you the necessary flexibility and expertise to add a crucial new dimension to your marketing and sales strategy: the ability to influence algorithms.

Four strategies to beat the commodity magnet

When working out your Day After Tomorrow strategy, it is vital to think carefully about ways to actively resist the pull of the commodity magnet. If you just allow your company to drift along on the tide of developments, you will soon find yourself stuck to the wrong corner of the magnet. There are four strategic pillars that can help you to avoid this unpleasant fate:

1. *Marketing for machines*: in the past, we talked about search engine optimization (SEO); today and in the future, we need to talk about algorithm optimization. Yesterday, you wanted to be found by a Google search; tomorrow, you want to be found by a Google Assistant.

2. *Non-comparable products*: if a product is easy to compare with its direct rivals, it is also easy for the algorithm to detect the differences between the products, which may not always work in your favour. If you can develop a product that cannot be compared with others, you will have a big advantage.

3. *A human touch*: in this book I have not talked much about the human aspect. This was covered in my previous book, *When Digital Becomes Human*.[102] The philosophy of using the human element as a differentiator remains valid. In fact, it is possibly the biggest differentiator of all in a digital world.

4. *Finding new markers of trust*: classic marketing communication no longer reaches large parts of the market. To influence people in the future, you need to find channels they know and trust.

1. Marketing for machines

Marketing teams are trained to influence people. An important new skill is the ability to influence machines. How? Use existing marketing knowledge and apply it to machines. Regard machines as a new target audience. This means that you need to do everything possible to help the new customer (= the machine) make the right choice: the choice for your product.

To help a customer, you first need information about that customer's needs. This is good news, because machines are much more predictable than people. If an algorithm is providing input for a comparison analysis, it is important to understand how that algorithm makes its choices. Once you know this, you can influence the algorithm by making small adjustments to your product. For example, lowering the price by a single eurocent can sometimes have a huge impact. Using other words to describe your product can also guide the algorithm towards different –

Use existing marketing knowledge and apply it to machines. Regard machines as a new target audience.

and more favourable – conclusions. This kind of algorithm hacking will become an important part of the marketing mix.

If you post a message on Facebook, YouTube or Instagram, it is important to know how the algorithm works. The marketeers who understand this best will gain most from their budget investment in these platforms.

Buzzfeed is an American digital media company. Started in 2006, and by mid-2016 its estimated value was 1.7 billion dollars.[103] Their expertise is the ability to portray news in a way that brings lots of visitors to their site. Right from the very beginning, the company believed firmly in the power of viral marketing. In an article for the *Harvard Business Review*, Duncan Watts, the founder of Buzzfeed, gave his views on how 'viral marketing for the real world' is created.[104] Viral campaigns start when content is spread by millions of ordinary people, not by a handful of influencers.

The secret of Buzzfeed's success? Marketing for machines! It cleverly exploits algorithms to obtain better results. Buzzfeed analyzes the behaviour of 100 million visitors to its site. The algorithm searches for the first signals of a successful piece of content. To do this it looks at visitor behaviour on its own host site, but also what happens with the content on other platforms, like Facebook. Once the algorithm sees that a certain article has attracted more than average attention, the machine places this specific article in a central position on the Buzzfeed site. Because Buzzfeed very quickly learns what the viral potential of a piece of content might be, they can make sure that their content scores optimally.[105]

This first strategy, marketing for machines, focuses very specifically on how you can use, exploit and manipulate algorithms to your advantage. The next three strategies ensure that the impact of people during the decision-making phase of the purchasing process remains significant. The bigger the impact of the customer in determining his choice for a particular product, the further away from the commodity magnet your company will remain. The marketing art consists of making the customer consciously opt for a specific brand.

2. Non-comparable products

Musical.ly is amazingly popular with young people. This new social network was launched in August 2014 and now (mid-2017) has more than 200 million active users.[106] You can use the Musical.ly app to make videos lasting between 15 seconds and a maximum of one minute. The videos are really a mix of karaoke and playback music clips. You choose a song and you make a clip. Some of them are semi-professional; some of them are just good for a laugh.

Nobody thought it was possible for a new social media site to find a place in the already overcrowded social media world. Facebook leads the way in this world, with more than two billion users (one in four people on the planet!), but sites like Instagram, Snapchat, WeChat, Twitter and LinkedIn also have hundreds of millions of users. You would think that the market for social networks is saturated, but apparently not. Along comes Musical.ly and somehow pushes its way in among the existing giants.

So how, exactly? The people behind Musical.ly were determined that they didn't want it to become just another Facebook or Instagram. So, they launched a completely new application targeted at a very specific niche group. What's more, the functionalities of the new platform are not so easy for others to copy, simply because they are so closely related to the niche. Facebook copied more or less everything on Snapchat, after the company refused to sell to Marc Zuckerberg. But it would be much harder for Facebook to replicate Musical.ly. Their lack of comparability with other players in the market has been the key to their success.

If a brand wants to differentiate itself from other players in the market, it is important to do something that others can't do. This, of course, is nothing new. It has been part of marketing strategy for years to try and find a blue ocean, rather than competing in a red ocean full of predators.[107] But the need to find something

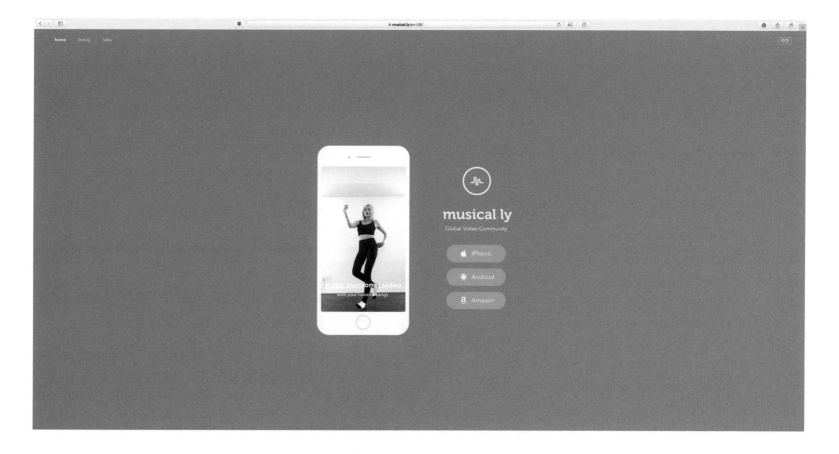

unique about your product or service will be of even greater importance in The Day After Tomorrow. As soon as a product or service can be compared with a rival, the influence of algorithms on the decision-making process of the customer automatically increases and the commodity magnet starts to pull.

Insurance products are an easy first victim for algorithms. The consumer doesn't care which company insures him, as long as he is insured. At the moment, the differences between the different insurance products are difficult to quantify for human customers. But give this task to a machine and the differences immediately become plain for all to see. In other words, insurers need to find ways to beat the commodity magnet and they need to find them quickly.

One company that has understood this is Centraal Beheer, an insurance brand in the portfolio of the Dutch Achmea group. Their roadside assistance insurance goes much further than just insuring. When your car breaks down, a Centraal Beheer operative will travel to the breakdown site to help you. In other words, the insurer solves the problem for you. You don't have to do anything, other than let them know where you are. What's more, there is huge flexibility with this type of contract. If you want to be helped everywhere at all hours of the day and night, you pay a fixed monthly fee (3.23 euros). If you prefer to pay for your help only when you need it, you can make use of Roadguard, which is Centraal Beheer's free app. When you are in trouble, you press a few buttons on your smartphone screen and help is on its way.

The strategy used by Centraal Beheer makes it very difficult for it to be compared with other insurers and insurance products. This increases the likelihood that customers will consciously opt for them. As a result, they escape from the algorithmic power of the commodity magnet.

3. A human touch

Anyone who read my previous book, *When Digital Becomes Human*, may well be asking by this stage how much of that book's theory will remain valid in The Day After Tomorrow? As far as I am concerned, it will remain as valid as ever. Perhaps even more so.

The '*When Digital Becomes Human*' philosophy is based on the old economic law of scarcity. If something is scarce, it increases in value. This is the simple operation of the principle of supply and demand. In future, the frequency of human contact with customers will decline in almost every sector. As a result, the human aspect will become scarcer and therefore more valuable

---

We cannot hope to beat computers at their own game, so we must supplement their digital strengths with our human strengths.

---

than before. For some people, this sounds like a paradox: the more digital the world becomes, the more important the human aspect will also become. In fact, this human aspect is potentially the biggest differentiator for companies in a commercial environment dominated by algorithms.

To use this human aspect as a differentiator, you first need to answer the million dollar question: what can people today still do better than computers? We cannot hope to beat computers at their own game, so we must supplement their digital strengths with our human strengths.

But what are those strengths? There is one in particular that stands out: people are still much better at the emotional aspect of customer relations than computers. In my previous book I spoke about empathy, passion and creativity as uniquely human characteristics. We are only three years further on, but we can already see erosion in the area of creativity. Computers have made giant strides forwards. When Google DeepMind beat the world champion at Go, it made moves that no human had ever made. It had studied the data from the past and added its own creative solutions for winning the game. I have already said that creativity is about trying something 10 times, 100 times or, if necessary, 10 million times, until you eventually find the answer you are looking for. On the basis of data iterations, computers can in many cases already do this better than humans.

Fortunately, passion and empathy can still serve as human differentiators. It always seems to me that passion and enthusiasm are

the human qualities most difficult for a computer to imitate. This is where we can still make the difference. Human enthusiasm is a powerful weapon against the commodity magnet. I often fly from Amsterdam to San Francisco with KLM. My experience is always good. Sometimes, it's fantastic. The difference between good and fantastic is not made by the type of plane, or by the food or by the in-flight entertainment. No, the difference is made by the crew. People can turn a commodity into something special. Afterwards, KLM always sends me a questionnaire about the flight. One of the questions is always: "Were the crew friendly?" That's the wrong question. KLM staff are always friendly. But 'just' being friendly is no longer enough: robots can be friendly as well. The question should be: "Were the crew enthusiastic?" or "Did the crew do their job with passion?" That's where people can still really make a difference. If the crew of a particular airline can make me feel their enthusiasm, I am happy to keep going back to that airline time after time. I won't be leaving that decision to a Google algorithm.

4. Searching for new markers of trust

Classic marketing channels are under pressure. It is costing more and more money to influence people using traditional methods. It is therefore crucial to discover which sources of information still remain credible with the target audience of your brand. Each consumer has sources of influence to which he/she attaches particular weight. For some people, this might be a newspaper article on a website. For others, it is a frequently shared message on Facebook or the posts of a handful of influencers on Instagram. Identifying these sources and knowing how they work can help you to limit the impact of algorithms on the choice processes of consumers.

The Belgian 'Kom op tegen Kanker' organization has applied this strategy successfully in its campaign to convince young people to give up smoking. Smoking continues to be one of the biggest causes of cancer, but is still also seen by many young people as a 'cool' way to rebel against parental authority. It's an easy option to explore new boundaries and one that doesn't seem to have immediate health risks, at least in the short-term. Young people understand rationally that these risks exist, but the emotional context is more complex. As a result, the classic anti-smoking campaigns of the past made little impact. If the communication is top-down, the youngsters just ignore the message. In addition, many of

This was one of the first campaigns where Kom op tegen Kanker reported a significant positive influence on changing the perception of smoking in young people.

this group take active steps to consciously avoid advertising of all kinds via adblockers and the like. Taking all this into account, Kom op tegen Kanker decided to work via vloggers. The organization made a conscious choice not to communicate its message as though it came from 'a higher authority', a government official or a traditional organization like itself, but used a channel that is used by young people themselves. A group of anonymous Belgian vloggers made 18 short YouTube clips about the 4,000 chemicals in cigarettes and cigarette smoke. Between them, the videos reached a total of more than six million impressions. 320,000 Belgian youngsters saw them. 97% of the feedback was positive. This was one of the first campaigns where Kom op tegen Kanker reported a significant positive influence on changing the perception of smoking in young people.[108] Working through a trusted channel increases impact on the behaviour of the target audience.

New and renewed expertise

The power of the commodity magnet is huge. Digital platforms are taking over the primary positions in the brand hierarchy. As a company leader, you can't just let this happen. Working together with the digital platforms has become inevitable, but at the same time you must rise to the challenge of maintaining the position of your brand, as best you can, against them. This is a very difficult balancing act.

Resisting the pull of the digital commodity magnet demands a new kind of expertise. The influencing of algorithms and marketing for machines involves many new techniques, but it is also necessary to redirect many existing ones. In particular, it is important to shift the weight of your marketing efforts towards people, but only in the areas where you know your brand can differentiate itself in the decision-making process of the customer. This means not only re-allocating budgets but also learning new skills.

The approach to product innovation needs to change, with a new focus on creating products that are difficult to compare. Likewise, you need to think about the interaction of your staff with customers. In the AI world, human contact during the purchasing process will become the exception rather than the rule, so it is vital to make best use of this scarce and valuable resource, which could be your key differentiator. You also need to identify the communication channels that your customers trust and focus your communication budget on these, if you want to lure them away from reliance on the cold logic of algorithms.

This axis of investment – fighting the commodity magnet – is not directly linked to the three key customer benefits of the future. It is a defensive strategy that will allow you to limit the impact of digitalization on your company and your brand, by revolutionizing your attitudes towards marketing, your new digital rivals and your increasingly demanding customers. And it is a necessary strategy if you want to hold on to a relevant role in The Day After Tomorrow.

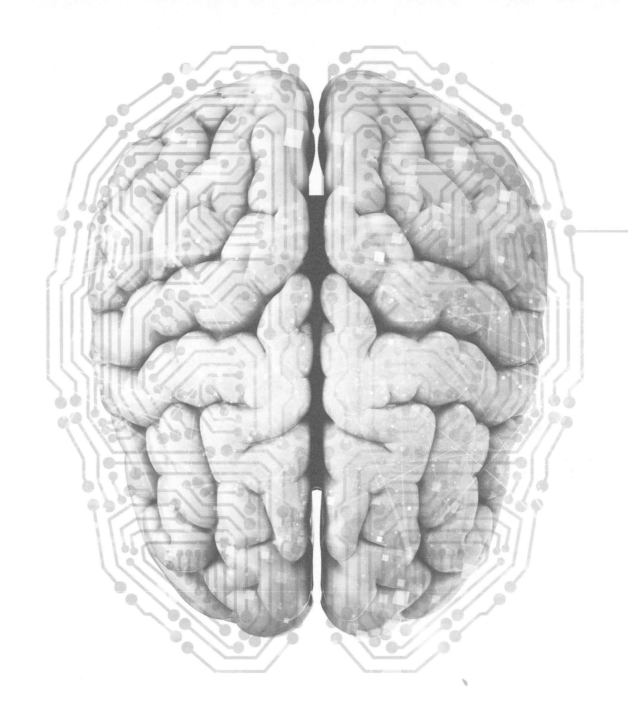

CHAPTER 8

INTELLIGENCE AUGMENTED

Artificial intelligence is more dangerous than nuclear weapons

Some of the most brilliant minds on earth have warned about the dangers of artificial intelligence. People like Elon Musk and Stephen Hawking potentially see the world coming to an end as a result of AI. In fact, Musk once posted a tweet in which he claimed that artificial intelligence poses a greater threat to mankind than the atomic bomb. If the human race dies out, they argue, this will in part be the responsibility of new technology. For the moment, humans still have a choice about the direction in which AI will develop. But this will not last. According to Hawking, artificial intelligence will either be the best thing mankind has ever created or the worst thing.[109]

Professor Stuart Russell is a researcher into existential at UC Berkeley and at the University of Cambridge research centre. Russell compares the research into artificial intelligence with the research carried out in the 1930s and 1940s for the development of nuclear weapons. In some respects, his conclusions seem to confirm the fears of Elon Musk and Stephen Hawking. In an interview with *Science* magazine, Professor Russell explained the similarities between the research into AI and the research into nuclear weapons: "The original purpose of investing in nuclear technology was to develop a limitless source of energy. Nuclear power would provide unlimited energy forever: that was the dream. Of course, everyone also saw the military potential, but the scientists thought that everybody would be sensible enough not to focus on this destructive power. The Second World War changed everything. In the short-term, the focus was switched from solving the world's energy problems to creating a weapon of mass destruction. With the consequences that everyone knows. There are many similarities between building an unlimited source of energy and an unlimited source of intelligence."[110] Other experts say much the same thing: "Today, everyone has the best of intentions with the potential of AI. But what if that changes one day?"

> **According to Hawking, artificial intelligence will either be the best thing mankind has ever created or the worst thing.**

Open AI

Elon Musk sees artificial intelligence as a threat for the continued existence of mankind. He doubts the good intentions of companies like Google DeepMind. Musk fears that the scientists are so enthusiastic about their work that they will one day discover 'by accident' something they can't control. This super-entrepreneur understands that the progress of AI cannot be halted. Consequently, he is looking for a way to surf on the wave of the hype, in the hope of being able to bring the story to a successful conclusion. With this in mind, in 2016 Elon Musk and a number of like-minded entrepreneurs started the Open AI platform. This is a non-profit organisation that is wholly dependent on its investors. The aim is to allow top scientists to collaborate on matters relating to AI, without the need to worry about quarterly results. Freed from commercial considerations, they are encouraged to create new AI applications that will benefit mankind. Whatever they invent will be shared free of charge with the rest of the world. In this way, the scientists are free to roam wherever their ideas take them. By sharing their knowledge, they hope that the rest of the world will also be motivated to develop positive AI uses. "Stopping AI is not possible. The only way to influence a positive final outcome is to be sitting behind the wheel of the car," says Elon Musk.

The biggest challenge when setting up this platform was to convince the top talents at the big technology companies to come and work for the new non-profit initiative. Top talents in commercial AI companies earn salaries comparable to top footballers. Nearly all of them work for Google, Facebook, Apple, Amazon and Microsoft. Greg Brockman, the former Chief Technology Officer at Stripe, was present at the initial meeting when the Open AI idea was first discussed. That evening, he made a list of the top ten AI researchers he would ideally want to recruit for the new platform. These ten scientists were invited one Saturday evening to attend a dinner in Napa Valley. Apparently, the atmosphere was amazing. Everyone was enthusiastic about the idea of conducting cutting-edge AI research for the benefit of mankind. In particular, they were attracted by the idea that they would be able to share their inventions with the rest of the world with no ulterior motive. At the end of the dinner, Brockman asked who was interested in taking part in the new initiative. He gave them three weeks to think about it. By the end of the three weeks, nine of the ten scientists had joined the platform. They gave up their highly paid jobs for the opportunity of working with the other top talents in their field for a noble cause.[111] Elon Musk and the other investors were willing to donate more than a billion dollars to make this dream possible and make sure that AI would not signal the end of life on earth as we know it.

The super AI myth

The world is divided into two camps. On the one side, there is the group with people like Elon Musk and Stephen Hawking, who are afraid of the power of AI. On the other side, you have the group of people for whom the development of AI can't go fast enough.

The second group contains people of a similar calibre to the first group, including people like Mark Zuckerberg (CEO Facebook) and Ray Kurzweil (founder of the Singularity University and a top researcher at Google). This second group only sees advantages in the rapid evolution of AI. In their vision, AI is the perfect partner for mankind.

In addition, there are also a number of voices who do not believe in the myth of an AI with superhuman qualities. In July 2017, an article was published by Kevin Kelly, the founder and editor-in-chief of *Wired* magazine, in which he describes in a masterful way the myth of an all-powerful, all-conquering AI.[112] His views are diametrically opposed to those of the group around Elon Musk and are worth summarizing. When people talk about 'superhuman AI', they generally make five assumptions that cannot be proven. These five assumptions are:

- artificial intelligence will become smarter than humans at an exponential rate;
- AI will develop general purpose intelligence, like humans;
- we can replicate human intelligence with silicon chips;
- intelligence can be expanded without limits;
- super-intelligent computers, once they exist, will solve all our most important problems.

Perhaps things will change in the future, but at the moment there is no evidence to suggest that we are nearing a point when there will be machines capable of taking over from humans. If the idea of a super-powerful AI is based on unproven assumptions, then it is more of a religion than a scientific argument. In

If the idea of a super-powerful AI is based on unproven assumptions, then it is more of a religion than a scientific argument. In short, it is a myth.

short, it is a myth. In contrast to these assumptions, the following five counter-arguments, put forward by Kelly, are scientifically verifiable:

- Intelligence has multiple dimensions. In other words, a phrase like 'smarter than people' doesn't really mean anything. There is no index for grading intelligence in a correct hierarchical order.
- People do not have general purpose minds, nor will AI. The human brain is not like a Swiss Army knife, with a wide range of functions of an average quality. Human beings are very good at some things and less good at others. AI will demonstrate this same kind of specialization. It will not be a Swiss Army knife that can do everything perfectly.
- The exponentially increasing curve of technological progress will eventually flatten out. In human history so far, there has never been an unending exponential curve in progress and it will be no different with AI. The idea of a limitless force is physically impossible. Speed and force are both finite parameters,

and the evolution of AI will eventually be constrained by their boundaries.

- The dimensions of intelligence are likewise not infinite. In the physical world, nothing is infinite. Temperature, for example, has a maximum and a minimum point. There is no proof to suggest that intelligence is an infinite parameter. This reality applies equally to computers.

- Intelligence is only one factor in progress. Thinking alone achieves nothing. A computer can read everything that has even been written about cancer research, but it will not be able to find a cure for cancer. There is a need for real physical research to make progress toward a final goal. If we hope to one day solve the world's major problems, a combination of humans and machines seems to be our best bet.

NOT SO FAST

STEPHEN HAWKING
Not afraid of black holes. A.I. is another story.

BILL GATES
First you'll lose your job. Then it gets scary.

STUART RUSSELL
Earth for the earthlings!

NICK BOSTROM
Prepare for "Disneyland without children."

MAX TEGMARK
Uh, can we talk about this?

DEMIS HASSABIS
Full speed ahead!

PETER THIEL
Will be a winner either way.

STEVE WOZNIAK
Resigned to being a robot's pet.

SAM ALTMAN
Sees intergalactic domination—or extinction.

ELON MUSK
Eyeing the next flight to Mars.

LARRY PAGE
Green-lighted Google Brain. 'Nuff said.

YANN LeCUN
Chill, people! We got this.

ANDREW NG
Trust the robot.

MARK ZUCKERBERG
Worried? Tell my A.I. butler.

RAY KURZWEIL
Eager to be a cyborg.

HIT THE GAS

"The greatest misunderstanding about artificial intelligence is to see intelligence as a single dimension," says Kevin Kelly. There is simply no scientific evidence for a kind of ladder of intelligence. Just try, for example, to rank the different levels of animal intelligence. If intelligence is a single-dimension, linear ladder, we should be able to order the intelligence of a parrot, a dolphin, a cat and a gorilla, but this is an impossible task. There are different dimensions to the intelligence of these animals. Some forms of intelligence are very simple; others are very complex. Some aspects of intelligence are located in particular niches. Some animals even have forms of intelligence and qualities that exceed human intelligence. In short, there is no 'ladder' that allows us to chart different levels of intelligence in the manner suggested by the detractors of AI.

It sometimes seems as if there is a general expectation that artificial intelligence will be able to solve all the problems we were never able to solve in the past. And it is indeed true that in the very near future, computers will be able to answer most questions faster and more accurately than humans. This leads to a tendency to assume that they are inherently cleverer than humans. But in reality, the processes that lead to this cleverness in computers are very different from our human way of thinking. Scientists are still not 100% sure how the human brain works, so how can it possibly be recreated from silicon chips? The super-computers will function in a totally different way from the human mind. When we build these machines, we will be building something that does not exist in the biological world. It is comparable with the invention of the aeroplane. When the Wright brothers wanted to build a machine that could fly, they did not try to imitate the flight of birds. Instead, they built something that did not exist in the world of nature. Nowadays, planes can fly further, faster and higher than birds. Does this mean that they are in some way like birds? Or better than birds? Of course not! And it is the same with computers and the human brain.

Artificial intelligence will certainly be able to solve some types of problem that are impossible for human intelligence to solve. Does that mean that a computer's processes are more intelligent than human thought? No, it is just a different kind of intelligence. This explains why the most likely source of continued progress in the future is an intense collaboration between smart computers and smart people.

This, at least, is the philosophical reasoning of the positivist camp. For the moment, the rest of the world is torn between hope and fear. Only time will tell in which direction we eventually travel.

The most important technology for the automation of work is natural language processing.

Robots steal our jobs, but less quickly than we think

A study[113] by McKinsey calculated that 49% of professional activities can be automated. This does not mean that 49% of our jobs will disappear. It means that in every job some aspects can be taken over by computers. Moreover, this 49% makes no allowance for future technological developments. This is the percentage of work activities that can already be automated with existing technology. This sounds like a doom scenario for the labour market, but the good news in that the same study also showed that only 5% of jobs can be fully automated. In other words, the vast majority of jobs will undergo fundamental change, rather than disappear. Other research confirms much the same. An OECD report estimates that 9% of jobs can be fully automated.[114] Forrester claims that 16% of existing jobs will be automated by 2025, but that 9% of new jobs will be created, making a net loss of 7%.[115] In fact, if you take all these reports together, 7% is also the average figure for the expected loss of jobs as a result of rapid automation. Even so, this still means that an awful lot of people are suddenly going to find themselves unemployed.

The most important technology for the automation of work is natural language processing. This technology makes it possible for computers to read and analyze huge volumes of text in the same way as people, but immeasurably quicker. The faster this technology is developed, the faster human tasks will be mechanized. This will include, for example, the routine work of accountants and lawyers.

This technology is already as good as available. Consequently, the automation process can begin, theoretically at least. But there is an important nuance. Technologists regard the moment when the technology becomes available as the moment when the jobs will disappear. In practice, however, in most companies there will be quite a lengthy adoption curve. The fact that the technology is available does not mean that everyone is immediately going to use it or use it 100%. Before the 1.7 million American truck drivers need to start looking for a new job, the scientists first need to refine the technology so that driverless lorries can operate safely in normal road conditions. This is estimated to be around 2025, but even that is not the end of the story. To replace all American lorries with self-drivers requires an investment of more than 1,000 billion dollars, a sum that is unlikely to be available overnight. In other words, the conversion is going to last for years, if not decades. And this scenario will be repeated in other sectors of the economy. The changes in the labour market are coming, and it would be foolish to deny it. We can even see which jobs are going to be most at threat. But at least we have a degree of time to prepare ourselves – as individuals and as a society – to cope with the worst social and economic effects. We need to use this time wisely.

Feeling threatened by automation? Learn new skills!

In the near future, automation will make it necessary for people and machines to work closely together. This means that the job description of every role is set to change drastically. Employees who are not prepared to learn new skills risk making things difficult for themselves and may find themselves no longer needed. Saying "I'm not really interested in digital" is the equivalent of saying "I'm not really interested in learning to read and write" fifty years ago. You immediately rule yourself out of the job mar-

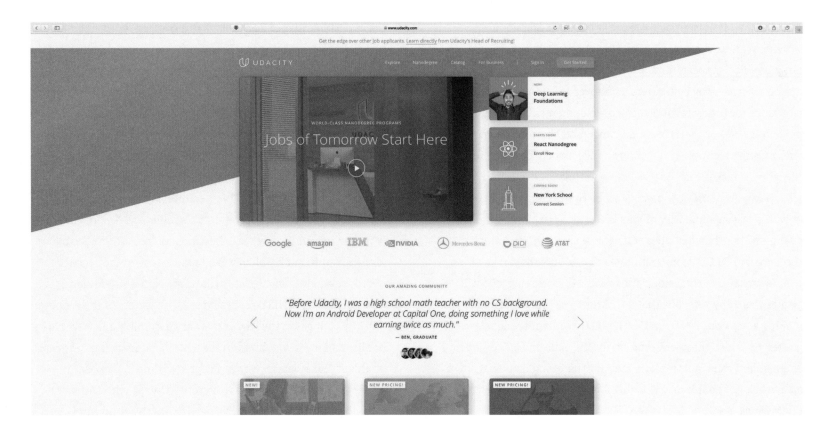

ket. The third phase of digitalization is the phase of automation. This means that many aspects of many jobs will be transferred to machines in the near future. We all have to accept that the day-to-day activities within your job are likely to change. Some of us may even have to accept that it means doing a completely different job altogether.

Fortunately, there are solutions for learning new skills. Udacity is a new educational platform. The company was founded by, amongst others, Sebastian Thrun, one of the pioneers of the self-driving car. Udacity grew out of two successful MOOCs (Massive Open Online Courses) at Stanford. In 2011, 160,000 students followed the free computer science lessons under Thrun. A further 90,000 registered for the introduction to artificial intelligence course. Sebastian Thrun was so amazed by these numbers that he decided to set up Udacity. The initial aim was to reach as many students as he could with his expertise. In the lecture halls at Stanford, he was teaching to just a handful of students. Via the MOOCs, he could inspire hundreds of thousands of people.

Shortly after he launched Udacity, Thrun came to the conclusion that the quality of his offering was not good enough, and that the impact of his large-scale online courses was insufficient. As a result, he decided to change strategy. Udacity has since evolved into a provider of nano-diplomas in highly specialized fields. For example, Udacity is the only training centre where you can follow a course in how to programme a driverless car. Today, Udacity also collaborates with large companies, putting together made-to-measure courses that allow employees to learn the new skills

they need in the most efficient manner. Via Udacity, people can even learn how to programme complex machines in just a few weeks. This kind of platform is the ideal solution for anyone who feels that their current job is threatened.

Bottleneck occupations? Send in the robots!

When it comes to employment, automation is often given negative connotations: "Machines are stealing people's jobs!" Of course, you can also look at it from a different perspective. What if robots can be used to solve the shortage of human candidates for certain jobs, and in this way, improve general provision of services? In his book *Industries of the Future* Alec Ross[116] cites the example of healthcare in Japan.

Japan has the highest average life expectancy in the world. Men live on average until they are 80 and women until they are 87 years of age. In the next 45 years, this is expected to increase to 84 and 91 years respectively. Today, 25% of the Japanese population is aged over 65; by 2050 this percentage will have risen to 39%. Self-evidently, the greater the number of older people there are in a society, the more younger health care personnel are required to care for them. In the past, it was the tradition in Japan that the elderly were cared for by their children, but nowadays there are too few grandchildren to maintain this tradition.[117] The Japanese government estimates that in the future it will need 4 million healthcare workers to look after its rapidly ageing population. At the moment, there are just 1.49 million of them.

In this situation, there is only one possible solution: robots. The communication robot Palro is already in use in many carehomes. This robot holds simple conversations with the residents and provides a number of basic entertainment programmes. Through these conversations, the robots can often establish whether a patient has a problem or not, and can pass this information on to their human colleagues, who therefore get a better picture of the current situation of each elderly person in the home.[118]

Toyota[119] is also building a nursing robot called Robina (named after Rosie, the robot housekeeper in *The Jetsons* cartoon series). Robina's task, like Palro's, is to reduce the workload of human nursing staff by talking to patients and entertaining them. Robina's 'brother' is called Humanoid. As the name suggests, he does look a bit like a human being (in the same way that CP3O did in *Star Wars*) and his task is to make it possible for the elderly to live longer in their own homes by performing simple household jobs that are not always easy for older people: doing the washing up, picking things up off the floor, opening the curtains, etc. This again reduces the need for human carers to perform this basic, unskilled and repetitive work. In addition to Toyota, Honda is also investing heavily in a similar robot with a similar purpose. Today, Japan is the world leader in robotics. 310,000 of the world's 1.4 million industrial robots were made in Japan.[120] The Japanese government supports the development of robots. They regard it as the only way to successfully meet the social challenges of the future.

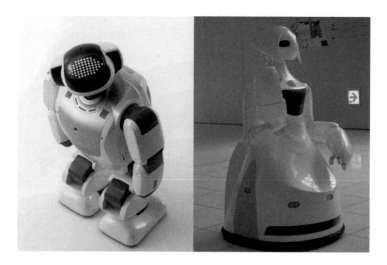

What if robots can be used to solve the shortage of human candidates for certain jobs, and in this way, improve general provision of services?

In term of the technical challenges, one of the biggest is to develop a system for robots that will allow them to carry out more complicated tasks in nursing care. For example, how long will it be before robots have the flexibility of movement to allow them to brush a patient's teeth? These kinds of skills will be necessary to further develop the collaboration between man and machine in the healthcare industry – and other industries – of the future. The robots will not replace nursing staff. The robots will assist nursing staff, by giving them the time they need to perform other more complex and more crucial duties in a more qualitative manner.

Intelligence augmented

The collaboration between man and machine has been providing benefits for society for many years. For example, by automating many elements in the manufacture of cars, they have become much cheaper and therefore much more accessible for a larger group of people. Telephone and email are much faster and cheaper means of communication than a courier service. And in a land like India, where the doctor/patient ratio is 1 to 1,600, technological support is the only way to ensure that Indian doctors can set the right priorities and see the right patients first.

In all these examples, the computer has provided added value, not only to the business world but also to society as a whole.

In the coming years, the collaboration between man and machine will be crucial in successfully meeting the expectations of customers. This will involve a transition from AI to IA: from Artificial Intelligence to Intelligence Augmented. Just as the machines of the Industrial Revolution helped us to overcome our physical limitations, the machines of the near future will help us to overcome our cognitive limitations. The more research reports I read, the more I become convinced that AI will 'only' initiate the process of fundamental change in the way we do our jobs, rather than eliminating those jobs completely. After all, that's more or less what has already been happening for the last hundred years or so. Progress during the past century has changed the nature of many jobs and, yes, it is true that some jobs have fallen by the wayside, but the vast majority of us still have work. It will be no different in the world of AI and IA.

Intelligence augmented is about offering technical solutions that will allow people to improve their performance. Personnel who are supported by the right technology can achieve higher levels of service than personnel who only make use of their human qualities.

The scaling-up of human skills

Every company dreams of being able to make the difference with its human component. That was the core of my previous book and in the previous chapter I also stressed the importance of the human interface. Unfortunately, however, you can't expect every person to have a perfect memory. You can't expect every person to immediately know what a customer is talking about when he/she asks a question. This is where intelligence augmented comes in. Intelligence augmented makes it possible to apply the human interface on a greater scale.

In recent years, we have organized three events at the W Hotel in Barcelona. The service on each occasion was fantastic. The W Hotel is without doubt one of my favourite hotels in Europe. In total, we have booked something like 270 nights for our different events. In other words, we are a good and loyal customer. About a month after our last event, I was back in Barcelona to give a lecture to a group of managers. When I wanted to check in, I was greeted with the words: "Good morning, Mr. Van Belleghem. Is this your first stay in the W Hotel?" When you are a good customer, that's not really what you want to hear. What you want to hear is: "Steven, it's wonderful to see you back again, and so soon!" Is this the fault of the receptionist? Not at all! Perhaps he had only been working there for a week. Even if he had been working there longer, you see thousands of guests pass through a hotel and you can't be expected to remember them all, can you? No, not as an individual employee you can't. But the hotel can – and should. Guest recognition software has been available for years and it's up to the management of hotels like the W Hotel to make sure that their staff have it at their disposal. With the right tech-support, hotels can make it easier for their staff to give loyal customers a special welcome. The loyal customer feels valued and thinks: "Wow! What a great hotel!" In my case, the W Hotel missed a good opportunity to score.

It is a useful exercise to think about what constitutes 'ideal' staff behaviour towards customers in your business. In particular, ask yourself how smart technology can help to make it possible for your people to achieve that ideal behaviour.

The starting point: customer service

Intelligence augmented will first make itself felt in customer service. In the chapter on new interfaces, we have already looked at the role for bots in customer service. If a computer programme is able to answer customers' routine questions, this frees up time for the human staff to deal with more complex matters. As a result, the overall quality of output for the customer is enhanced. Intelligence augmented will quickly become a reality in customer service, because this is a part of the overall business processes for which lots of data exists as most companies already use software programmes to record all their customer interactions. This data is the required raw material for the computer/bot to do its work.

One of my favourite companies in this field is Digital Genius. It was started in 2014 and already has a number of top brand names as customers. During the preparation for my book, I had a conversation with their Chief Strategy Officer and founder, Mikhail Naumov. Once again, you can see our full discussion on my YouTube channel (*www.youtube.com/stevenvanbelleghem*). The

Digital Genius philosophy perfectly matches the idea of intelligence augmented. They use software to maximize the performance of customer service agents. The companies that become their customers give Digital Genius their customer service data for the past two years. The Digital Genius software 'eats' this data and translates it into algebra. This makes the software language independent. The input can be in different languages, but the final output is a mathematical model. If a customer (of the customer company) asks a question, this is also translated into a mathematical model. It makes no difference in which

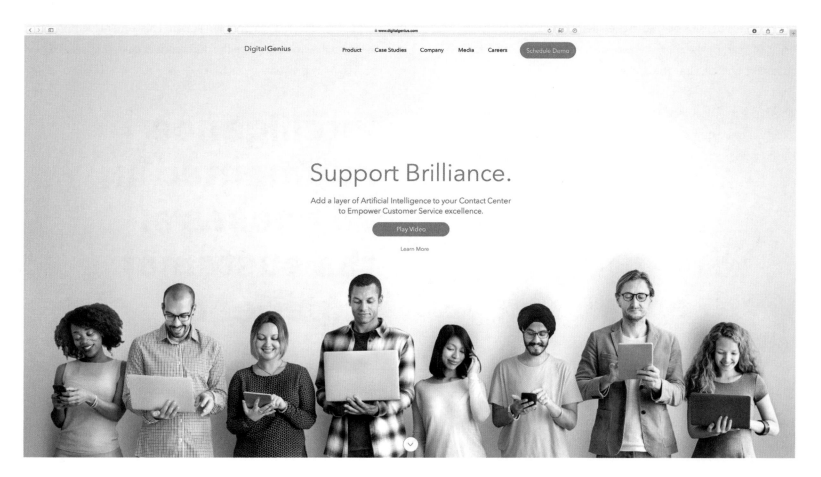

language the question is asked. The mathematical formulas are compared with each other, and on the basis of this analysis, the Digital Genius software suggests an answer to the customer question. The computer-generated answer is accompanied by a probability score. This score is the computer's estimate about the likely accuracy of the answer. If the score is higher than 95%, the answer is sent automatically to the customer. If the score is lower than 95%, the suggested answer is first sent to a human customer service agent. This operative then decides whether or not to use all or part of the suggested answer in the final answer to the customer, and also has the option to personalize it.

This has a double effect. The customer gets an answer to his/her question more quickly and the answer is also personalized. For the customer and for rival competitors, this is invisible technolo-

CAN [0.1341, −0.5896, 0.5789]

YOU [−0.1231, 0.8596, 0.3798]

REBOOK [0.9578, 0.2357, −0.8897]

MY [0.5587, −0.2221, 0.5794]

FLIGHT [0.8998, −0.2396, 0.4793]

Converted to word vectors for the Deep Learning Model

gy. KLM is one of Digital Genius's customers. KLM's own customers therefore receive quick and personal responses to their questions. As a result, their natural reaction is to think: "KLM has really good staff, better than any other airline." KLM does indeed have very good staff, but so do many other airlines. The difference is that KLM also has smart software that allows the performance of its staff to be taken to a higher level. Or to put it another way, the intelligence of their staff is taken to a higher level. Intelligence augmented in action. This kind of 'behind-the-scenes' software will make the difference in customer service provision in the years ahead.

Intelligence augmented in all phases of the customer experience

Thanks to intelligence augmented, staff will be able to provide a better service in all phases of the customer experience. The way in which Apple uses Apple ID in their stores is a good example. Once a member of the sales team enters an Apple ID into his/her smartphone, he/she can see the entire Apple history of that customer. In other words, the Apple sellers know what products you have, when you bought them, where you bought them, etc. In other words, their service levels are immediately personalized.

In pre-sales, staff can also benefit from technological assistance to better help customers during the purchasing process. If you want to buy a new car, you are likely to have done extensive research on the car manufacturer's website before you visit a showroom. Wouldn't it be interesting for the sales team in the showroom to know which models and options you have already looked at? This would save time and allow the sales conversation to carry on from where your website visit left off. Similarly, during a return visit to a restaurant, it would be useful if the restaurant could call up details of any allergens you may have mentioned during your first visit. In this way, you don't need to repeat yourself and the restaurant can offer you allergen-free menu options that it knows you will be able to eat.

Intelligence augmented can be applied in all business situations where data is available about the customer, and where the customer interacts with a human member of staff. As soon as data is stored about a particular aspect of the customer experience, that data can be used to improve staff performance.

For policemen and policewomen intelligence augmented can mean the difference between life and death. It can mean the difference between preventing a terrorist attack and counting the number of casualties afterwards. International security services make extensive use of software and data to support their people in the field. A professor at the Carnegie Mellon University has recently developed a piece of technology that makes it possible to identify suspects at a distance using an iris scan.[121] In concrete terms, this means, for example, that police travelling behind a suspect car can establish the driver's identity from the moment he glances in his rear-view mirror. This gives them time to assess the situation in safety and decide what resources are needed to deal with it.

Investing in intelligence augmented

Intelligence augmented is no longer science fiction. As a company, it is important to think about ways you might be able to use IA in the context of your business to raise the potential of your people to a higher level. What technological support do they need to meet, and even exceed, the expectations of modern consumers? This is the final axis of investment you need to follow if you want to secure the key customer benefits in The Day After Tomorrow:

- *Faster-than-real-time customer service:* if service agents have the right data, they can set the right priorities. Doctors can see information that allows them to help someone before it is too late. Airline staff can inform passengers about important aspects of their flights.

- *Hyper-personalization*: knowing exactly who the customer is and making use of that information makes the human interface more personal. If a shop recognizes a customer, the sales team is better able to help that customer to find what he/she is looking for. The right tech-tools can make human staff seem like Amazon algorithms, but more personal!
- *Convenience*: having the right information about a customer makes it possible to serve that customer quicker and more easily. You don't have to repeat your allergens when you return to a restaurant. You don't have to explain that this is actually your fifteenth visit to a hotel. Data helps staff help customers.

A top team of 60 researchers at Facebook are working on a device that will allow you to post Facebook messages directly via your brain.

Cyborgs!

Intelligence augmented improves the performance of people through technology. For the time being, this means technology external to the body. But to finish this chapter, let's take a little look forward into the future. What are the possibilities for further augmenting human intelligence by inserting technology into (or at least connecting it with) the body?

Many futurists see this as the next step: the evolution from human to cyborg. Cyborgs are the physical integration of man and machine. With cyborgs, human performance is not enhanced by software, but by technological adjustments made to the body. Neil Harbisson[122] is now generally regarded as the first human cyborg. Neil is a 33-year-old artist who was born completely colour-blind. He can only see the world in different shades of grey. To correct this, an antenna has been inserted into his skull that converts light into sound. For Neil, the antenna is like having an extra sense, a sense that allows him to feel the power of light. In other words, it adds an extra dimension to the way he sees the world. Since the British government agreed that the antenna could be included in his passport photograph, Neil is officially the first cyborg.

This is another area where Elon Musk wants to innovate. Since 2017, he is not only the founder of Tesla, Open AI and Space X, but also of Neuralink. With Neuralink, Musk wants to develop brain interfaces. The aim is to link artificial intelligence to the human intelligence locked inside our heads. It is another part of Musk's fight against the machines. "By allowing people to function at a higher level, we will be able to continue competing against smart computers."[123] The first Neuralink products seek to help people with brain damage. They hope to cure conditions like Parkinson's and epilepsy with an extension in the brain.

As always, Elon Musk's ambitions are sky-high, but this time he has come in for considerable criticism from the scientific community. Antonio Regalado[124], the biomedicine editor at the *MIT Technology Review* has no faith in the project. Elon Musk's timeline is just 8 to 10 years, which Regalado regards as wholly unrealistic. Neuralink plans to use brain implants, but at the present time, medical science still knows too little about the brain to make this possible. Equally, there are not too many otherwise healthy people who would be willing to take the risk of having their brains opened up. Such techniques may become possible in the very long term, but not in the coming decades.

Yet notwithstanding criticism of this kind, more and more tech companies are looking at ways to develop augmented human intelligence. A top team of 60 researchers at Facebook are working on a device that will allow you to post Facebook messages directly via your brain.[125] When, for example, you are dining in a restaurant, you will no longer need to reach for your smartphone to contact your friends; you just 'think' your message and it will automatically be posted online. The Facebook plan doesn't involve the use of implants, but relies on a device attached to the outside of the skull.

The timeline for all this is pretty vague. Some people expect cyborgs on a large scale by 2030. Others see it as a much longer-term evolution. One thing is certain. At the moment, an awful lot of very clever people are spending an awful lot of money to find ways to raise human potential to a higher level. And at some indefinable point in the future, it is highly likely that they will succeed.

How far along are you?

After reading chapter 8, the time has come to pause and reflect. Ask yourself how well you are currently scoring on the four axes of investment. Have you already made a start? If so, where? What other projects do you have in the pipeline? Are there axes where you have done nothing so far? How can your business achieve the key customer benefits for The Day After Tomorrow? Take your time to think about and answer these questions. Decide on a list of priorities and start implementing them now. Before you know it, The Day After Tomorrow will have become Today.

THE
DAY
AFTER
TOMORROW
CONSEQUENCES

CHAPTER 9

ORGANIZATIONAL MODELS FOR THE DAY AFTER TOMORROW

In the last section of the book, I described the four axes of investment you need to follow if you wish to realize the key customer benefits in The Day After Tomorrow. Everyone can see the possibilities. Everyone has ideas. So the core question now becomes: "How can we organize ourselves to turn our ideas into reality?"

Often it will not be possible for large companies to make the crucial innovations for The Day After Tomorrow within their existing structures. For this reason, I am delighted that my business partner and good friend Peter Hinssen has agreed to look at this problem as a guest author. Peter has studied the ways in which large companies are organizing themselves to meet the challenges of The Day After Tomorrow in great detail, and in the next chapter he offers his conclusions about the different organizational models that can help to bring the four investment axes to life.

How successful companies are preparing for The Day After Tomorrow

By Peter Hinssen, founder and partner at nexxworks

Steven and I go way back. Before he became my business partner at nexxworks, we organized numerous innovation tours together and became great friends, in spite of our different backgrounds. Or maybe just because of it. As a marketing inspirator, he is always looking at business through the lens of the customer, whilst I have been preoccupied with the impact of technology on both society in general and organizations in particular. We have always been perfectly complementary that way.

Lately, our visions have converged even more, because – travelling together to the most disruptive hubs on our tours – we have come to see that the most successful companies of today are the ones that dare to think *very long-term*. Those that are creating a radical Day After Tomorrow that will reshape not only their markets, but how they interact with their employees and their customers. That's why both of our new books, my *The Day After*

Tomorrow and Steven's *Customers The Day After Tomorrow* have been written as a complementary series. That's why we both wrote a chapter in each other's books. And that's why our company nexxworks exists.

More than anyone I know, Steven deeply understands how everything starts and ends with our customers. The technology we use or design, our company culture, our business model, even up to our most boring business processes: they all revolve around them. So that's also the case for radical innovation and extremely long-term thinking: the consumer is the only constant at the centre of our organization's potential futures. Customers are our compass in The Day After Tomorrow.

I love how Steven writes that companies should always start with the customers, and the experience they deserve, and work your way back from there to stay ahead of the curve. When it comes to our Day After Tomorrow, I believe we'll have to think big – huge even – to catch these increasingly demanding customers, and reiterate from there until today with a realistic roadmap.

Above all, I'm excited about technology becoming invisible and how this evolution is going to impact our Day After Tomorrow relationship with the customer. Especially with smart bots like Google Home or with the Internet of Things. These technologies are both ubiquitous *and* invisible at the same time: always on, but barely noticeable. They have the power to "make shopping disappear", to use Daniel Rausch's words when he described Amazon Dash. Just think about their consequences for the

customer experience, the buying cycle and even the concept of a customer itself. Because, if you just have to ask for something to get it – without any actual payment process – should we still call it shopping? Try to think about that, and then work your way from there to now.

So, the chapter that follows is an adapted excerpt from my own book *The Day After Tomorrow*, which was published earlier this year. What follows describes how the most successful and agile companies out there organize their innovation, and which models they use. You will immediately notice how quite a lot of them have a powerful focus on their customers, which is a matching addition to Steven's story, I believe.

Haier, for instance, has a brilliant 'zero distance to customers' rule. Mastercard innovates together with its customers, through co-creation. Deutsche Telekom's hub:raum start-ups receive direct access to their customers. Autodesk collaborates with pollutants – pioneering customers with extreme demands – to create its Day After Tomorrow. You'll see that the customer and his needs are never far away.

So, here goes. I hope you'll enjoy the ride.

Patterns of The Day After Tomorrow

Over the past few years, I've had a privileged view of radical innovation as I had the chance to follow some of the largest corporations in the world very closely during our nexxworks innovation tours: on their journey to re-invent, re-generate, re-boot or re-think their very core existence. In the next few pages, I'll present the innovation approaches of some of the companies that stood out: those who have successfully tackled their Day After Tomorrow.

Don't be mistaken: this is *not* by any means a cookbook with ready-to-follow recipes, but rather an inspiration smorgasbord. It's a set of patterns of The Day After Tomorrow for you to compare and ingest, to see if it could serve as stimulation for your organization, for your company, for your future. That's because there is no silver bullet when it comes to organizing your innovation.

The truth is that there are as many innovation methods as there are companies. But if you look closely at some of the pioneers I describe in the following examples, patterns emerge with the basic ingredients of corporate innovation.

PATTERN #1: The remote silo

Many have tried to shield their Day After Tomorrow 'magic' in a separate silo. They create a removed 'division' where they can – in splendid isolation – invent the future. Their Day After Tomorrow team is neatly separated from the Today people, and the 'shit of yesterday'.

It's an incredibly alluring idea. But it proves incredibly difficult to pull off.

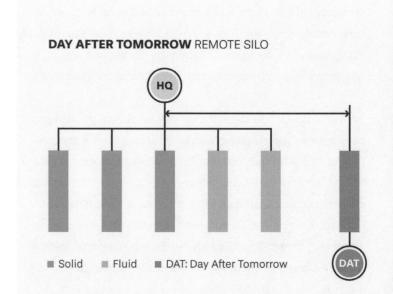

DAY AFTER TOMORROW REMOTE SILO

■ Solid   ■ Fluid   ■ DAT: Day After Tomorrow

The most magnificent and inherently tragic example of this approach is that of Xerox PARC: the birthplace of modern computing as we know it. Ethernet, the personal computer, laser printing, the graphical user interface (GUI), object-oriented programming, ubiquitous computing: they were all developed there. But Xerox made one vital mistake. PARC was too much of a 'silo'. Geographically, culturally and commercially. So much so that it became disconnected from the mothership's core activities. And that is why Xerox never commercialized any of its brilliant and earth-shattering creations. Truly tragic. Xerox could be 'Apple *and* Google combined' today. Instead, it is a shadow of its former self. If you develop The Day After Tomorrow and can never bring it into the spotlight, you run the risk of essentially destroying any fundamental value creation.

Going the distance

One of my favourite examples of radical innovation is what is being developed at Johnson & Johnson: one of the largest health-care product companies, providing the world with everything from baby shampoo, to band-aids and state-of-the-art pharmaceuticals to tackle schizophrenia.

Its Day After Tomorrow labs are not inside the mothership either, which is on the east coast. They are safely tucked away in places like La Jolla, San Diego, where brilliant former Head of Innovation Diego Miralles was, until recently (he became President of Adaptive Therapeutics), running a team of about 200 people whose sole purpose was to focus on The Day After Tomorrow.

Diego Miralles once jokingly told me that he would probably have been spending 95% of his time on corporate politics, had his team been located near the headquarters of his company. But he was lucky enough to be three time zones away. This distance empowered him to focus exclusively on The Day After Tomorrow. Instead of spending his time on corporate politics, he was able to dedicate 95% of his time on The Day After Tomorrow.

He had all the benefits of the power and investments of the J & J brand, without the drawbacks of corporate and risk-averse meddling. It was what enabled his team to create things that were groundbreaking, radically pioneering and capable of really reinventing their organization and business model. This radical silo approach allowed them to think about how the company could serve its patient-customers in a smarter, more convenient and personalized manner: by evolving from reactive sick-care –

which is the only way to describe a business model that profits more from sick people than from healthy people – to actual proactive healthcare.

So, isolating your Day After Tomorrow efforts in a separate unit inside your company is a good idea. But make sure you do not completely disconnect the entity. If it's too far removed – like PARC was from Xerox – it can backfire. The isolation of the remote silo can lead to frustration if the mothership doesn't pick up. It will be very difficult to cycle the innovation back into the mainstream of the corporate entity, as Xerox has shown. Perhaps it is the remoteness, perhaps the jealousy of the corporate body, or the lack of oversight and governance, or the combination of all of these. But, as J&J will show, there is an 'optimal distance' where the remote silo can indeed invent The Day After Tomorrow, and still influence the mothership to act on those insights.

Isolating your Day After Tomorrow efforts in a separate unit inside your company is a good idea. But make sure you do not completely disconnect the entity.

PATTERN #2:
The separate entity

The biggest challenge of large corporates is balancing an existing business model with another one that operates on the flip side, and might even cannibalize the core business. They have to level out the solid (focused on exploiting) and fluid (focused on exploring) parts of their organization and keep both fully functional. Ambidextrous organizations – as the authors Michael Tushman and Charles A. O'Reilly III call them – solve this conundrum by separating the existing business from the emerging one. The

reason is that the management structures, processes, mindsets and skills that are used to sustain the business tend to clash with those needed for radical innovation.

One solution, as described above, is working with a radical Day After Tomorrow silo inside a company. But sometimes this does not work because there is a severe integration problem. In such cases, cutting the umbilical cord is really the only solution.

A wonderful example of such a radical separation is that of CLAAS tractors – one of the top players in the EU market. When I heard the story behind this family-owned business, I was really fascinated by the capability of this organization to keep reinventing itself. Today, the company, founded in 1913 by her grandfather, is owned and run by Cathrina Claas-Mühlhäuser. She was only 35 when she was handed the reigns of a thriving 4 billion euro business with more than 11,000 employees.

Agriculture as a service

The machines that CLAAS builds are incredibly intelligent: the pinnacle of 'precision agriculture', where big data meets self-driving. They make the Google cars pale by comparison in their autonomous capabilities. The farmers are only required to take the vehicles from one field to another. That's it. The tractors can do all the rest pretty much by themselves.

But Claas-Mühlhäuser didn't stop here. She dared to ask the courageous question: 'Is the future of agriculture less about selling

DAY AFTER TOMORROW **SEPARATE ENTITY**

HQ

SEPARATE

■ Solid ■ Fluid ■ DAT: Day After Tomorrow

DAT

tractors than it is about providing agriculture as a service?' If the answer was 'yes', it would kill her existing business model in the long run. She was smart enough to put herself in the shoes of her customers in The Day After Tomorrow, and work her way back from there.

Today, the business of CLAAS consists of building complex machines and selling them to farmers. The future of agriculture, however, will more than likely be about fleets of self-driving tractors and harvesters. The latter would allow CLAAS to play a whole new role in the agricultural value chain, but would need them to radically rethink their business model.

Never lose touch with the outside world and not with management either. And that is the tricky part, which a lot of organizations get wrong.

Therefore, they conceived a company called 365FarmNet, which allows farmers to completely manage their farming and agricultural activities in a cloud-based solution. All kinds of sensors gather information about the farm in one single programme: from cultivation planning to harvesting, from field to stable, from

documentation to operating analysis. That's a radical move away from the tractor world of physical products to the world of bits and software. One that requires a very different set of capabilities, talents and processes.

It should not come as a surprise that the gap between the hundreds of tractor engineers and the much smaller team of software developers focusing on this radical Day After Tomorrow farming service was too big to be bridged. So, after a while, it was decided to take 365FarmNet out of CLAAS and make it a subsidiary with a high level of independence. Today, it is located in Berlin, surrounded by a great number of like-minded Internet of Things start-ups, where it is really making a dent. This approach gives the former intracompany start-up the best autonomy and maximum speed and flexibility to grow.

Though not all of the most successful radical innovators out there use this method, separating their core business from their radical innovation efforts – inside (like J & J) or even outside (like CLAAS) your organization – can be very effective. Just make sure it's a protected yet connected kind of isolation. Never lose touch with the outside world and – if we're talking about an in-company silo – not with management either. And that is the tricky part, which a lot of organizations get wrong.

PATTERN #3:
The 'catapult'

One of my favourite radical innovation examples comes from the airline industry, where the International Airlines Group (IAG) – the parent company of Aer Lingus, British Airways, Iberia and Vueling – is performing a radical experiment in Day After Tomorrow thinking. These innovation exercises – called 'catapults' – are headed by the brilliant Glenn Morgan.

During these catapults, eight senior executives – each from different business divisions – participate in an intense eight-week programme. Throughout that time, they are put in an innovation 'pressure cooker': bombarded with all kinds of eye-opening experiences and fed with all sorts of disruptive ideas, concepts, technologies and start-ups. The aim is that – using agile mechanisms – by the end of the experiment, they figure out one or more possible Day After Tomorrow initiatives that are truly radical. They have to come up with projects that have the potential to change the course of their industry. Not just add-on innovations, but built-in innovations that have the potential to really become billion-dollar businesses. And then they have to present them to the board.

Pressurizing it

Although the eight IAG executives are a permanent part of the existing business, they are separated from their own teams for these eight intense weeks. The reason is that they need to be able to fully concentrate on their Day After Tomorrow thinking, steering clear of the 'shit of yesterday' that gets in the way of any kind of innovation endeavour.

Another crucial ingredient of these kinds of catapult approaches is time pressure. I think that the clearcut timeframe of eight weeks is essential for providing a crystal-clear sense of purpose, keeping the passion and dedication alive and, at the same time, makes sure the project evolves fast enough to keep it relevant. Decision inertia tends to be a major obstacle in siloed organizations and this catapult disruption is a very efficient manner to beat this challenge.

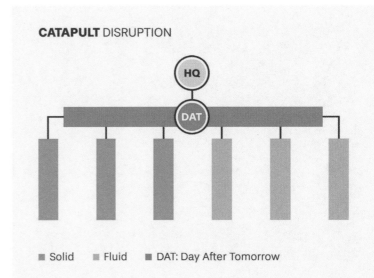

CATAPULT DISRUPTION

■ Solid　　■ Fluid　　■ DAT: Day After Tomorrow

The best part of the catapult exercise has to do with ownership because, at the end of this exercise, one of the executives is actually going to have to lead the initiative. This intense catapult disruption is a brilliant way to cover all the different silos and to involve every single one of the different businesses. As Glenn himself puts it: their approach is focused on 'built-in', not on 'bolt-on'.

Catapults tend to work really well in large siloed organizations because they have the potential to close unhealthy gaps between certain teams and their endeavours. But they can only work if the innovation team has the right DNA, and if – regardless of their day-to-day work – they are unafraid to adopt radical decisions and are then truly empowered to test and implement the radical Day After Tomorrow experiments they came up with. If these conditions are met, this type of method can truly work wonders.

PATTERN #4:
Customer co-creation

One of the most efficient ways to keep in touch with increasingly complex markets and look ahead at a company's Day After Tomorrow is to use co-creation with customers. Ideas coming from outside the organization tend to meet with less resistance than when they are originated by employees with similar ideas. It's a strange form of bias, but it is the reason that valuable suggestions are too often ignored.

One of the best examples in co-creation comes from the international payment technology company, MasterCard, and its success-

Co-creation stimulates us to focus on emerging business – on Day After Tomorrow thinking – instead of obsessing about the status quo and company politics.

ful innovation labs, which are run by Garry Lyons. The concept starts with MasterCard working with their customers or partners to identify a well-defined problem. MasterCard then brings a multidisciplinary team of designers, developers and product experts from their labs – augmented by subject-matter experts from the relevant parts of MasterCard – to come up with a radical idea to solve the challenge in just one week. That's right: one week. At the end of the week they have a working prototype, a video advertorial of the solution and a full-blown go-to-market plan.

Many of the MasterCard customers that are involved in the labs projects are obviously banks. But one of my favourite examples is the collaboration with Maytag. In the US, Maytag is the largest supplier of washing machines that are used in laundromats. The problem is that all these washing machines and dryers in laundromats typically operate on coins, which is a hopelessly outdated approach in a dematerializing world.

Watching clothes spin

Maytag came into MasterCard labs and in just one week they built a prototype of an app called Clothespin. The app allows customers to use the laundromat 'coin-free', paying directly with their mobile phone. If they want, they can enjoy a drink at the coffee bar next door while their laundry is being processed, because they are notified when the wash is done. I absolutely love the feature that for 50 cents extra, you can follow a webcam that continuously shows your spinning clothes, so that you are sure no one is stealing your socks.

The most impressive part of MasterCard labs is not just that they open a continual dialogue with their customers. It's also the speed at which the projects evolve. In just one week the project owners are able to evolve from idea to prototype, which can then be re-evaluated or actually scaled to a real-life product or service. There is no time for the projects to grow 'stale'. The innovation teams are empowered. Management is on board. And MasterCard's culture has a big part to play in that.

But co-creation is not just about keeping a close eye on a fast-evolving market. One of its lesser known characteristics in purely neuroscientific terms, as explained by Judith Glaser in *The Huffington Post*, is that listening to 'outsiders' – customers – without judgement and with a fresh perspective triggers our prefrontal cortex or executive brain to access higher-level

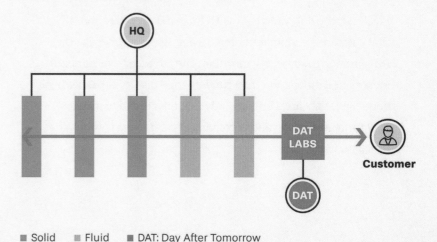

CUSTOMER CO-CREATION DAT LABS

■ Solid   ■ Fluid   ■ DAT: Day After Tomorrow

capacities. This enables us to access new ways of thinking and to handle gaps between reality and aspirations. Without this part of the brain activated, Glaser warns that we tend to fall back into positional thinking and fight for our vested interests.

In other words, co-creation stimulates us to focus on emerging business – on Day After Tomorrow thinking – instead of obsessing about the status quo and company politics. Glaser continues by saying that as the co-creators develop a bonding experience (oxytocin rush), they start to open up new conversations about 'what ifs'. They imagine new possible collaborations, even fostering higher risk-taking and openness. Co-creation opens the 'infinite space' where our minds need to be free to connect with others in new ways. It is not just about two different parties sharing ideas with each other that they would never have thought of on their own. It is just as much about the individual parties being more open, alert and innovative themselves, because of the impact co-creation has on their brain.

I feel that the only drawback with this kind of co-creation lab is that they are sometimes not radical enough to survive The Day After Tomorrow of an organization. They tend to be more about incremental innovation than fundamental disruption. But when done right, they are a brilliant way to innovate and to instill a new form of thinking and perceiving at a company, through the lens of your customer.

PATTERN #5:
The portfolio organization

In my previous book, *The Network Always Wins*, I launched the concept of 'corporate thermodynamics', where some companies have the possibility to combine superfluid, fluid and solid parts of the organization in pursuit of that fabled 'triple point' where all of these different states can coincide at the same time. One of the largest experiments in such a portfolio innovation strategy is how Google re-organized its entire corporate structure under the umbrella company Alphabet Inc., while keeping the engine revving.

The move from Google to Alphabet is anything but a simple cosmetic name change. It's a very clever portfolio exercise for The Day After Tomorrow, creating a new holding company that is composed of independent operating units, each with a separate and strong management. There has been a lot of speculation about Google's motives for this extreme move. Some say the new organizational structure was created to keep nurturing and attracting the best talent on the market. Others say that it had to do with providing clarity to investors. But I believe that the main reason is that even Google – by many perceived as the epitome of organizational agility – had to come to terms with the fact that it was not immune to the impact of its rapid growth. Or as Larry

Page wrote in a memo explaining the move: "As you 'age' – even when you're still a teenager like Google – you have to work hard to stay innovative."

Google realized that it had become too big to stay as fast, open and pioneering as it had been. Like with any other large company, some parts had logically become solid. So, it duly parked its older root businesses – search, advertising, Google Maps, YouTube, Chrome and Android – under Google Inc. These are all about optimizing operations, implementing lean strategies, consolidating structures or streamlining processes. About efficiency and revenue. Its advertising business, for instance, amounted to about 67 billion dollars in 2015. This solidity is obviously needed to generate enough cash to invest in radical Day After Tomorrow

experiments. But other parts of the organization have to remain fluid and 'untouched' by the solid parts, if a company is not to become rigid and die.

The radically innovative and superfluid ventures are separated from Google Inc. and fall under the larger Alphabet umbrella: like X (the research and development facility) and DeepMind (the AI division). The X lab is, for instance, equipped to run radical tests and experiment on crazy ideas, and attracts brilliant researchers and entrepreneurs. When ideas are starting to scale, they 'graduate' from the X lab, and can be spun out. The same goes for the fluid parts, like Verily or Google Ventures, which look at the next new technologies on the horizon. Each part is managed quite similarly to how a venture capitalist would cope with a portfolio of investments.

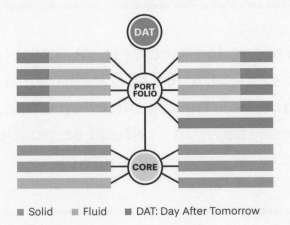

DAY AFTER TOMORROW **PORTFOLIO** ORGANIZATION

■ Solid ■ Fluid ■ DAT: Day After Tomorrow

The move from Google to Alphabet is a very clever portfolio exercise for The Day After Tomorrow: creating a new holding company that is composed of independent operating units, each with a separate and strong management.

One size fits none

What's fascinating is how Google realized that if it wanted to maintain the huge potential for the future, a 'one-size-fits-all' approach would not do. And that's why Alphabet was created: a portfolio of superfluid, fluid and solid parts of the organization that are kept at a safe distance from one another, because the capabilities, processes and structures needed by the (super)fluid and solid parts are so different that they would antagonize each other if they overlapped and intermixed.

To have this kind of restructuring and separation of the different parts of the organization work successfully, one critical component is essential: culture. Everybody at Google and now Alphabet clearly feels the same engagement and purpose. They feel that they are part of the one company and share the same culture. These very powerful shared values are what allows far-reaching autonomy for the divisions without losing the interaction between the parts that are necessary for survival. Alphabet has successfully created this precarious balance between belonging and feeling that you are part of something but, at the same time, admitting that there are clear differences between the superfluid, fluid and solid parts of the organization.

Alphabet

Calico
Fights age-related disease

Google X
Working on big breakthroughs

Fiber
Providing super-fast Internet

Google Ventures
Funding for "bold new companies"

Google Capital
Invests in long-term tech trends

Nest
"Smart home" products

Google
Android · Search · YouTube · Apps · Maps · Ads

To have this kind of restructuring and separation of the different parts of the organization work successfully, one critical component is essential: culture.

PATTERN #6:
The accelerator

Many companies that are trying to tap into the fountain of eternal youth are setting up corporate 'accelerators'. In these accelerators, they are encouraging young (digital) start-ups to speed up their development by offering them mentoring, funding and access to corporate resources. The philosophy is that these young start-ups could be instigators for radical change in the mother company. The enthusiasm of these 'young guns' could inspire a cultural change in the mothership, and perhaps one of them could be the pot of gold to lead them to The Day After Tomorrow.

I love the example of Bayer, which is one of the biggest pharma giants in the world: with more than 115,000 employees, and more than 46 billion euros in revenue in 2016 (before they acquired Monsanto). Bayer is also old. They were founded in 1863, and were one of the very first pharmaceutical giants. Bayer was the one to develop and trademark Aspirin. (Even today more than 40 thousand tons of Aspirin are produced each year.)

Though Bayer is big and old, it keeps innovation at the core. The world of chemicals and pharmaceuticals is a world where you have to be able to look at The Day After Tomorrow. The patent on a compound, a molecule, is usually twenty years. So when a company like Bayer decides to try and build the new Aspirin, they are engaging billions of dollars on a 20-year journey in order to reap the rewards at the end.

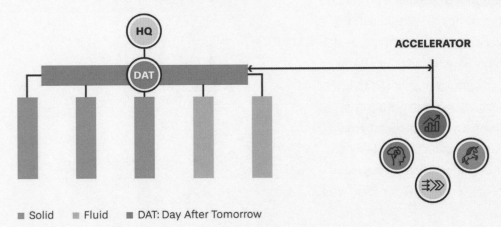

STARTUP ECOSYSTEM **THE ACCELERATOR**

■ Solid ■ Fluid ■ DAT: Day After Tomorrow

Jesus is a (Cuban scientist) DJ

But even an innovative company like Bayer realizes that they need to look outside if they want to keep their edge. They realize that there could be start-ups out there that are dreaming up things that the scientists in the Bayer environment could never cook up. Especially in the world of digital, which is likely to have a huge impact in healthcare but is not the traditional habitat of Bayer folk.

So they decided to set up a digital accelerator. And they chose the perfect person to run it: the flamboyant Cuban, Jesus del Valle. He was trained as a biological scientist, but kept his lifelong passion for music, and he's a pretty amazing DJ. A Cuban scientist DJ who can throw a mean party is obviously the perfect person to run a corporate accelerator. Needless to say, Bayer is thrilled to have Jesus on their side.

His accelerator is called Grants4Apps: a three-month programme promising to help digital-health start-ups get 'accelerated'. The carefully selected chosen few receive 50,000 euros in cash, and are located for three months on the Bayer campus. But the most important thing they get is not the cash or premises. It's the mentorship. The selected start-ups get access to the top executives at Bayer, who open up their network to 'accelerate' the growth of these fledgling companies. "That is incredibly valuable," says Jesus. The enthusiasm of the top Bayer executives is very high, and they see the start-ups for half an hour every week.

Originally started in Berlin, the concept of Grants4Apps (G4A), has spread around the world, and is now active in Singapore, Moscow, Tokyo, Barcelona and Shanghai. The reason Bayer runs its accelerator is not just to invest in the start-ups, but to learn to understand The Day After Tomorrow and interact with radical new business models.

The accelerator also contributes to the positive image of Bayer as an innovative company, even in the burgeoning digital health space. And, ultimately, it aims to build a more entrepreneurial start-up spirit within the Bayer culture, so they can spread some of that disruptive magic inside the company. Last, but not least, the top executives who mentor these young start-ups are excited and really feel the possibilities, which can trigger a tremendous top-down culture shift in the organization.

PATTERN #7:
The corporate garage

The problem with accelerators is their limited impact, because the time during which they actively engage with the start-ups is very constrained. In the case of Bayer, three months of a start-up's life is often too short to have a lasting impact on the mothership.

In the Silicon Valley start-up myth, the 'real' magic happens in a garage. Apple started life in a garage. Google started in a garage. Hewlett Packard started in the original mother of all garages. Basically, if you're a young entrepreneur and you or your parents don't have a garage, you're screwed. That's why many corporates, too, are building 'corporate garages' where start-ups can be hatched. And these often have more impact, greater influence and a longer effect than the standard 'short-lived' accelerators.

Deutsche Telekom's 'hub:raum' in Berlin is a good example of this kind of approach. It's a huge company, with more than 73 billion euros in revenue in 2016, whose origins lie in the federal German

STARTUP ECOSYSTEM **THE GARAGE**

post office. When it started to evolve into telecoms, the company grew spectacularly both in revenue and geography. Today, it boasts a global business ranging from mobile telephony like T-mobile, and IT integration like T-systems, with about 220,000 employees worldwide.

Leveraging the network

hub:raum was first created in Berlin and today they are also active in Poland and Israel. The aim was to attract start-ups that have the potential to fundamentally transform major markets for Deutsche Telekom. When start-ups join hub:raum, they get the standard offering: financing to help grow the business and prove market traction, a co-working space in the heart of Berlin, and mentoring to help the start-up grow and mature. So far, nothing spectacular, but the beauty is in the last offering: leverage.

The start-ups that join hub:raum are carefully selected to be able to leverage the Deutsche Telekom operating environment. There are specific areas that Deutsche Telekom wants to expand, and in which to branch out, like the Internet of Things. When the selected start-ups begin to develop their product and service offering, they get access to the Deutsche Telekom network.

This is a huge advantage, as the technology start-ups could only have dreamt of using the vast technical platforms, systems and networks of Deutsche Telekom to build their offering, had they been on their own. It gets even better: when the start-up's products are commercially ready to scale, they can rely on the Deutsche Telekom salesforce to help them contact and convince their own customers.

It's a win-win-win. The start-up wins because the technical and commercial benefits are massive. Deutsche Telekom wins because they can showcase innovative products and ideas faster, and remain on the cutting edge of innovation. And the final winner is the customer: they get early access to disruptive services and offerings.

If done right, the hub:raum could work wonders for Deutsche Telekom. It could develop their service offerings, help them keep their innovative edge, entice their customers and receive some great financial returns from their investments in those start-ups that become successful.

Calling intrapreneurs

Deutsche Telekom also extends this 'garage' approach to internal employees in a corporate intrapreneurship programme that is called UQBATE. The company fully understands that it would be a mistake to think that only the outside world is capable of starting a company. You need to nurture that kind of entrepreneurship inside your company as well, with internal talent accelerators. That's because many employees are faced with so much pressure on the 'today' and 'tomorrow' focus, that it's very difficult to have them focus on The Day After Tomorrow. As Seth Godin once put it so well: "So busy doing my job, I can't get any work done." That's why programmes like UQBATE are essential to help corporates like Deutsche Telekom tap the potential of their own existing team.

PATTERN #8:
The network organization

Haier's networked model is one of the most inspiring cases of audacious Day After Tomorrow strategic thinking that I have ever come across. It completely challenges the hierarchical command and control strategic thinking and, instead, radically empowers employees to take risks and seed out the future.

Haier's innovation story proves that the typically 'move fast and break things' Silicon Valley start-up approach can be successfully translated to a large corporate in the completely different Chinese culture, and in one of the most traditional sectors out there.

DAT NETWORK
ORGANIZATION

And it all started with Zhang Ruimin. When he started his career at the Qingdao Refrigerator Plant in 1984, he found a company in ruins. Though it had the reputation of being one of the worst-run factories in the entire Chinese economy, he was determined to completely transform the dying fridge factory into one of the world's biggest white goods companies. Today, Haier has 73,000 employees and generates 30 billion dollars in revenue (2015). It is considered to be one of the most innovative leading quality players in the field of appliances ranging from washing machines, microwave ovens and refrigerators. Ruimin is still the CEO.

The transformation was massive, and should earn Zhang Ruimin a Nobel Prize for corporate turnarounds, if ever there was such a thing. The quality of the products that the then dying company was churning out was so incredibly bad that when Ruimin took over the factory in 1984, he performed a legendary demonstration that made a very strong statement.

A dissatisfied customer had brought a faulty refrigerator back to the factory and showed it to Ruimin. Ruimin and the customer then went through his entire inventory of more than 400 refrigerators on the production line, looking for a replacement. In doing so, he discov-

The beauty of Haier's competitive and networked innovation approach is that only a certain type of 'gutsy' and entrepreneurial employee will be drawn to the company, which will reinforce its innovation culture.

Haier

ered that there was a 20% failure rate in all of the merchandise produced by the factory.

Hammer-time

Furious, Ruimin ordered 76 faulty refrigerators to be lined up on the central hallway of the factory floor. He also issued sledge-hammers to his employees and ordered them to destroy all of the refrigerators. At first, the workers didn't dare touch the machines. The cost of one such refrigerator was almost two years' worth of their wages. But Ruimin told them: "Destroy them! If we put these 76 refrigerators up for sale, we'll be continuing a mistake that has all but bankrupted our company." After he led by example himself, all 76 machines were smashed to pieces. One of the hammers is still on display at company headquarters as a reminder to posterity.

The rest is history. With an almost obsessive focus on quality, Zhang Ruimin was able to completely overhaul the company. It started to produce quality products, grow extremely quickly, and to expand geographically. Soon, Haier was giving companies like Whirlpool and GE a run for their money.

By 2015, Haier was one of the largest companies in the world, and Ruimin was recognized by *The Financial Times* as one of the '50 most respected business leaders in the world'.

But he was still not satisfied. He wanted, yet again, to take it one step further. Over the years, he had studied every management technique and operational improvement approach known to man. But to really take his Haier to The Day After Tomorrow, he wanted to go where no CEO had gone before.

He wanted to engender a culture of entrepreneurship by copying and transferring the rules of the outside market inside his company. The result was a highly competitive, even uncomfortable and chaotic environment, but one that yielded tangible results.

The unsteady crew

One of the first measures Ruimin took was to eliminate middle management and chop his 73,000-employee workforce into hundreds of internal micro-companies with their own profit and loss account. He transformed his company into a fast flowing and competitive network with hardly any hierarchy. Employees were empowered to propose new ideas, which were then put to the vote. The winner would then become the project leader and could 'recruit' employees for his venture (who were free to join or leave at any time). In other words, these micro-companies functioned just like actual start-ups.

Zhang Ruimin also introduced 'catfish' to keep everybody on their toes: shadow managers who follow the micro-entrepreneurs and ruthlessly report on missed targets and lost opportunities. These are anything but traditional command and control managers. Haier's system is a lot cleverer than this: the catfish is the person who had a rival idea that came second in the voting, behind the intrapreneur he's supposed to help and carefully watch.

The 'catfish management' metaphor comes from the fishing industry. Fresh sardine is delicious and succulent. But it loses its taste if you transport it in a tank. Unless you put its natural enemy, the catfish, in the tank as well, so that the latter can keep the sardine sharp, alert and ultimately very tasty. Zhang Ruimin cleverly used this 'catfish management' technique to counterbalance the natural chaos created by his micro-enterprise network philosophy.

One of my favourite parts of the Haier approach is its 'zero distance to customers' rule. Everything begins and ends with the end-user. They are the 'bosses' of their micro-entrepreneurs. In fact, Haier employees do not receive a fixed salary: it's the customers who 'decide' upon their remuneration. Again, this works just like in a real market, where entrepreneurs are completely at the mercy of the customer for their income.

When asked how he managed to strike the right balance between the chaotic entrepreneurial energy within his company and the need for corporate control at the top, Zhang's answer was simply: "We don't need to balance! An unsteady and dynamic environment is the best way to keep everyone flexible."

Let me be clear. I'm not saying that this highly competitive approach will work for every company. But I do believe that radical innovation needs an environment that's a little bit on the edge and even seems a little dangerous. It needs a little pressure. The beauty of Haier's competitive and networked innovation approach is that only a certain type of 'gutsy' and entrepreneurial employee will be drawn to the company, which will reinforce its innovation culture. It's a perfect circle.

But perhaps the best result of the Haier culture is how its employees get used to continual change, which reduces the usual fear that is associated with change in most companies. If companies want to stay alive and even thrive in an accelerating market, they have to embrace continuous evolution and innovation, and one of the biggest obstacles to that is 'fear of change'. But Haier's culture is organized in such a manner that people always expect change. And that's a big enabler for Day After Tomorrow thinking.

PATTERN #9:
Integral disruption

From time to time, I have the extreme privilege to observe a company that has 100% pure and undiluted Day After Tomorrow DNA. SpaceX is a perfect example of such an enterprise.

Unless you have been living under a (Martian) rock for the past few years, you'll know a thing or two about Elon Musk. As a young man, he amassed his fortune by successfully selling PayPal to eBay for 1.5 billion dollars. But instead of retiring to the Bahamas, he wanted to reach higher. Much higher. With 100 million dollars of his early fortune, Musk founded Space Exploration Technologies, or SpaceX, in May 2002.

He did not set out to make rockets at first. He 'just' wanted to land a miniature experimental greenhouse on Mars, a project he called Mars Oasis. This obviously entailed a need for rockets to send materials and supplies into space. He contacted the European Space Agency, which turned him down. Then he flew to Russia to meet with companies such as the International Space Company Kosmotras, which offered him one rocket for 8 million dollars. Musk was so appalled at the price that he stormed out of the meeting room.

On the flight back from Moscow, Musk decided to start a new company that would build him the rockets he needed. He came up with a revolutionary plan to completely change the cost equation of rockets. Instead of burning up the rocket in the atmosphere – which is how it had been done up till then – he wanted them to land vertically so he could recover them. That approach would cut the launch price by a factor of ten and allow Musk to enjoy a 70% gross margin.

The progress of the company was phenomenal. They launched their first rocket, the Falcon 1, in 2008. Only four years later they were the first commercial company to send a spacecraft into space that successfully docked with the International Space Station (ISS). This got the company the lucrative NASA contract to fly supplies to the ISS, which had been done by very expensive Russian carriers since NASA had abandoned its own Space Shuttle project.

Occupy Mars

When you walk around SpaceX, and talk about the NASA contract, you will hear: "Ah, that's just to pay the bills. What we really want to do is colonize Mars." The first time I heard that I thought they were joking. But then you look around and everything in the company just shouts out this massive ambition. The coffee mugs in the cafeteria carry the slogan 'Occupy Mars', the workers in the factory wear T-shirts with 'Occupy Mars' printed on them, the doormat on which you wipe your feet reads 'Occupy Mars'.

Musk revealed his plans to start flying missions to Mars in 2016. It seemed strange, weird and just plain unrealistic. It still does. But then again, his idea of landing rockets vertically to recover the cost of the spaceships seemed strange, weird and unrealistic in 2002. Today, SpaceX has done what no other organization in the space industry has done before: launch a rocket and let it land again. The result is that he can launch rockets 90% cheaper than anyone else before him. Yes, there have been (major) failures, among which was the explosion of the Falcon 9 rocket during a propellant fill-operation. Yes, he was almost bankrupt a few times. Yes, Musk has been ridiculed a lot for his extreme ideas. But he carried on. He believed. And, in the end, he succeeded.

If any company can make it to Mars, it will probably be SpaceX. Having such a burning, wildly ambitious dream as a company mission is the hallmark of truly disruptive, 100% pure Day After Tomorrow companies.

Pure Day After Tomorrow companies are rare, but they exist. Elon Musk has created an environment where his burning ambitions are being realized. He once said in an interview: "I want to die on Mars." When we visited SpaceX, his collaborators told us that the full quote sounded a bit different: "I want to die on Mars, but not on impact." It's people like that – with ambitions so big that they'll sound crazy to most of us – who will eventually end up changing the world. They are the ones who will solve the huge problems humanity is struggling with. Wouldn't you like people to say that about you?

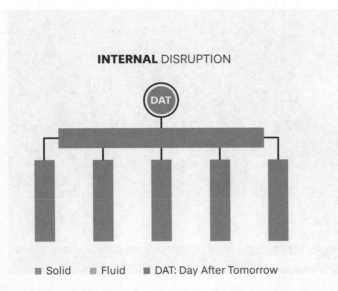

INTERNAL DISRUPTION

DAT

■ Solid   ■ Fluid   ■ DAT: Day After Tomorrow

PATTERN #10:
The pollutants strategy

The ever-smiling design thinker and Chief Pollutant at Autodesk, Mickey McManus, is one of the smartest people I know. I love how he keeps pushing Autodesk towards The Day After Tomorrow with the wonderfully extreme Pier 9 research lab. When people hear 'Autodesk', they tend to think of the number one software product for architects: AutoCAD. It's true, the rise of the company Autodesk had a lot to do with the stellar growth of this particular software. More than 90% of all buildings in the world are designed with it. And more than 90% of all automobiles are designed with it as well. It's the de facto tool for designing products.

But a couple of years ago, the company felt that it had achieved pretty much everything it set out to be. Monopoly tends to breed complacency and Autodesk realized it was perhaps getting a little stale. The engine was revving, but not much truly disruptive innovation was in the pipeline. The company was desperate for a radically new approach to re-invent itself.

McManus's challenge was not to make AutoCAD just a little bit better. Or to make AutoDesk, the parent company, a little more

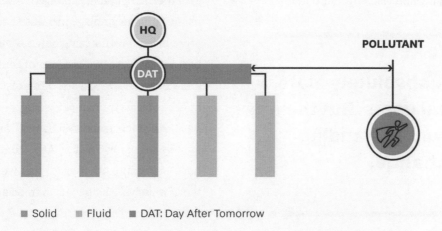

STARTUP ECOSYSTEM **THE ACCELERATOR**

HQ

DAT

POLLUTANT

■ Solid   ■ Fluid   ■ DAT: Day After Tomorrow

efficient. Or a little faster. Nope. The challenge laid out for McManus was to help this company rekindle the innovative power they had unleashed back in 1982, when their original approach disrupted the way we think about drawing and designing. He saw that he would not be able to do this if he were to just extrapolate the past. In The Day After Tomorrow philosophy, 'tomorrow' is often the 10% better version of 'today', but if he wanted to shape The Day After Tomorrow – the 10x disruptions – McManus knew he had to follow the outliers, or the 'pollutants' as he calls them: those users who are trying to do things radically different. The ones who are trying to accomplish 'crazy' things that have never been done before. These 'pollutants' will look absolutely 'nuts' to 99.99% of normal users. But they are essential to understanding radical change.

James Cameron is one of the most influential filmmakers of our day and age. Movies like *The Terminator*, *Titanic* and *Avatar* have changed the way films are made, as well as altering the entire industry. Not just in their storytelling and visualization, but also

in their use of technology. Few know that Cameron is also one of the 'pollutants' of AutoDesk: a radical crazy outlier who has helped AutoDesk to become smarter, better and more disruptive.

One of his biggest and most extreme accomplishments was the 2009 movie *Avatar*. Cameron had been dreaming about making it for a very long time – since 1994, in fact – but the virtual technology he needed to create an entirely new world from scratch was far out of reach for a very long time.

From start to finish, software from Autodesk played a pivotal role in helping Cameron pioneer new methods of virtual moviemaking for *Avatar*. A 'SWAT-team' of Autodesk software engineers built completely new systems just for Cameron and his crew, because they knew that he was the outlier who would show them The Day After Tomorrow for their company and thus transform their industry.

Together, they literally changed the way movies are made by using digital technology in a way that was impossible just a few years before. *Avatar* came out in 2009 and, when it did, finally beat *Titanic* (also by Cameron, of course) as the highest-ever grossing movie, with a box office of 2.8 billion dollars.

As Mickey McManus says: "James Cameron helped us shine a light in an area of The Day After Tomorrow that we wouldn't have looked into otherwise. What we learn from these encounters is massive. It's up to us to translate what these pollutants want into our Day After Tomorrow."

Pollutants will look absolutely 'nuts' to 99.99% of normal users. But they are essential to understanding radical change.

The Day After Tomorrow canvas

So that's it? That's the whole list? A meagre ten approaches?

Hell, no! There are many more ways companies can accelerate and boost their innovation ventures in order to thrive in their Day After Tomorrow. The success of each approach will always depend upon its match with the size, culture, structure and type of customers of the organization.

Some will seclude their innovation teams to protect them from corporate suffocation. Others use short but highly inclusive sprints to make sure that the entire organization is involved. Some will co-create with customers, some will seek pollutants, and some will submerge the entire organization into the Kool-Aid of The Day After Tomorrow.

But there are as many ways to find The Day After Tomorrow as there are companies, employees and customers. I'm truly sorry to disappoint you if you were looking for a ready-to-follow recipe. Just as life is not simply the sum of all the atoms in our body but an emergent property, so radical innovation is an emergent quality of all the ingredients in your company. So, no. No sure-fire recipe. But there are ingredients that can stimulate this emergence, provided you respect the DNA of your company and dare to experiment with things that may even seem 'unnatural' to your industry.

I've tried to paint a canvas of how different initiatives could play out in becoming Today, Tomorrow or Day After Tomorrow-driven (on the horizontal axis). The more to the left, the more they will lean towards 'solid' approaches; the more to the right, the more 'fluid' they will prove to be.

The vertical axis separates 'internal' initiatives within the company and 'external' initiatives outside of the organization. In between, you'll find the concept of an 'ecosystem' of innovation.

> **The success of each approach will always depend upon its match with the size, culture, structure and type of customers of the organization.**

Today

When companies innovate with a Today lens, internally they will tend to focus on a 'research & development' activity. They might also reach out to the community around them by, for example, outsourcing activities or sourcing innovations from the community. On the outside, they will likely have an investment arm that, for example, will provide capital for private equity transactions.

Tomorrow

When we start to move up to the Tomorrow lens, in a more fluid set-up, companies will set up intrapreneurial activities and platforms to stimulate internal ventures. Like the UQBATE example of Deutsche Telekom. Many of the co-creation labs, like the MasterCard labs case, are good examples of fluid companies trying to reach out – in this case to customers – to invent the future. As we discussed earlier, many of these initiatives might not be utterly disruptive. They will rather tend to be incremental fluid innovation. And, on the outside, they could set up accelerators and incubators, like the Bayer Grants4Apps or the Deutsche Telekom hub:raum.

Day After Tomorrow

When we move to The Day After Tomorrow lens, we see the truly disruptive labs inside companies. Setups like Google X, or JLabs in Johnson & Johnson. These are the places where the future is being made today. They tend to reside inside the bosom of the mothership, but remain far removed from corporate politics and guidelines.

Other companies are trying to invent the same Day After Tomorrow philosophy by building completely new ecosystems. General Electric, for instance, is reinventing itself for the age of the Internet of Things. It believes that the machines they produce today, from gas turbines to jet engines, will wake up, become smart and start to communicate. So they came up with Predix, the software

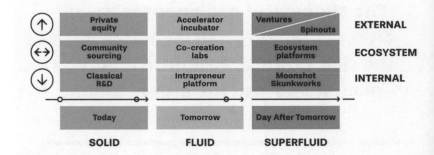

platform for building and managing industrial IoT apps, for both GE and non-GE assets. In doing so, they are creating an ecosystem where others can build new business models on information for the age of trillions.

And finally, there are the companies that are radically trying to invent The Day After Tomorrow on the outside. Brilliant examples are investment vehicles like the Google Ventures and CLAAS, which has spun out its farming concept into 365FarmNet.

I believe that you shouldn't just choose one spot on this Day After Tomorrow canvas in which to be active. Many large companies will have multiple initiatives spread over this canvas in order to maximize their chances for The Day After Tomorrow. I'd advise you not to put all your talent and money in just one Day After Tomorrow moonshot, because this kind of radical far-ahead thinking is always an experiment and never a sure thing.

I hope these examples and this canvas will give you inspiration to start acting on your Day After Tomorrow. To help you gear up your company and engender your culture for radical innovation.

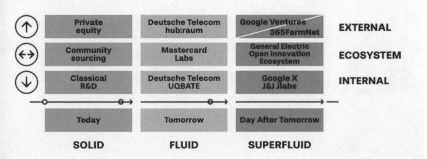

CHAPTER 10

ETHICS IN THE DAY AFTER TOMORROW

Society in The Day After Tomorrow?

This final chapter is not directly concerned with customer relations in The Day After Tomorrow. It is more about the broader social implications of Day After Tomorrow developments. It is an appeal to business organizations and government authorities to open a debate about the societal impact of powerful new technologies on the way we live. If we can proactively make the right ethical choices, AI can offer fantastic added value for individuals, the business world and society as a whole. But if we continue to evolve at lightning speed without conducting this debate, it is much less clear where the future might lead us.

As I mentioned before, I am a born optimist. I am enthusiastic about the prospects for the decades ahead. At the same time, we need to recognize that the great potential of artificial intelligence also brings with it potential dangers. Having said that, I am optimistic about this as well. I am convinced that customers in The Day After Tomorrow will expect – will insist – that companies make choices that are good for both consumers *and* society. The questions I am most frequently asked after my lectures are not about customer relations, but about the wider social context. It is something that worries many people – and this is not necessarily a bad thing.

A world of limitless ambition

If you are one of today's billionaires, how can you make a difference? What are you going to tell the other billionaires when you bump into them in Monaco or Dubai? That your fortune has grown from 44 to 50 billion? That won't cut much ice. That you are planning to conquer death or give away 99% of your fortune to good causes? Yes, that might make a bit of an impression, even in billionaire circles. At the moment, there seems to be almost like a kind of competition between the world mega-rich to set the most far-reaching positive ambitions.

Google do indeed effectively want to solve the 'problem' of death. Mark Zuckerberg does indeed intend to give 99% of his Facebook shares to projects aimed at improving the world. Bill Gates has been setting a good example for decades with his Bill and Melinda Gates Foundation. Salesforce is building children's hospitals everywhere. Microsoft wants to eradicate cancer by 2026. But the biggest show-off of all is Elon Musk, who not only wants to solve the world energy problem, but at the same time save mankind from destruction by AI, or at the very least fly the survivors off to Mars.

Does this sound cynical? It's meant to: because that's the way many people react. If Mark Zuckerberg wants to put his Facebook shares into a foundation, then it must be for fiscal reasons, mustn't it? Perhaps, perhaps not. But whatever the truth, the fantastic ambitions of the world's wealthiest people are something that fill me with enthusiasm. If they want to use their fortunes to make the world a better place, surely that can only be a good thing? If Mark Zuckerberg wishes to make best use of the fiscal system to launch world-improving projects, then I would much rather he did that than use his riches to further feather his own nest.

Ambitions create enthusiasm. People want to work for Elon Musk because it gives them the feeling that they can change the world. Open AI pays its specialists much less than Google or Facebook do, but they have still managed to attract the cream of the world's top AI talent. Why? Because of Open AI's wider ambition and vision.

What are you going to tell the other billionaires when you bump into them in Monaco or Dubai? That your fortune has grown from 44 to 50 billion? That won't cut much ice.

The greatest comeback ever!

Showing ambition, and having the willingness to declare it, is an important part of making people enthusiastic for The Day After Tomorrow. Sometimes people are reluctant to demonstrate ambition, for fear of being branded as arrogant or even worse. But there is nothing wrong with being ambitious and from time to time ambitions need to be expressed, even if they sound hopelessly unrealistic.

On 14 February 2017, Barcelona lost 4-0 away to Paris Saint Germain in the quarter final of the Champions League football competition. Barcelona were outplayed from start to finish and nobody gave them a chance for the second leg in Camp Nou. Nobody, that is, apart from the players and staff of F.C. Barcelona. After the debacle in Paris everyone connected with the club spoke with a single voice: "We're going to put this right in the home game." In the post-match press conference, the Barcelona coach, Luis Enrique, was equally adamant: "If a team can score four goals against us, we can score six against them.[126] I warn our fans: stay to the end of the game, otherwise you will miss the greatest comeback in history!" During the return game, these unlikely ambitions became a reality. Barcelona won 6-1 and qualified for the semi-finals. The determination and the will to express this ambition had much to do with the result. If you believe in something hard enough, anything is possible.

Not just ambitious billionaires

The billionaires and the digital giants are not the only ones with ambitious ideas. One of the most interesting ones comes from Volvo. Volvo wants there to be no more fatalities from accidents involving Volvo cars after 2020. This perfectly matches the Volvo DNA, which has been focused on safety for decades. Will they achieve their ambition? Perhaps not by 2020. But maybe – probably – by 2030. In the meantime, the expressed ambition generates pride, purpose and motivation among Volvo's many thousands of employees.

There are also laudable and impressive ambitions in the field of customer relations. The CEO of the Dutch insurer Centraal Beheer expressed his desire to achieve a Net Promoter Score of 50 for the company. No-one believed him, not even his own staff. An insurer with an NPS of 50? Never! Most insurers have a negative NPS: more detractors than promoters. But the CEO persisted in his dream and continued to persuade people that it was possible. And he was right, at least in part. Within a year, Centraal Beheer had indeed achieved an NPS of 50 for some aspects of its service. Not all, admittedly, but general customer satisfaction with the company had never been higher.

Companies with bold ambitions are attractive for customers, for employees, for shareholders and for the press.

Homo Deus

Ambition is fine, but there is a shadow side. You can't put ambition before everything. It has to keep you moving in a positive direction. In our present context, most ambitions rely on technology to make them possible. However, the rapid evolution of technology has the potential to fundamentally change society as we know it. The book *Homo Deus*[127] by Yuval Noah Harari is a must-read for everyone. *Homo Deus* offers insights into the future of the world based on our past history. In the past, technological revolutions resulted in advancement for society as a whole. Over the centuries, technology has improved both our quality of life and life expectancy. It makes it possible for us to live in relative comfort and safety. As a result, more people now die from eating too much than from not having enough to eat. Notwithstanding all the doom scenarios, for the majority of us the world is generally a nice place. The logical conclusion of this thinking is that because the technology of the past made the world better, the technology of the future will do the same: the positive ambitions of the tech-giants and the billionaires will have a positive effect.

According to Harari, this is a flawed conclusion. In the past, it was also in the interests of the people at the top of the social hierarchy that everyone should enjoy the benefits of technological advancement. The muscle power of the masses was needed for both military and production purposes; to fight wars, tend fields and man factories. But what if 21st century technology and automation can do away with the need for the 'labouring' masses? What if wars can be fought and production maintained by smart computers operating at a distance? Once we reach the tipping point when machines know more and can do more than the average person, at that point there is no longer any reason for the government and the social elite to make new technology and its benefits available to everyone. Social empathy will be swept aside by the powerful forces of greed and automation.

Once automation is operating at optimal capacity, a group of people will be created who no longer have any value to society: a useless class. *Homo Deus* does not make light reading. It describes a vision of the future that no-one wants, but even so, some of the grimmer scenarios still have an unmistakable tinge of realism about them. Imagine that a form of technology is developed that can increase human intelligence. It is not inconceivable that a

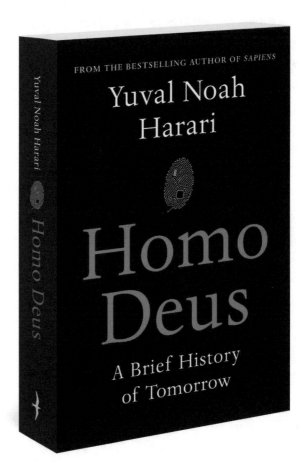

select elite will want to keep this to themselves. The masses will be kept in the dark, while the elite use the technology to become a 'superior' intelligent class. History offers us plenty of chilling examples of what can happen when one groups feels superior to another. But Harari goes a step further. He points out that humans as a species have elevated themselves to a position of superiority over all other 'inferior' species on the planet. As a result, they use these other species for their own purposes. They breed them, they deprive them of their freedom and natural behaviour, they use them for labour, they kill them and eat them. Who is to say that a new super-breed of 'superior' humans would not treat the 'inferior' useless class in much the same way?

Fortunately, we have not yet arrived at the future predicted by *Homo Deus*. We are still in a position to make choices about the way the world develops. Initiatives like Open AI still make technological advances freely available to all. This massive availability of technology is necessary not only to allow everyone to benefit from its gains, but also maintain and strengthen the societal empathy that can prevent *Homo Deus* from ever becoming a reality.

A world full of technological filters

In recent history, there have already been a number of serious problems caused by smart technology. Think, for example, of the influence of the Facebook filter on the last presidential election in the United States. The Facebook algorithm knows what you like to see and ensures that this is exactly the kind of information you get. Our information filter is no longer our own brain, but the computer systems of the major technology companies. Google and Amazon will soon decide which products are 'suitable' for us. Facebook will decide which information is relevant. We are increasingly finding ourselves in a world full of filters, supported by algorithms.

In the past, I used to be naive. When people asked me what I thought about the Facebook filter, I answered: "Of course, we're all subject to the whims of the Facebook filter, but there's always Google. If you need to know something really important, you can always look it up on Google. That way, consumers can get around the Facebook filter." My eyes were opened in June 2016, just a few days after the Brexit referendum. The day after the British had voted to leave the EU, Google published an interesting report. It revealed that the most frequent search request *after* the referendum result was known was "What is the EU?" In the days before the referendum, almost no-one had made this kind of search.[128] Once the damage was done, people wanted to know exactly what they had voted for.

Technology filters have a huge impact on the thoughts and opinions of the population. It sometimes seems as though our brains are mass programmed by algorithms. As a marketeer, this is an opportunity too good to miss. What better way to influence people to buy your products!? But this is not a healthy evolution for society.

Technology filters have a huge impact on the thoughts and opinions of the population. It sometimes seems as though our brains are mass programmed by algorithms. As a marketeer, this is an opportunity too good to miss.

Fake news? You ain't seen nothing yet!

Facebook did more than just apply its information filter to news selection during the US presidential election. It was also a very useful channel for spreading fake news. During the months before voting day, there were more fake news posts on the social media site than genuine ones. Smart propaganda machines made grateful use of the Facebook algorithms to spread what were in effect lies to influence public opinion.

If you think that this is bad enough, brace yourselves: the worst is yet to come. At the moment, fake news only comes in written form. In The Day After Tomorrow, there will also be fake news in the form of video and sound clips. By the time of the next US election, it will be almost impossible to distinguish real news reports from false ones, no matter what form they come in: written, spoken or filmed! The Canadian start-up Lyrebird can already imitate any voice digitally. If you give the Lyrebird algorithm 60 seconds of spoken text by anyone in the world, its software can make that person say anything. Their website has a demo that imitates the voices of Barack Obama, Donald Trump and Hillary Clinton perfectly. These politicians helped in no way with the demo, but their voices have been copied so well that you can't tell the real from the fake.

Professor Pieter Abbeel predicts that the next step in fake news will be false video clips. In the near future, computers will be able to simulate 3D images. This will make it possible for the computer to fabricate videos of things that never happened in reality. In the future, we will potentially see videos that seem to show politicians in a bad light, but it will all have been faked by a computer. This means that there is a need for strict ethical rules in the world of 3D image copying and manipulation. The role of Facebook and YouTube in allowing people to distinguish between reliable and unreliable sound and video clips is crucial if these platforms wish to continue serving as news sources for billions of people.

The current privacy discussion is the wrong discussion

We are at the start of phase three of digital evolution. However, the privacy and ethics discussions of governments usually relate more closely to the second phase of digitalization. For example, the European Commission is not happy about the advertising model of Facebook and Google. In June 2017, the Commission hit Google with a massive 2.4 billion dollar fine, because it felt that the company was giving more advertising opportunities to its own products than the products of others. This is like fining a supermarket because it gives more publicity to its own house brands than to the brands of its competitors. It doesn't make sense.

Similarly, lots of privacy commissions in different countries get very agitated about Facebook's use of cookies. Facebook can follow people's behaviour over different websites. They do this by leaving small data files (cookies) in the browsers of the digital devices used by surfers. Even if you are not a Facebook user, your online behaviour can be monitored by the social network sites. Once you have clicked on a Facebook image on, say, a news site, Facebook can follow your every digital move. In this way, they theoretically have the ability to track every internet user. Of course, you can discuss whether this is a good thing or not. Opinions vary, but in reality Facebook's use of cookies has only limited consequences for society and the daily lives of consumers. In essence, all it does is decide what kind of advertising you get (or don't get) to see, and it allows them to already know who your family and friends are the first time you log on to the site. Some people call this creepy; others call it user-friendly.

The debate should be about impact. The impact on society of the elements for which Facebook and Google are punished is minimal. It almost seems like some kind of sport for the privacy commissions to find new ways to give both companies a rap over the knuckles. However, this type of privacy discussion really belongs to the second digital phase and has too little impact to seriously worry or excite the vast majority of people. It is time to move the privacy discussion into the third phase.

The real discussion should not be about following people online with cookies. It should be about the sensors in our telephones. It should be about the power of artificial intelligence when armed with our data. It should be about the use of the information that virtual assistants collect about us. If you have Google Home or Amazon Echo in your house, you probably talk for 15 minutes a day with a machine. But guess what that machine does for the remaining 23 hours and 45 minutes. Exactly! It listens. And not only does it listen, it also records. Every word you say. One of the very first examples in my book was about the use of Amazon Echo in a murder trial, but at a more prosaic level Amazon says it uses the data collected in this way to learn more (amongst other things) about dialects. But the amount of data held by Amazon (and the other tech-giants) is staggering and once unsupervised computer learning becomes possible, all this mass of data will become proactively useable. The essential debate should therefore be about what we, as a society, want to happen with this huge source of knowledge. Although if you've bought a smart TV from Samsung, it's already too late. Their privacy statement explicitly includes the following disclaimer: "Be careful you do not say things of a personal or sensitive nature around your television, because all this information will be recorded and sold on to third parties." Yet everyone agrees to this privacy statement without batting an eye-lid! At the moment, Samsung doesn't do much with this data, but once personalized advertising on TV becomes feasible, the data will become highly relevant. If you are discussing with your partner in your living room what make of new car to buy, within seconds you will get an advert on TV for the brand you have just mentioned! There will be no such thing as coincidence in the third phase of digitalization.

In short, we would do better to devote our time and energy to discussing those elements that have a greater impact on society. How will we deal with the potential loss of jobs? How are we going to prepare for the greater need for digital skills? How are we going to adjust our education system? What do we want AI to do for us? What is the role of virtual personal assistants in our homes?

Brands with convictions

The most recent results of the Edelman brand study show that 60% of people expect brands to do something positive for society.[129] Yet at the same time, our behaviour as consumers is becoming more and more opportunistic. Just two years after the great emissions scandal, Volkswagen is selling more cars than ever before. In fact, VW is now the largest car manufacturer in the world.[130] It is important for companies to make the right ethical choices. But you must not make these choices just for your customers. You must also do it for yourself, your employees and for society as a whole. It is part of the responsibility you have as a business leader.

Just passively observing the problems of the world is becoming less and less of an option for companies. The Edelman study looked at several brands that have recently participated in the societal debate. The more successful ones not only try to change market opinion, but also seek to actively engage the public in the debate. They start a discussion. They force people to think. They give them a chance to have their say. Of course, it is important that the theme is a relevant one in the context of the company. Brand activism must be credible and convincing: brands need to prove their engagement in the long term.

In the past, brands used to steer clear of political debate. The election of President Trump has changed things. After the United States pulled out of the Paris climate agreement, numerous American companies reaffirmed their own commitment to its terms. When the president announced his ban on certain Muslims from entering the country, several leading companies once again publically criticized the decision. Viewed from a European perspective, such actions often seem like a no-risk strategy, because there is an assumption that almost everyone in the US is opposed to the president's policies. But this is patently not true. Roughly half the American population was in favour of the Muslim ban.[131] Nike was one of the most outspoken business critics of the ban. Nike is also a brand that sees almost everyone as a potential customer. This means that Nike has millions of American customers who voted for Donald Trump during the election.

Taking a political standpoint is never without risk for companies. Nevertheless, Nike felt it could not remain silent, even at the risk of offending the 50% of the population – in other words, the 50% of its target group – that elected the president.

In the years ahead, some brands will change from being mission-driven to activism-driven.[132] Activists seek to achieve through words and deeds objectives they believe are positive for society. Activism is therefore more 'hands-on' and involves more risk than having a mission. Starbucks has promised to give at least 10,000 refugees a job. Airbnb has also found free accommodation for refugees. Lots of people think this is fantastic. Lots of others think the refugees should stay in their own country and therefore disagree with the choices made by Starbucks and Airbnb. Backing a particular conviction always means that some people will be for you and others against. The alternative is to say nothing, but this simply leads to your brand becoming greyer and greyer.

In the future, you will be expected to make your company's standpoint clear in the public debate in your sector.

Almost every company is linked in one way or another to the social debate. Some are linked through health issues (Coca Cola, McDonald's, hospitals, etc.), others through climate (energy companies, car manufacturers, etc.), yet others through the need for sound finance (banks). The challenge is to be more than just customer-oriented. Making good products for your customers is not enough. In the future, you will be expected to make your company's standpoint clear in the public debate in your sector.

Explicit ethical choices

In a study[133] carried out by the Dutch supermarket chain Albert Heijn, a group of young people and 65-plussers were asked to describe their expectations for the supermarket of the future. As you can imagine, there were many differences between the two groups, but amongst the similarities were terms like 'sustainable', 'aware' and 'healthy living'. Both groups expect Albert Heijn to make the right ethical choices for society.

Tony Fadell, the founder of Nest and one of the creators of the iPod and the iPhone, says that he is kept awake at night by the ethical dilemmas attached to his innovations.[134] "Did we really bring a kind of new nuclear bomb of information into the world, which can blow up people's minds and re-programme them?" This is his fundamental question about his contribution to history. "Addiction has been designed into our devices – and it's harming the newest generation. If you take technology away from today's teenagers, it's like you're tearing a piece of their person away from them. Looking back, the iPhone was perfectly developed for the needs of the individual, not for what's best for the family and society," says Fadell.

In an interview with *Fast Company*,[135] Fadell adds: "Silicon Valley is a group of mainly young male designers who don't have kids. There is too little diversity in the design teams, so that choices are made specifically for that one target group. In this way, greater individualism is forced on the rest of society, with less attention for family and the larger community."

Fadell wants to develop an ethical code of conduct for programmers, similar to the Hippocratic Oath for doctors. Doctors need to publically affirm that they will abide by the rules of their profession. The power of AI, and the explicit ethical choices its use involves, makes such a code necessary in the technological field, according to Tony Fadell.

These ethical choices are real. If a bank is going to use bots to sell investment products, how is that bot going to be programmed? Does the bot do what's best for the bank or what's best for the customer? True, these same questions can also be asked of human investment bankers, but with humans it is possible to say things (or not say things) implicitly in a briefing. As a result, the ethical choices are less pronounced. But a computer needs clear guidance about the things programmed into it. By automating many of the communication aspects of the customer relationship, many ethical choices will need to be made more explicit. The same evolution will also be seen in relation to customer data. As companies gather ever-expanding oceans of data, there is a need for an explicit company vision about what can and cannot be done with that data. This must become one of the central pillars of the ethical debate.

It is not unreasonable for people to expect companies to always behave ethically. But technological evolutions in the years ahead will put this expectation under greater pressure. As a result, it may be a good idea in the third phase of digitalization for companies to make their ethical choices public. Transparency in the market about digital choices can only increase public trust in a company. Communicating these choices to the outside world also increases commitment to their proper implementation.

How far can technology go?

The most important debate is about the role of artificial intelligence in the world of The Day After Tomorrow. That world will be awash with oceans of data. This data will allow computers to make a major impact on many aspects of our lives. Consider, for example, the role of virtual personal assistants. We know that these machines not only carry out tasks on our behalf, but also listen to every word we say. To what extent should these machines be allowed to influence our lives? Imagine that Google Home hears that a man is about to hit his wife. What should Google do with that information? In June 2017, the police received a call from a Google Assistant in similar circumstances. A man had attacked his girlfriend and was waving a gun around, threatening to kill her. The young woman had somehow managed to activate the device, so that it could send out a distress call. The police arrived just in time to save her life. In this instance, it was the woman who took the initiative to activate the virtual personal assistant. But what if that had not been the case? What should we expect of this kind of AI device in the future? Should Google automatically phone the police? Or should it try to talk the man out of doing anything foolish? Just how far can technology go? If artificial intelligence can predict when somebody is going to commit a crime, should that person be punished simply for his/her intention to commit that crime? Are we moving towards the world depicted in the film *Minority Report*, where crime prevention is proactive rather than retrospective?

Another important area of debate is the evolution of health care. It will soon be possible to change human DNA. This potentially opens up remarkable possibilities for eradicating illness and disease. But it also means we can order 'made-to-measure' babies. Do you want a son with brown or blond hair? How smart would you like your daughter to be? If or when this becomes possible, it is open to question whether or not it is societally beneficial. If we fail to conduct this and other similar debates proactively, we will wake up one morning to discover that the future has already arrived – and then it will be too late.

Imagine that the Chinese government manages to develop a strain of smarter and stronger people. The United States will immediately see this as a threat to its military and economic position. In addition to an arms race, we will also find ourselves in a race to develop a new breed of superhumans. Science fiction? Perhaps, but the American Army is already conducting tests to see if brain manipulation will allow their soldiers to learn new skills more quickly. For example, they are using AI to examine the brain-wave data of their best snipers, to provide output that can be used to increase the analytical capabilities of other soldiers. The brain race is already underway, before the societal debate about its ethical acceptability has even started.

In the years to come, technology will be able to do many remarkable things. But not all of these things will be positive for society. We need to start talking about the possible implications. And we need to do it now.

Towards a collaborative model?

So who should initiate this ethical debate? This is a difficult question for governments to answer. It is hard to pin down the development of AI to a specific place. It is a global phenomenon.

Even so, governments must still try to take a guiding role. And the major digital companies of the business world must also play their part. In this respect, there are positive signs. In mid-2016, Facebook, Amazon, Google and IBM set up a combined AI development group,[136] similar to Elon Musk's Open AI project. The aim of both initiatives is to ensure that artificial intelligence continues to move in the right, societally beneficial direction.

But what the ethical debate really needs is a collaborative model. For the time being, too many governments and companies are working against each other, rather than with each other. Governments tend to see themselves in a strict monitoring and regulatory role, so that more often than not they end up picking fights with the technology giants rather than trying to understand the problems – ethical and otherwise – they face. Making the right ethical choice will only be possible if the public and private sectors learn to work hand in hand.

This is the final and most important question for your company: what ethical choices are you going to make? What contribution will your company make to the necessary social debate? What point of view will you take? How can your technology be used to make society and the world a better place? And how can you work together with other stakeholders to maximize the impact of those choices?

FINALLY...

Dream of the future, but use what is available today

Wow! You've made it to the end of my book. Congratulations!

Hopefully, you have obtained some new insights and discovered some new ideas during your reading. Perhaps some aspects of the AI revolution have filled you with enthusiasm, while others have made you feel a bit apprehensive. Thinking about the future always produces this double-sided emotion.

Many of the things discussed in my book are still in their infancy. But if you look carefully at the cleverest technological innovations of today, you can already see the future taking shape. And once you have seen the future, you keep on seeing it. Closing your eyes to it is no longer an option. When we take groups to Silicon Valley, they return as changed people. They look at the world in a different way and feel a responsibility to do something with this new vision. I hope that reading this book has helped to change the way you look at things. And I hope you feel that same sense of responsibility.

I would like to end with one last tip: dream of the future but use what is available today. Whether your company is large or small, there are many applications that will already allow you to start your journey along the four investment axes that lead towards a new era of improved customer relations.

I wish you every success. Please let me know what you think about our story via *Steven@VanBelleghem.biz*. Feedback from readers is crucial!

Many, many thanks for journeying with me on the road to The Day After Tomorrow.

Dream big!

Steven

THANK YOU!

Writing a book never becomes routine. This is now my fourth management book and I found it just as exciting as when I wrote my first, *The Conversation Manager*, back in 2009. Each time you reveal a little piece of your soul. Each time you hope that readers will feel inspired by your new story. The journey involved in writing a book is a long and intense one. It is a journey that I was fortunate to make with many other people alongside me, all of whom deserve a big thank you for their help and guidance.

First of all, thank you to my colleagues and partners at nexxworks and Snackbytes. Thank you for all the energy and inspiration I draw from our collaboration. Thank you in particular to my good friends Peter Hinssen and Sam Berteloot. You are both a fantastic source of new and creative ideas. Peter, thank you also for the great chapter you wrote for my book!

In addition, I would also like to thank my colleagues at the Vlerick Business School. The academic network helps me to further refine my ideas. Thank you especially to Marion Debruyne for her friendship and our wonderful collaboration.

My former colleagues at the wonderful InSites Consulting also continue to help me develop my story. A big thank you to Kristof De Wulf and Tim Duhamel for their support, friendship and years of fruitful collaboration.

I would like to thank my mentor, Professor Dr. Rudy Moenaert (Tias Business School) for the years and years of support. Rudy is the man who taught me how to create better presentations, and to look at the world from a critical perspective. Thank you, Rudy!

Thank you to my publisher LannooCampus for the years of marvellous co-operation.

In preparation for this book, I visited hundreds of companies. I would like to thank each of them for their openness. In addition, I was able to interview a number of people with specific themes in mind, and they too are deserving of my grateful thanks: Davy Kestens (CEO Sparkcentral), Mikhail Naumov (CEO Digital Genius), Pieter Abbeel (Professor at UC Berkeley), Fons Jurgens (CEO Efteling), Tom Debruyne (CEO Sue Amsterdam), Daniel Ropers (former CEO Bol.com), Mickey McManus (forward thinker at Autocad), Joeri Van den Bergh (managing partner at InSites Consulting) and Jonathan Reichental (CIO Palo Alto). Joeri and Jeremiah Owyang were also kind enough to write pieces as guest authors for my books: thanks, lads!

I would also like to thank the group of people who gave open and honest feedback that significantly enhanced the quality of my book. They read the drafts and helped me to dot all the i's and cross all the t's. Thank you to Marc Michils (CEO Kom op tegen Kanker), Peter Hinssen (nexxworks), Sam Berteloot (CEO Snackbytes), Marjolein Mens (Efteling), and my dad, Pol Van Belleghem.

But my biggest thanks go to my family. Evi is my most fervent supporter and tower of strength. She is also my first reader. All my texts must pass her careful scrutiny and her literary skills help to make them more readable. She is also my business partner in our company. Even more importantly, she has been my life partner for the last 16 years, a fantastic mother to our children and my very best friend. A big, big, big thank you, sweetie! And what can I say about the important role of our two fantastic sons, Siebe (8) and Mathis (6)? Siebe already knows that he's going to be an inventor when he grows up and Mathis is crazy about all the latest gadgets. It looks like both of them have got the AI virus! Every day, their energy and love gives me the inspirational drive and determination to keep on moving onwards and upwards. Thanks, little friends!

Last but not least, I would like to thank each and every one of you. Thank you for reading my book. Thank you (perhaps) for following me on Facebook, YouTube, Instagram, Snapchat, Twitter or during one of my many presentations. The energy I get from the public is one of my biggest sources of creativity and motivation. Thank you so very, very much.

Thank you,
Steven

PHOTO CREDITS

p. 12   http://media.corporate-ir.net/media_files/IROL/17/176060/AmazonEcho/062315/AmazonEcho.jpg

p. 24   © ScientiaMobile

p. 25   © Company Filings/Management Commentary/BTIG Estimates

p. 30   © Google DeepMind

p. 32   https://deepmind.com/blog/deepmind-ai-reduces-google-data-centre-cooling-bill-40/#image-437

p. 33   https://qz.com/870708/uber-is-taking-its-self-driving-cars-from-san-francisco-to-arizona-on-self-driving-trucks/

p. 55   © Catwalker/Shutterstock.com

p. 66   © Winni Wintermeyer

p. 76   © Jeremiah Owyang

p. 78   http://www.tecnoandroid.it/wp-content/uploads/2017/02/Entregas-de-UPS-con-drones-Si-es-verdad-722x445.jpeg

p. 82   https://www.zembro.com/wp-content/uploads/2015/09/header4.jpg

p. 85   https://27s2ym2rovnf2lsmdx18fml1-wpengine.netdna-ssl.com/wp-content/uploads/2016/01/Disney-MagicBands-Park-Ticket.jpg

p. 89   https://prowly-uploads.s3.amazonaws.com/uploads/landing_page_image/image/27127/Joeri_van_den_Bergh.jpg

p. 96   © Google Maps

p. 98   https://www.quicktapsurvey.com/blog/wp-content/uploads/2016/04/Mcdonalds-2.jpg

p. 102   © Chonlachai/Shutterstock.com

p. 105   https://upload.wikimedia.org/wikipedia/commons/6/6b/Jeff_Bezos%27_iconic_laugh.jpg

p. 107   © Jaguar PS/Shutterstock.com

p. 112   http://static.digg.com/images/d5a45331fe264371ba860836ce07541d_7d03ceb7564d49f58617949bc903374f_header.jpeg

p. 138   http://images.businessfinancenews.com/bfn/960-alibaba-baba-needs-youku-for-one-more-push-into-online-entertainment.jpg

p. 144   © Markables/hbr.org

p. 168   © BI Intelligence/company statements/TechCrunch/Forbes

p. 170   https://upload.wikimedia.org/wikipedia/commons/0/09/Sundar_Pichai_at_Google_IO_2017_Keynote.jpg

p. 179   https://venturebeat.com/wp-content/uploads/2017/07/img_1409.jpg?fit=1920%2C1080&strip=all

p. 197 https://www.vanityfair.com/nems/2017/03/elon-musk-billion-dollar-crusade-to-stop-ai-space-x, Photos by Anders Lindén/Agent Bauer (Tegmark); by Jeff Chiu/A.P. Images (Page, Wozniak); by Simon Dawson/Bloomberg (Hassabis), Michael Gottschalk/Photothek (Gates), Niklas Halle'n/AFP (Hawking), Saul Loeb/AFP (Thiel), Juan Mabromata/AFP (Russell), David Paul Morris/Bloomberg (Altman), Tom Pilston/The Washington Post (Bostrom), David Ramos (Zuckerberg), Getty Images; by Frederic Neema/Polaris/Newscom (Kurzweil); by Denis Allard/Agence Réa/Redux (LeCun); Ariel Zambelich/ Wired (Ng); © Bobby Yip/Reuters/Zuma Press (Musk).

p. 202 © Fuji SoftInc.

p. 202 https://upload.wikimedia.org/wikipedia/commons/0/03/TPR-ROBINA.jpg

p. 216 © Saflot, Vera Ponnet/nexxworks

p. 217 https://upload.wikimedia.org/wikipedia/commons/thumb/5/52/Parcentrance.jpg/1200px-Parcentrance.jpg

p. 217 https://upload.wikimedia.org/wikipedia/commons/e/e8/PARC-logo-color.png

p. 219 © Saflot, Vera Ponnet/nexxworks

p. 220 https://upload.wikimedia.org/wikipedia/commons/thumb/1/19/Claas_Logo.svg/2000px-Claas_Logo.svg.png

p. 221 © Saflot, Vera Ponnet/nexxworks

p. 223 © Saflot, Vera Ponnet/nexxworks

p. 225 © Saflot, Vera Ponnet/nexxworks

p. 226 https://nl.wikipedia.org/wiki/Alphabet_Inc.#/media/File:Alphabet_Chart-vector.svg

p. 227 © Saflot, Vera Ponnet/nexxworks

p. 229 http://www.tijd.be/dossier/startups/OPROEP-Pitch-je-start-up-via-De-Tijd/9828837

p. 232 https://upload.wikimedia.org/wikipedia/commons/thumb/6/64/Haier_logo.svg/2000px-Haier_logo.svg.png

p. 232 https://upload.wikimedia.org/wikipedia/commons/9/91/Haier_Industrial_Park_Qingdao_Panoramic_View.JPG

p. 236 © Saflot, Vera Ponnet/nexxworks

p. 237 © Saflot, Vera Ponnet/nexxworks

p. 240 © Saflot, Vera Ponnet/nexxworks

p. 241 © Saflot, Vera Ponnet/nexxworks

p. 245 © Maxisport/Shutterstock.com

p. 247 http://beeld.boekboek.nl/WP_Omslagen/BBBB/ddi9789400407237.png

NOTES

1   http://www.bbc.com/news/world-us-canada-39587853

2   https://techcrunch.com/2017/03/07/amazon-echo-murder/

3   https://techcrunch.com/2016/11/22/googles-ai-translation-tool-seems-to-have-invented-its-own-secret-internal-language/

4   https://www.geekwire.com/2017/amazon-passes-10m-alexa-powered-echo-devices-sold-survey-says-with-more-models-on-the-way/

5   2001, The Disney Way, Bill Capodagli.

6   2006, The Ultimate Question, Fred Reichheld.

7   2010, Delivering Happiness, Tony Hsieh.

8   Scientia Mobile 2017

9   https://www.statista.com/statistics/272014/global-social-networks-ranked-by-number-of-users/

10   Gartner, customer experience survey 2017.

11   Accenture, 2016; https://www.accenture.com/us-en/insight-retail-customer-experience.

12   Bain and Company, Harvard Business Review

13   Zenith's "Top Thirty Global Media Owners" report

14   http://www.smartinsights.com/traffic-building-strategy/integrated-marketing-communications/many-connected-devices-use-toDay-chartoftheDay/

15   https://www.statista.com/statistics/471264/iot-number-of-connected-devices-worldwide/

16   http://nordic.businessinsider.com/googles-400-million-acquisition-of-deepmind-is-looking-good-2016-7/

17   https://qz.com/877721/the-ai-master-bested-the-worlds-top-go-players-and-then-revealed-itself-as-googles-alphago-in-disguise/

18   http://www.nytimes.com/1997/07/29/science/to-test-a-powerful-computer-play-an-ancient-game.html?pagewanted=all

19   https://www.wired.com/2017/01/mystery-ai-just-crushed-best-human-players-poker/

20   http://www.popsci.com/ai-pilot-beats-air-combat-expert-in-dogfight

21   http://ftw.usatoday.com/2016/02/eldrick-robot-hole-in-one-scottsdale-save-the-humans

22   https://www.theverge.com/2016/7/21/12246258/google-deepmind-ai-data-center-cooling

23   https://arstechnica.co.uk/information-technology/2017/03/deepmind-national-grid-machine-learning/

24   http://tech.eu/features/15574/latvia-autonomous-car-europe/

25   https://www.theverge.com/2017/5/9/15596366/south-korea-self-driving-car-test-site-worlds-biggest

26   http://www.pewresearch.org/fact-tank/2016/02/29/5-facts-about-online-dating/

27   http://www.wired.co.uk/article/ibm-watson-medical-doctor

28   http://www.nytimes.com/2013/05/14/opinion/my-medical-choice.html

29   http://www.telegraph.co.uk/news/science/science-news/11340166/Facebook-knows-you-better-than-your-members-of-your-own-family.html

30   https://www.cigionline.org/internet-survey

31   https://www.forbes.com/sites/walterloeb/2017/03/20/these-21-retailers-are-closing-3591-stores-who-is-next/#34fccbfa4854

32   https://www.digitalcommerce360.com/2017/01/23/amazons-us-echo-sales-top-8-million/

33   https://www.experian.com/innovation/thought-leadership/amazon-echo-consumer-survey.jsp

34 https://www.forbes.com/sites/jasonbloomberg/2017/06/23/amazons-whole-foods-strategy-its-not-what-you-think/#1e3a5001a822

35 https://www.gartner.com/imagesrv/summits/docs/na/customer-360/C360_2011_brochure_FINAL.pdf

36 http://www.adweek.com/digital/facebook-now-makes-84-of-its-advertising-revenue-from-mobile/

37 Facebook's financial results.

38 http://pwcartificialintelligence.com

39 http://www.mckinsey.com/business-functions/mckinsey-analytics/our-insights/how-artificial-intelligence-can-deliver-real-value-to-companies

40 http://www.mckinsey.com/industries/semiconductors/our-insights/smartening-up-with-artificial-intelligence

41 https://media.ford.com/content/fordmedia/fna/us/en/news/2016/08/16/ford-targets-fully-autonomous-vehicle-for-ride-sharing-in-2021.html

42 https://www.technologyreview.com/s/607841/a-single-autonomous-car-has-a-huge-impact-on-alleviating-traffic/

43 https://ai100.stanford.edu/sites/default/files/ai100report10032016fnl_singles.pdf

44 https://www.wsj.com/articles/how-artificial-intelligence-will-change-everything-1488856320

45 http://www.bbc.com/future/story/20160701-historys-greatest-technopanics

46 https://skift.com/2015/02/04/disneys-mymagic-wristbands-are-magic-money-makers/

47 http://www.orlandosentinel.com/travel/attractions/universal-orlando/os-universal-volcano-bay-queueless-water-park-20160627-story.html

48 https://www.fastcodesign.com/3066933/how-the-minds-behind-disneys-magicband-are-remaking-a-38b-cruise-giant

49 http://www.wiley.com/WileyCDA/WileyTitle/productCd-1118176073.html

50 http://www.cnbc.com/2017/06/20/mcdonalds-hits-all-time-high-as-wall-street-cheers-replacement-of-cashiers-with-kiosks.html?utm_content=buffer95a4b&utm_medium=social&utm_source=facebook.com&utm_campaign=buffer

51 https://www.genome.gov/sequencingcosts/

52 http://www.marketingdive.com/news/study-71-of-consumers-prefer-personalized-ads/418831/

53 *How Brands Grow*, Byron Sharp.

54 L2 Inc., research retail report

55 https://www.reuters.com/article/us-bmw-autonomous-idUSKBN13T0ZH

56 http://fortune.com/2016/06/03/walmart-lyft-uber/

57 https://www.statista.com/statistics/255778/number-of-active-wechat-messenger-accounts/

58 http://www.businessinsider.com/amazons-cloud-business-hits-over-12-billion-in-revenue-2017-2

59 https://www.forbes.com/sites/shephyken/2017/06/17/sixty-four-percent-of-u-s-households-have-amazon-prime/#3453b1264586

60 http://www.telegraph.co.uk/science/2016/09/20/microsoft-will-solve-cancer-within-10-years-by-reprogramming-dis/

61 https://www.technologyreview.com/s/545416/could-ai-solve-the-worlds-biggest-problems/

62 https://www.wired.com/2016/10/president-obama-mit-joi-ito-interview/

63 https://en.wikipedia.org/wiki/Azure_Window

64 *The Day After Tomorrow* by Peter Hinssen

65 https://hbr.org/2016/11/the-best-performing-ceos-in-the-world

66 https://www.euromoney.com/article/b13pw3kq954nl6/world39s-best-bank-transformation-2017-kbc

67 https://www.inc.com/kevin-j-ryan/insurance-startup-lemonade-california-90-percent-of-americans.html

68 http://www.economist.com/news/finance-and-economics/21718502-future-insurance-named-after-soft-drink-new-york-startup-shakes-up

69 http://www.amweb.nl/branche/nieuws/2017/3/knab-wil-ook-verzekeringen-gaan-aanbieden-10192915

70 http://www.mckinsey.com/business-functions/digital-mckinsey/our-insights/the-case-for-digital-reinvention

71 http://www.mckinsey.com/business-functions/digital-mckinsey/our-insights/the-case-for-digital-reinvention

72 http://www.themeparkinsider.com/flume/201707/5631/

73 Addiction by design http://press.princeton.edu/titles/9156.html

74 https://www.wsj.com/articles/alibaba-reaches-deal-to-buy-youku-tudou-1446814345

75 https://developers.facebook.com/case-studies/onefootball/

76 *The industries of the future*, Alec Ross, 2016

77 *Harvard Business Review*, April 2015. 'Why strong customer relations trump powerful brands' by Christof Binder, CEO of Trademark Comparables, and Dominique Hanssens, Professor of Marketing at the UCLA Anderson School of Management

78 https://www.statista.com/statistics/250934/quarterly-number-of-netflix-streaming-subscribers-worldwide/

79 https://thenextweb.com/insider/2016/03/20/data-inspires-creativity/#.tnw_OoQECP8K

80 https://medium.com/netflix-techblog/its-all-a-bout-testing-the-netflix-experimentation-platform-4e1ca458c15

81 https://en.wikipedia.org/wiki/Ant_Financial_Services_Group

82 https://hbr.org/2012/10/data-scientist-the-sexiest-job-of-the-21st-century

83 http://www.businessinsider.com/a-professor-built-an-ai-teaching-assistant-for-his-courses-and-it-could-shape-the-future-of-education-2017-3

84 http://www.who.int/mediacentre/news/releases/2013/health-workforce-shortage/en/

85 http://www.businessinsider.com/98-of-iphone-users-have-tried-siri-but-most-dont-use-it-regularly-2016-6

86 https://www.experian.com/innovation/thought-leadership/amazon-echo-consumer-survey.jsp

87 https://intelligence.businessinsider.com/google-assistant-outperforms-alexa-whatsapp-aims-to-become-one-stop-shop-nigerian-tech-startup-shows-telco-promise-2017-6

88 http://fortune.com/2017/05/16/singapore-car-vending-machine-worlds-tallest/?xid=soc_socialflow_facebook_FORTUNE

89 McKinsey/Finalta benchmarking van 2016

90 https://arstechnica.com/information-technology/2017/04/how-amazon-go-probably-makes-just-walk-out-groceries-a-reality/

91 The explanation of Blockchain is based on: http://www.watisblockchain.nl/wat_is_blockchain.php

92 https://intelligence.businessinsider.com/the-evolution-of-robo-advising-report-how-models-are-adapting-to-suit-the-realities-of-the-automated-advice-market-2017-4

93 https://newsroom.accenture.com/news/majority-of-wealthy-investors-prefer-a-mix-of-human-and-robo-advice-according-to-accenture-research.htm

94 https://intelligence.businessinsider.com/uk-fintechs-defy-brexit-concerns-goldman-bucks-slowdown-in-online-lending-another-blow-for-zenefits-2017-6

95 http://www.investopedia.com/articles/financial-advisor/042516/how-vanguard-dominating-roboadvisor-arena.asp

96 http://www.digi-capital.com/news/2017/01/after-mixed-year-mobile-ar-to-drive-108-billion-vrar-market-by-2021/#.WVqs2GVDDZg

97 L2 Inc. research retail report

98 Raymond James Research

99 *Harvard Business Review*, 'Beating the commodity magnet', June 1994

100 https://www.engadget.com/2017/07/12/ai-lawyer-help-thousand-legal-issues/

101 http://www.hbs.edu/faculty/Publication%20Files/14-055_2ef21e7e-7529-4864-b0f0-c64e4169e17f.pdf

102 *When Digital Becomes Human*, Steven Van Belleghem, 2014

103 https://www.recode.net/2016/10/20/13352900/nbcuniversal-buzzfeed-investment

104 *Harvard Business Review*, 'Viral marketing for the real world', Duncan Watts and Johan Peretti, May 2007

105 http://www.businessinsider.com/heres-how-buzzfeed-works-2010-6

106 http://www.billboard.com/articles/business/7776302/musically-apple-music-partnership

107 *Blue Ocean Strategies*, W. Chan Kim and Renée Mauborgne, 2005.

108 Input via the Kom op Tegen Kanker marketing team and CEO Marc Michils

109 https://www.theguardian.com/science/2016/oct/19/stephen-hawking-ai-best-or-worst-thing-for-humanity-cambridge

110 http://www.dailymail.co.uk/sciencetech/article-3165356/Artificial-Intelligence-dangerous-NUCLEAR-WEAPONS-AI-pioneer-warns-smart-computers-doom-mankind.html

111 https://www.wired.com/2016/04/openai-elon-musk-sam-altman-plan-to-set-artificial-intelligence-free/

112 https://www.wired.com/2017/04/the-myth-of-a-superhuman-ai/

113 http://www.mckinsey.com/global-themes/digital-disruption/harnessing-automation-for-a-future-that-works

114 http://www.oecd-ilibrary.org/social-issues-migration-health/the-risk-of-automation-for-jobs-in-oecd-countries_5jlz9h56dvq7-en?crawler=true

115 http://www.huffingtonpost.com/entry/ai-powered-customer-service-needs-the-human-touch_us_58b88046e4b0ffd61787bd3d

116 *Industries of the Future*, Alec Ross, 2016

117 https://www.linkedin.com/pulse/could-our-future-nurses-caregivers-robots-alec-ross

118 https://america.cgtn.com/2016/07/29/japan-use-robotics-to-help-ease-burden-in-health-care

119 http://www.toyota-global.com/innovation/partner_robot/family_2.html

120 https://ifr.org/ifr-press-releases/news/world-robotics-report-2016

121 https://www.theatlantic.com/technology/archive/2015/05/long-range-iris-scanning-is-here/393065/

122 http://news.nationalgeographic.com/2017/04/worlds-first-cyborg-human-evolution-science/

123 http://www.wired.co.uk/article/elon-musk-neuralink

124 https://www.technologyreview.com/s/604254/with-neuralink-elon-musk-promises-human-to-human-telepathy-dont-believe-it/

125 https://www.theguardian.com/technology/2017/apr/19/facebook-mind-reading-technology-f8

126 http://www.espnfc.com/blog/the-match/60/post/3076900/barcelona-make-the-impossible-possible-in-historic-champions-league-comeback-vs-psg

127 *Homo Deus*, Yuval Noah Harari, 2017

128 http://fortune.com/2016/06/24/brexit-google-trends/

129 http://www.edelman.com/post/brands-take-stand/

130 https://www.ft.com/content/63b368b0-fabf-11e6-9516-2d969e0d3b65?mhq5j=e1

131 http://www.slate.com/blogs/the_slatest/2017/01/31/reuters_ipsos_muslim_ban_poll_finds_support_for_order.html

132 https://www.fastcodesign.com/3066981/the-radical-future-of-branding

133 http://www.marketingonline.nl/nieuws/zo-ziet-de-supermarkt-van-de-toekomst-eruit-volgens-albert-heijn?utm_source=NB_MOL_mol_dag_20170712&utm_medium=email&utm_term=&utm_content=&utm_campaign=12-07-2017&mt=js6oQjmAHe6An9Ojr6mKUw&vk=8WuFPhstqnZTjjydRP2vWA&pub=1002

134 https://www.fastcodesign.com/90132364/nest-founder-i-wake-up-in-cold-sweats-thinking-what-did-we-bring-to-the-world

135 https://www.fastcodesign.com/90132364/nest-founder-i-wake-up-in-cold-sweats-thinking-what-did-we-bring-to-the-world

136 https://www.theguardian.com/technology/2016/sep/28/google-facebook-amazon-ibm-microsoft-partnership-on-ai-tech-firms